Anthem Quality

Anthem Quality

National Songs - A Theoretical Survey

Christopher (Kit) Kelen
University of Macau

intellect Bristol, UK / Chicago, USA

First published in paperback in the UK in 2015 by
Intellect, The Mill, Parnall Road, Fishponds, Bristol, BS16 3JG, UK

First published in paperback in the USA in 2015 by
Intellect, The University of Chicago Press, 1427 E. 60th Street,
Chicago, IL 60637, USA

A catalogue record for this book is available from the British Library.

Cover designer: Ellen Thomas
Copy-editor: MPS Technologies
Production manager: Claire Organ
Typesetting: Contentra Technologies

Print ISBN: 978-1-78320-472-4
ePDF ISBN: 978-1-78320-368-0
ePUB ISBN: 978-1-78320-369-7

Printed and bound by Short Run Press Ltd, UK

FSC
www.fsc.org
MIX
Paper from responsible sources
FSC® C014540

I know very little about the Stock Exchange. I know, of course, that stockbrokers wear very shiny top-hats, which they remove when they sing 'God Save the King', as they invariably do in a crisis.

– A.A. Milne, 'High Finance'

Dulce et decorum est pro patria mori, sed dulcius pro patria vivere, et dulcissimum pro patria bibere. Ergo, bibamus pro salute patriae.

– anonymous nineteenth-century toast

Patriotism is the virtue of the vicious.

– Oscar Wilde

The dead shall live, the living die,
And music shall untune the sky.

– John Dryden, 'A Song for St Cecilia's Day'

Contents

Acknowledgements

With thanks to my collaborators on various anthems-related projects: Sasa Pavkovic, Merima Didjarevic and Ruth Jordana Pison.

Thanks also to Benedict Anderson, John Hines, Andrew Sewell, Paisley Livingston, Matthew Gibson, Glenn Timmermans and Carol Archer for their advice on various aspects of the work.

The author acknowledges the assistance of the University of Macau for sabbatical leave in 2011–2012 and for funding research trips contributing to the production of this book: to Australia in 2002, to the Philippines in 2009, and to the Balkans in 2010 and 2011.

The Loyal Toast – A Personal Introduction

Gather yourselves together, yes, gather together, O nation not desired;
Before the decree bring forth, before the day pass as the chaff,
before the fierce anger of the Lord come upon you,
before the day of the Lord's anger come upon you.
Seek ye the Lord all ye meek of the earth, which have wrought his judgement;
seek righteousness, seek meekness:
it may be ye shall be hid in the day of the Lord's anger.

(Zephania 2: 1–3)

When I was a primary school boy (in the sixties), perhaps as just recompense for the half pint of milk (warm or cold, depending on the season) that the crown provided, I was expected to perform certain demonstrations of fealty on a regular basis. I had to say the Apostle's creed and the Lord's prayer; I had to salute the flag with the Union Jack in the corner. I had to stand to attention and I had to sing various songs, the most regular of which was 'God Save the Queen'. The stanza of the song, which we sang and which must be firmly committed to memory by any Australian today over the age of forty, was:

God save our gracious Queen,
Long live our noble Queen,
God save the Queen;
Send her victorious,
Happy and glorious,
Long to reign over us:
God save the Queen.

(Bristow, 576)

Australian boys got a chance at independent practice of drinking habits in the playground with the milk at recess (play lunch or little lunch depending on your state of origin). Boys could polish off the surplus the more sheepish girls left behind. The duties of the wrist (saluting, sculling) seemed to coalesce in the lyrics of what was then an Australian patriotic song, 'Advance Australia Fair': this was 'wealth for toil'. Ours truly was a land of plenty, with often enough more milk than any of us could drink. Raising the wrist in this patriotic manner connected us in a way we were not yet up to imagining, with a long continuity, perhaps beginning with William Charles Wentworth's famous Anniversary Day (26th January) toast of 1825: 'the land boys, we live in' (Manning Clark, 1968, 55). Truly, we were drinking our inheritance, albeit in commendable (bone and tooth strengthening) fashion.

Toiling at being a primary school pupil and getting paid in milk was training for life's later rewards-for-the-diligent. The theme of guzzling down your entitlement, as a kind of proof of toil and the rights it establishes, was echoed more dramatically in the last lines of that iconic *outback* song 'The Overlander'/'The Queensland Drover' (depending on which refrain you prefer): 'And a full year's cheque pours down the neck/Of many a Queensland drover' (Radic, 1983, 29). Six o'clock closing, with all that attended the all-male consumption of as much beer as possible in less than an hour, was still a thing of the recent past. In that world the working day finished at five, the pubs closed at six. Public bars were built to be hosed out. The ladies had a ladies' lounge. Enough said.

The milk and the beer: these dreams of, and realizations of, plenty had in common an unofficial if not subversive element. Here was the frenzied moment at the trough. Here was the repressed, bubbling up to be requited. This was the moment no convict overseer or teacher could properly control. In terms of Manning Clark's insistent dichotomy throughout his six volume history of Australia, here were the workers and the underlings wresting their carnival moment from the Protestant ascendancy. A dream of plenty as icon of national identity did not quite constitute an other-than-British self-conception. The picture of a feed (or a drink or a smoke) as something to share was however an echo of pioneering days which the Depression and the privations of the Second World War had done nothing to diminish: 'Eat what's on your plate', my generation were forever being told by our depression-and-war generation parents. Now there is plenty on the plate and the dutiful nation tends a little to obesity.

So much for the milk accompanying the song. I make no claims for my precocity as a student of culture in noting that, before the words were fully *automatised* for me, I did find myself wondering a few things about 'God Save the Queen'. Principally I recall wondering from what it was this queen needed saving? I am sure that mine was not the only childhood troubled this way. Did she need saving from death? Was a monarch a kind of demi-god; one capable of immortality if only given some moral support? Or failing that would the singing thing be generally helpful from the point of view of regal longevity? Did she need saving from the foreign hoards? Or might that have been the case until recently? Or might it still be the case, elsewhere? Was she or had she been under real personal threat, in the line of carrying out her duties? As time went on and no news came from the front, this seemed less and less likely.

Cynically one might have wondered if she needed saving from herself, from her silly situation, from our dreadful singing? Did she need saving from God; being there by the grace of God, as it said around her head on the back of the coins (D.G. = *Dei Gratia*). The God in the Old Testament would certainly have been able to remove her, being the kind who smites and does all sorts of vengeful things. It was possible that she needed various kinds of saving, from herself and the natural wicked proclivities of humans in general. In other words she needed saving because she was like us. Saving from sin: that would have to be the guiding theme. The power of redemption is there to save you from yourself. This sounded more New Testament. It might seem paradoxical that such an exemplary character would need to be saved from her own sinfulness. Until of course you realised that this was part of her exemplariness: it was not *save this poor sinful queen*, it was *even the queen needs saving*, viz. even the best of us needs redemption via the forgiveness of a Saviour. Lucky thing that the queen happened to be head of the church!

Reflecting on these arrangements, all these years later, it seems that we, the singers of 'God Save the Queen', down on the lowest rung, are asking or telling God to look after the queen. Does she need that kind of support? Does God need to be told to look after those he has appointed? This 'divine right' angle on the story surely had to do with fairy-tale royalty. It had to do with a *reified* feudal conception of society such as one met in storybooks. Here one is reminded of Benedict Anderson's first paradox of the national: the faux antique of nations (1991, 9–46 passim). Our idea of how we are or ought to be governed owes more to children's storybooks than most imagine. Perhaps reminded of the evildoings to be overcome by the partisans of the natural orders of the storybook, there remained the nagging feeling that the queen needed to be rescued; the sort of thing, after all, that knights in shining armour could be relied upon to do.

The song was a kind of prayer; an instruction to God to look after the queen. I do not think it occurred to me that there was any element of self-interest here, a long reign making for stable society, or anything of that nature. It was just that we the subjects had a genuine and benevolent interest in the welfare of our queen. Something reciprocal was no doubt implied. Because the queen on the wall in the classroom was the picture of benevolence. Her eyes were with you even if the teacher were out of the room.

The lyrics of 'God Save the Queen' provided an interesting lesson in pride and humility and their mysterious balance. Here we were virtually praying (for the soul, for the body?) of this person (not personally known to us) who had accumulated the most remarkable collection of epithets pointing to virtue: this lady had to be gracious, noble. A strange kind of job description for work you inherit, but then grace and nobility could run in the family. 'Send her victorious': that always seemed odd; because the queen as picture-hanging-from-the-wall seemed like the sort of quasi-person who really did not need to go anywhere. She *was* everywhere: her empire, commonwealth, whatever it was, the sun never setting and so forth. This pointed to one of the amazing properties of the queen, a god like property – omnipresence. I am sure it never occurred to me that all this singing and saluting might be the trick required to keep up that omnipresence. Singing and saluting were, like the milk and the beer, the ritual facts. Questions hung over their immediate application perhaps (*Why this song? Why the queen? Who is she?*). When you are learning who you are in the first place, you naturally have no points of comparison with other possible identities and you lack the tools to disable the order of abstraction the ritual facts establish. Hence you are unlikely to ask: *Why a queen? Why the singing en masse, here and in other places like this?*

For me personally though there was something which brought this queen down to earth somewhat, something which cut her down to size. But it was secret: my father had taught her and her sister to play table tennis when they were just wee slips of princesses. In the thirties, that was, when my father could not really speak English. It was probably for about half an hour or so; an afternoon at the palace, but I bet most of it was spent waiting to be shown into the presence of the royal ping pong table. But the best thing was: these princesses were no good at table tennis. I was not allowed to tell anyone. But I did.

***

This is a book about the lyrics of national anthems, in general. Its aim is to theorise the general meaning of an *inter*-national social phenomenon – the words we sing together with our compatriots when we assert ourselves to be national subjects. Like all social phenomena, the singing of an anthem is an event with a context. The persistence of an anthem, the changing of an anthem, the meaning of an anthem – these things have a subjective basis that an honest analysis needs to disclose. In other words, there is no way to approach this kind of topic except as a participant-observer. There will also be no single disciplined approach from which anthems can be exhaustively, or even summarily, understood. Anthems are texts but they are also forms of human behaviour. Anthems are a political/historical, sociological/linguistic, cultural/literary/musical phenomenon and so require and deserve analysis from many complementary angles. One further, perhaps painfully obvious observation, to frame the project: although anthems might notionally be of every language, in fact they are of the languages that dominate the territory in which they are sung – the national territory. In scholarship too, we speak of territory and it is no accident that this book is written in English, by a native English-speaking student of poetry, who writes and teaches in English. Most of what we know internationally about nations, states and anthems is in English (either originally or through translation). The English language today dominates this and many other academic fields and so some bias towards the English language's ways of seeing the world will be unavoidable. Heroic struggles to overcome such a bias may be worthwhile and they will commence with the effort to acknowledge it.

I hope in this introduction to have shown my reader who and where I am, and what motivates the critique continuing through these pages. And perhaps I should also at this point apologise to my reader in advance for an inevitable bias in emphasis towards three songs important in the definition of Australian identity. These particular songs are of interest to me in terms of my understanding of who I am, in the national sense.

Chapter 1

Identification of the National Subject

the idea of the anthem in the world today

Music falls on the silence like a sense,
A passion that we feel, not understand.

The enlarging of the simplest soldier's cry
In what I am, as he falls. Of what I am, […]

The cry is part. My solitaria
Are the meditations of a central mind.
I hear the motions of the spirit and the sound
Of what is secret becomes, for me, a voice
That is my own voice speaking in my ear.

(Wallace Stevens, 298)

In the twenty-first century, new empires, virtual networks and (multinational) corporate governance notwithstanding, ours remains a world of nation states. Space in today's bounded geography is divided into nations, and nations are marked off from each other by lines on the map that may or may not coincide with, or deliberately ignore, divisions in terms of race, language, religion, ethnicity. The world's nations have been classified along various lines to account for that fundamental difference in orientation[1]; the division of the world into national spaces remains the pre-eminent fact of human geography. One may sit at a computer communing through the internet in Manuel Castells' 'space of flows' (181–2), but if one wishes to physically present oneself at a border for the purpose of crossing to the other side, then one is unavoidably reminded that the world's real physical space is national and that national space is typically defined in terms of some kind of attitude towards difference in terms of race, language, religion, ethnicity. The definitional rubric is something along the lines of – *it matters or it doesn't* – the 'we' of the national entity includes and excludes others at least partly on the reflexive basis of whether we see ourselves as the kind of people able to include or exclude persons who could be considered 'others'.

In his seminal 1983 work *Nations and Nationalism*, Ernest Gellner defined nationalism as a political principle 'holding that the political and national unit should be congruent'. As a sentiment then, nationalism, for Gellner, 'is the feeling of anger aroused at the violation of the principle, or the feeling of satisfaction aroused by its fulfilment' (1). How nation and nationalism are related in such a political principle is the subject of Gellner's and many subsequent scholarly works. These investigations, and the whole field of nationalism studies is of relevance to the present work, but this book concerns itself with the operation of national sentiment or feeling, rather than politics or principle. The writing and standing up for and the singing of anthems must be closely connected with (personal and collective) sentiments of the national kind. It would appear, *prima facie*, that national feeling generates self-sustaining cultural phenomena, and conversely, that symbolic/affective machinery is available for the purpose of generating and nurturing national feeling. As Anthony D. Smith writes, in accounting for what he describes as the postmodern conception of nation: 'the nation is a communion of imagery', 'only in [...] images or cultural constructs does the nation possess any meaning or life' (1999, 170). I shall forego the chicken-and-egg speculation that begs a rather persistent question as to the naturalness as opposed to the manufactured-ness of sentiment of the national kind. One notes though that it is by way of such a disagreement that Smith is able to divide the field of nationalism studies among, on the one hand, primordialists and perrenialists and, on the other hand, modernists and postmodernists (1999, 3–27 *passim*). Nationalists themselves, of course, are among those who harbour few doubts as to the naturalness of (at least their own) national affiliation.

Nations are relational and bounded phenomena, with tangible existence and effects, and yet, as Benedict Anderson has famously theorised in his 1983 study *Imagined Communities*, the feelings of solidarity and identity that national subjects associate with their nation and fellow citizens demand collective imaginative effort. That kind of effort is necessary because of the scale of national community; it is possible because of the technology available to states and their supporters. The relationship between state and nation is crucial to the infrastructural basis for the existence of nations as we know them today.

Then how are nations and states related? To some extent we may take nation and state to be the one phenomenon viewed in different aspects, as suggested by the appellation – 'nation state'. The nation is the territorialised (or de-territorialised) population aware of itself as such; the state is the institution that exercises power over all others, within and beyond the national territory, on behalf of the national entity, and with whatever violence it deems appropriate/acceptable and without regard to type of government.

But how did nations and states arise and how are these ideas related in theory and in practice? One might look for the Western origins of the concept of nation in the Old Testament. And one might seek the original notion of state power and its exercise in Plato's *Republic* (and perhaps in other-than-Western texts such as the *Analects* of Confucius). It would be interesting to trace the intertwining evolution of state and nation. With a view to the kinds of analyses we associate with, for instance, Michel Foucault and Pierre Bourdieu, it would be possible to gather institutional evidence of each; likewise to look at the ways in which cultural capital is invested in institutions of state and nation, their interdependence and the way in which they (dis/concertedly) generate patterns of belief and identity, power and discipline.

Gellner writes that the state is a necessary though not a sufficient condition of nationalism (4). In modernity (shall we say, of the last two centuries at least) the two have come to be normatively fused. As the age of empire waned, nations assumed state power; as per Weber's definition: 'A nation is a community of sentiment which would adequately manifest itself in a state of its own; hence, a nation is a community which normally tends to produce a state of its own' (Gerth and Mills, 1970, 176). Perhaps more importantly, the state is, for Weber, that societal agency distinguished by its possessing a monopoly of legitimate violence within a particular territory, the territory that today we overwhelmingly associate with nations in particular (Gerth and Mills, 1970, 78). Today, state and nation are conflated to the extent that they may, in many circumstances, be used as interchangeable terms. Smith writes:

> In the modern world only one form of political unit is recognised and permitted. This is the form we call the 'nation-state'. [...] Nation-states have frontiers, capitals, flags, anthems, passports, currencies, military parades, national museums, embassies and usually a seat at the United Nations. They also have one government for the territory of the nation-state, a single education system, a single economy and occupational system, and usually one set of legal rights for all citizens, though there are exceptions. (In some federal systems, there may be citizenship rights for all members of the nation-state, but also communal rights for members of particular communities.)! They also subscribe, tacitly or openly, quietly or vociferously, to a single ideology which legitimates the whole enterprise – nationalism. Indeed, the whole system of states is built on its assumptions, even if its practice does not often conform to nationalist precepts. We even call it the '*international*' system.
>
> (Hall, 109–137)

There are many situations today in which we may take state and nation to be close synonyms, with this connotative difference: that the use of 'state' emphasises power and authority, whereas the term 'nation' emphasises an appeal to the 'natural' facts of who and where people are. What the nation demands of its people will have a more powerful emotional pull than what the state demands. The state is associated with the kinds of obligations citizens endure through such phenomena as taxation and conscription; the nation is most powerfully associated with a people's sense of 'who we are', the feeling for instance that there are borders to defend. We may take the conflation of state and nation to be part of the process on the world scale by which political entities reify themselves and through the institution and regulation of an official culture, make themselves appear permanent and necessary. Anthems then are a part of that official, regulated culture through which state authorities appeal to the nation as their emotional constituency.

As relational entities (i.e. as items in a series), nations behave according to rules determined by precedent, expectation, and by their relative power and especially by their capacity to wage or threaten violence they see as legitimate, beyond their borders. The very existence of the United Nations may be taken as suggesting a consensus among nation states that the violent propensities of nations constitutes what might be considered a permanent problem for the *inter*-national system as we know it. And the UN also suggests by its existence that nations are like-enough entities to find common ground or means of adjudication necessary to peace. So there is, in late- or post-modernity, a sense in which, for all their necessary (defining) differences, nations are members of a club in which rules of decorum and standards of self-efficacy need to be followed. 'Pariah' states are those that fail to live up to the inter-*national* norms. Despite the idea of an ethnic core to nation in the modern sense (Smith, 2008, 28–48 *passim*) and the obvious examples of this phenomenon in cases such as those of China and Japan, the modern nation as site-of-identity-investment is familiarly seen (and often portrays itself) as transcending divisions we associate with race, language, religion, ethnicity. That is because, I would argue, in ideological terms the notion of nation has been skewed towards the multi-ethnic model we find in the settler societies of 'new Europes' and most particularly because of the dominating exemplar of the US The influence of the US model and the geopolitical pre-eminence of the US bring into focus key contradictions of modernity/post-modernity and the national basis of international relations in the world today. The world's biggest economy is the key node in the network of global flows through which capital and information pass on their mysterious path, and this passage appears by the minute to diminish authority of the national kind and test geopolitical frontiers. Still, at the time of writing, we have very little indication of what might succeed the age of nations; nor is there any such prospect in sight. The US, circa 1776, was the first apparently *ex-nihilo* nation, a polity founded on principles that may be associated with modernity. The age of (notionally equal-footed) nations has notionally succeeded an age of (avowedly world dominating) empires; the ethnic/religious basis of identity and identification has notionally given way to a set of enlightenment inspired ideals, centred today on the idea of universal human rights – the endowment of civilisation that nations, in general, have a responsibility to guarantee for their citizens.

Yet nations are entities demanding loyalty and inspiring devotion in a manner analogous, in important ways, with demands made on members of religious communities in the pre-national past. Gellner comments, 'Durkheim taught that in religious worship society adores its own camouflaged image. In a nationalist age, societies worship themselves brazenly and openly, spurning the camouflage'; Gellner's exemplar for the phenomenon is Germany at the Nuremburg rallies (56). The extreme manifestation we see in Nazism though perhaps belies the more commonplace quasi- or pseudo-religiosity of national devotions. In *The Cultural Foundations of Nations*, Anthony D. Smith writes, 'As "secular religion of the people", nationalism was able to combine a purely human and terrestrial compact with public worship of the nation' (xv, 2008). Smith further contends that, in the West and elsewhere, 'it is impossible to grasp the meanings of nation and nationalism without an understanding of the links between religious motifs and rituals and later ethnic and national myths, memories and symbols' (8). This continuity is demonstrated by the use of the generic category 'anthem'[2] for the kind of song that allows the subject of state or religion to express devotion through unison.

Anthems are sites of powerful collective affect and are remarkable for being the key narrative means of identification – the words – held in common as sacred (or nearly sacred) by national subjects. Strikingly under-theorised, the lyrics of national anthems are among the best known poems in the world today. So how does the study of anthems stand in relation to a more general effort to understand nations, nationalism and their meaning for identity and identification of individuals and populations? Jonathan Hearn concludes his 2006 book *Rethinking Nationalism* with ten summary theses, the third of which is as follows:

> Understanding the role of the emotions in the constitution of nationalism is important, but so far under-theorised. There is a tendency to simply draw attention to the use of symbols, and then assume their emotional efficacy. A more sophisticated understanding of both how symbols do (and do not) work, and how human beings are emotionally constituted, needs to be developed and then brought to bear on nationalism.
>
> (230)

This book can be read as part of the project foreshadowed in Hearn's third thesis. As Hearn argues in his tenth thesis (232), symbolic processes are part of a more general ideological pattern in which social power is organised. The making and mending of anthems, the singing and standing to attention anthems demand – understanding these phenomena will help us to understand the emotional efficacy of the symbolic processes and the general ideological patterns that shape identity in the world today.

Anthem and Nation, the Idea of Anthem Quality

I have already broached the question as to why it is nations have anthems. Perhaps such a question is rarely asked simply because national, like religious, devotion depends on articles of faith not amenable to scrutiny of any fundamental ('why is this happening at all?') kind. Singing and singing together go back such a long way in the human story that it seems natural collective identity would have always been sung by those who saw themselves as belonging to a particular group. Song has always played a part in human community, and nothing in history thus far has broken the continuity of the central role of song in culture. Song is perhaps as old as speech, nor is it inconceivable that speech evolved from song. In the third chapter of this book I will devote some effort to finding suitable ways of classifying anthems, but for now, before going any further in seriously attempting to answer such a fundamental (and perhaps unanswerable) question as why there is such a phenomenon as the anthem in the national sense, it will be a good idea to determine what kind of a song we are dealing with. In her article in *The Routledge Companion to Philosophy and Music*, Jeanette Bicknell places anthems in a three part classification of songs, as follows:

> First, while any song can be performed in front of an audience, some songs are 'works for performance,' specifically intended to be performed, often in a formal setting. These include art songs, songs in opera and music drama, jazz standards, and the songs recorded by professional singers for a mass media audience. Second are songs intended for 'participation-performance' or communal singing. The 'audience' and the performers

> are one in this case. Such songs include national anthems, hymns, campfire songs, and many folk songs. Even when only one person performs such a song, he or she does so less *for* an audience than *on behalf* of an audience. Finally, some songs are best understood as 'functional' songs because they serve specific practical or cultural purposes. Examples include lullabies, mnemonic songs, work songs, and laments.
>
> (Gracyk and Kania, 438)

Although this classification places our object of investigation in the 'participation-performance' category, anthems would appear to blur somewhat the lines Bicknell has drawn: often performed in formal settings where most of the audience would not be in a position to sing (for instance at international sporting events), anthems can also serve 'specific practical and cultural purposes'. Culture, very generally conceived, is a kind of dreaming together and it might not be much of a stretch of the imagination to think of anthems as lullabies for adult populations. Certainly anthems have mnemonic functions in teaching citizens or helping them to remember how and who they are. Upon reflection, Bicknell's 'classification' begins to look more like a functional continuum, and anthems are a kind of text which travels that continuum, according to the particularity of function being served in a set context.

Compare Bicknell's classification with Edward T. Cone's (1974) four-part classification of songs. For Cone there are 'simple' (unaccompanied) songs, 'art' songs that combine vocal line with instrumental accompaniment, 'natural' songs like ballads (where the particularity of authorship and audience have little relevance) and 'functional' songs in which singers express themselves as members of a community: the classical example of this fourth kind of song would be 'Happy Birthday' (Cone, 49–52). In Cone's classification, clearly an anthem is a functional song, and whether it is also an art song or a natural song would be an issue up for case-by-case debate.

In Chapter 3 I will explore the sociolinguistic notion of speech function along with the generic classification of anthems; however, given that song is a fundamental cultural form, it might be useful from the outset to make a brief comparison of the idea of function in relation to song and in human language more generally. Consider Bicknell's and Cone's categories in relation to Jakobson's famous six part classification of speech functions,[3] which one might gloss as follows: the referential function (dealing with contextual information), the poetic/aesthetic function (where the reflexive focus is on the message itself), the emotive function (where self-expression is to the fore), the conative function (focussed on addressing a receiver), the phatic function (focussed on ensuring the channel of communication is working), the metalingual function (focussed on ensuring the code is working) (Sebeok, 1960, 350–377). Where does song, in general, fit in relation to Jakobson's categories? The answer, again case-by-case, is anywhere or everywhere. Songs refer, are of a context, songs express emotion address parties; songs (like other texts) may unconsciously or reflexively test whether channels and codes of communication are working.

Leaving aside the question of whether song could or should be considered a form of speech (or vice versa), one key difference between song and speech is that monologue and dialogue. The salient point for the study of anthems is that the act of singing together, which we call unison, is a means of expressing identity-in-common: those who could be turn-taking in conversation instead take a turn together, to be of one mind/heart/soul. Anthems we can say, utilise a fundamental component of human culture in which assumed agreement is expressed, and so a common identity is more or less unconsciously asserted. As Bicknell writes, 'singing is linked with the human desire for recognition and the obligation to recognise others' (Gracyk, 444).

Why is it necessary to say who we are in this (self-convincing) way? Unison is a defence against the erosion of self and community brought about by the action of time. Lost in the moment of music, we claim a place in an eternal order (or in an order that appears unalterably out of time, as in the Platonist's time as the 'moving image of eternity' [Plato, 450]). Singing together is more than a passive recognition of place; it is an assertion of presence; it makes vital the here-and-now of who we are. Then perhaps nations have this singing-together phenomenon we call the national anthem because the song inspires the devotion the nation requires and because the nation inspires the devoted to make this kind of music together. There is a lot of chicken-and-egg-and-which-came-first (?) in this equation and the fact is well expressed in the tautological character of many anthem lyrics.

Scholars and citizens alike may be inclined by temperament to consider phenomena such as anthems and the sentiment they generate as either natural (spontaneous outpourings of popular feeling) or as manufactured by political elites for defined and self-interested purposes. And surely there is truth to both of these views. Mark Pagel's (2012) book *Wired for Culture* explores the biological/evolutionary basis of community and its relation to culture in presenting, as per the book's subtitle, a 'natural history of human cooperation'. Pagel proposes that evolution has duped us with a 'group thinking' emotion that makes us act 'as if for the good of the group, an emotion that brings pleasure, pride, or even thrills from coordinated group activities'. Artefacts such as national anthems may well exploit this kind of feeling: 'an emotion that by encouraging coordinated group behaviour has brought our ancestors and us direct benefits' (98). Pagel's thesis is that 'our facility for culture is the key to our success as a species'. Until recently the human story had been one not only of population explosion but of the proliferation of cultures. For Pagel, propensity for culture, and its concomitant possibilities for cooperation, has played a key (and under-recognised) role in the evolution of the species. Flags and anthems and other ritual objects and processes of identification are a key to understanding the relationship between culture and cooperation and their concerted role in creating society on every level. So humans have a biological propensity to relate to each other through such means as song and unison, and that capacity (like many others) is available for political manipulation.

A key fact of modernity is that in a world principally organised on a national and international basis, people see who they are as defined by their *national* sense of belonging. They express, assert and renew such affiliations by doing what humans have always done to assert who they are – that is, by singing together. The problem with easy answers to questions like 'Why do nations have anthems?' is that (however much truth they contain) they make the particular circumstances of particular people in the world today seem universal, eternal and inevitable. Whenever social phenomena appear to be universal, eternal and inevitable, it will be advisable to ask how and why they came to appear this way.

Paul Nettl commences his classic post-war work study, *National Anthems*, with the observation:

> Love of country has always been among the strongest of man's impulses. Nationalism and patriotism are a sort of collective self-confidence. The pride a man takes in his noble descent or in his personal work corresponds in another sphere to the pride he takes in being a member of his nation and the love he feels for his country.
>
> (1)

This hypostasisation of the call of patriotism as eternal and therefore universal is achieved only at the expense of a de-historicising move that forecloses a question as to the nature of the relationship between pride in one's noble descent and pride in one's nation, likewise a question as to the relationship between pride of place (or love of land) and patriotism. Elided in this process of foreclosure is the issue as to the legitimacy of rights. By what rights – and at whose expense – is land or nation or noble lineage claimed? The claim is made while the player to whom it is addressed has her or his eye off the ball.

This particular de-historicising move is conveniently answered by Benedict Anderson in his introduction to *Imagined Communities*:

> [N]ationness, as well as nationalism, are cultural artefacts of a particular kind. To understand them properly we need to consider how they have come into historical being, in what way their meanings have changed over time, and why, today, they command such profound emotional legitimacy.
>
> (4)

Anderson's argument is that 'nation' as we now know it is an artefact of late eighteenth-century provenance, 'the spontaneous distillation of a complex "crossing" of discrete historical forces', which, once in existence, were able to be transplanted to various political climates. Anthem for Anderson is part of the imagined reality of the nation artefact (81). Although there is a sense in which anthems-as-we-know-them predate nations-as-we-know-them, our sense of what a national anthem is is governed by our concept of nation.

Over the nation-and-nationalism territory Anderson has critically explored, theorists have in recent decades argued long and hard. As has already been mentioned, scholars like Anthony D. Smith have divided the antagonists, for convenience, into such camps as primordialists, perennialists and modernists, postmodernists. One could see the field as divided more fundamentally between those, on the one hand, who essentially (however piercing their analysis may be) feel good about the idea of nation and their own possession of a national affiliation (those for whom 'nation per se is not the problem') and those, on the other hand, who approach their work (as a matter of course) with critical consciousness in mind and with the aim of developing a critique of nation and nationalism along the lines of a 'thesis eleven' assumption that 'humanity can do better'. Where does the present orthodoxy lie? Smith is unhappy with the fact but himself acknowledges that 'the western conception of the *modern* nation has become the measure of our understanding of the concept of nation per se, with the result that other conceptions become illegitimate' (2008, 14). The orthodoxy thus is that nations as we know them are an invention of modernity; in Anderson's terms, nations are phenomena made possible by the advent of print capitalism (1991, 37–46).

As scholars like Smith are keen to demonstrate, very many nations have pre-modern origins, and it will be interesting to trace (and compare) historically the nature of particular national affiliations. Perhaps the more salient point in today's world is that scholars of nationalism are like other world citizens today, national subjects; that is to say their sense of who they are is in some large part determined by national affiliation. A scholar's efforts at objectivity will always be laudable, but that kind of exertion should include a reflexive effort to acknowledge his or her own interests in the subject in question. In the case of the study of nationalism, there is no avoiding a participant-observer approach because all involved in studying the field are themselves national subjects. In fact the field is and has long been dominated by Anglo-American scholarship, and so one may go so far as to say that a particular notion of nation is normatively to the fore in the hearts and minds of those undertaking the study (as is demonstrated by the key selection of scholars already cited in this chapter). It is typical of the reflexive turn in postmodernist scholarship that, from time to time, we see the persona self-presenting in the work's *trompe-l'oeil*. To counter the pseudo-objectivity that is a present and real danger to all social scientific research, part of my method throughout this book will be to disclose my own interests where these are relevant to the enquiry. I hope that my 'personal introduction' has set this reflexive process in motion.

Nation and Benedict Anderson's Paradoxes

I have already given some consideration to the historically evolving relationship between nation and state. Still, as this is a book mainly about devotion to nations as expressed in the words of *national* anthems, it will be helpful, early on, to have a working definition, specifically, of nation. Anthony D. Smith provides seven principal criteria for the purpose of defining nation in the modern sense, a list of necessary conditions: nations have well-defined territory, constitute a legal and a political entity, have a citizenry and a mass public culture, have sovereignty, participate in inter-national relations, and legitimise themselves through a nationalist ideology (2008, 12–13).

Smith has a problem with what he sees as ethnocentrism in an 'extreme' modernist position, where the assertion of the modernity of the nation becomes 'no more than a tautology, one which rules out any rival definition of the nation outside of modernity and the West' (2008, 14). Clearly, there are acute dangers of anachronism attending any effort to describe the organisation of societies throughout the world and through human history in terms that allow comparison. It may well be ethnocentrism to claim that a concept like nation can have universal meaning or application. There must be, and must have been, many societies that have no use for a term like 'society', and yet, writing of them will be difficult without recourse to such an idea. Notwithstanding these doubts, I think Smith's list of necessary conditions may be taken as universally applicable today. Nations lacking in terms of one or more of Smith's criterial conditions are under just that sort of a cloud. Still, the problem with the 'industry definitions' of nation and nationalism is that they tend over time to drift from the common parlance, becoming progressively more opaque from the point of view of those who are not, in this case, nationalism theorists. And so, for the purposes of understanding the idea of the anthem, I think it is important to remain in touch with the common understanding of what a nation is. The second (1991) edition of the *Oxford English Dictionary* (OED) gives as its main entry for the definition of nation:

> An extensive aggregate of persons, so closely associated with each other by common descent, language or history, as to form a distinct race or people, usually organized as a separate political state and occupying a definite territory.

In smaller type we are told that, 'In earlier examples the racial idea is usually stronger than the political; in more recent use the notion of political unity and independence is more prominent.' The Old Testament of the Bible is peppered with references to 'nations'; but we may sensibly read nation in this sense as a synonym for tribe – perhaps a tribe with special, even proto-national, aspects. The Israelites may have had a covenant with their God, but nations of the Old Testament have little in the way of what we could today call 'state apparatus'; nor did they have aspirations of that kind in the way a modern nation-in-waiting (Palestine, Kosovo, South Sudan) might. In the naming of modern Amerindian 'nations' as such ('the Cherokee nation'), there appears to be a conceptual hybrid of nation in the ancient and in the modern sense.

In his 1976 work *Keywords* (178–180) Raymond Williams tracked the historical overlap of the old use of 'nation' as indicating racial affiliation, against the newer 'political' definition, which we take as the norm today when we refer to the Australian, Sri Lankan or Peruvian nation. One way to make the distinction clear is to acknowledge that there is no such thing as national-*ism* in the biblical sense.[4] Although 'nation' was used in the unitary political sense from the seventeenth century to indicate a contrast between the people considered as a whole and any particular (for instance racial) sub-grouping, the overlap between the old and the new idea is of continuing significance. If today, dispossessed indigenous peoples borrow legitimacy by passing off the old idea of nation in aspiring for the new, then they are only adopting a par-for-the-course rhetorical strategy of the acknowledged nations containing them. If the rhetoric seems fanciful or desperate that is because indigenous claims press beyond the conceptual limits of de-colonisation.

From Europe's point of view we can say that before the age of empire there were nations everywhere, but only in the biblical sense. After empire there are nations everywhere in the modern sense, and there are accompanying atavistic echoes, the ghosts of nation in the former sense. That biblical sense remains important because it bolsters the appeal of modern nations to an eternity of rights presupposed by 'primordial ties' (cf Billig, 7, for a critique of these). The paradox of this appeal and of the present world-wide spread of nation in the modern sense lies in the fact that the nation-state system as we know it is unprecedented in history. Today, the world's land surface consists almost entirely of national territory (as does much of the sea), nations routinely ask us to presume that they will last forever and they mystify their origins in the hope that citizens and strangers will feel that they have always existed. Part of the hypostasisation strategy of nations in general depends on the anthropomorphism to which I have succumbed in the last sentence: 'nations ask us' or the 'your country needs you' rhetoric. Nations in particular, self-positing as entities *sui generis*, render the anthropomorphism difficult to avoid; their relationship to the citizen of whom devotions are expected is, *in loco parentis*, as of an entity venerated by a religionist. The assumption is that future generations will carry on with what the venerating past generations have done. Yet the myth of the eternity of nations was exploded in the earliest phase of nationalism studies by Ernest Renan, who in 1882 wrote, 'Nations are nothing eternal. They had a beginning and they will have an end [...] The existence of a nation is a plebiscite of every day, as the existence of the individual is a perpetual affirmation of life' (Kohn, 135–140). In recent decades, along with (and perhaps at least partly because of) a resurgence of nationalism as an ideology, the world has witnessed the expiry of many national/state entities.

So nation as we know it today is a relatively young concept, but it is one for which pretensions at long tradition are essential. The mythic figure of Britannia, the eagle that represents the United States: each of these icons of temporal authority harks back to the symbolisation of Roman imperial power. It is the authority of a certain kind of story – the written kind that declares the bond between territory and people and the abstract forms of relation linking them. The bounded nation-in-the-modern-sense we might regard as the apotheosis of written law. Its people are defined in terms of a jurisdiction with spatial, but notionally without temporal, limits. Nation is the territory – physical and moral – within which a law is sanctified as sovereign possession. To participate in a nationality as a citizen is to mythologise and to de-historicise one's identity (processes national histories are made to serve). It is to imagine an eternal and arbitrary set of facts in place of a motivated story. And it is to imagine one's self-image as founded in a difference (*my* nationality as opposed to *theirs*), based on a much more powerful identity (the common worldwide investments of nationhood and citizenship).

Benedict Anderson's *Imagined Communities* drew attention to three key paradoxes of the national. The first concerns the contrast between the objective modernity of nations and the subjective claims to unbroken tradition that characterise the sentiments of nationalists. Consider for a moment the lyrics of the Greek National Anthem:

I shall always recognise you
By the dreadful sword you hold,
As the earth, with searching vision,
You survey, with spirit bold.

'Twas the Greeks of old whose dying
Brought to birth our spirit free.
Now, with ancient valour rising,
Let us hail you, oh Liberty!

(Cartledge's translation, Bristow,[5] 237)

The connection of modern with ancient Greece is highly plausible from a general Western point of view. The Romantic Byronic cause was an update on the Crusader mentality. From the northern European point of view, that cause was more or less the redemption of the home of classical antiquity from the heathen conqueror. How much does the formation of the modern Greek (Orthodox) state and its separation from the Ottoman Empire have to do with the pagan cities of antiquity and with their struggle against, for instance, Persian invaders of the fifth century? The connection may be spurious but the myth of such a continuity was nation-making at the time of the composition of the lyrics, which were written by the twenty-five year old Dionysios Solomos. The making of these lyrics immediately followed the Greek Revolution of 1821 (against the Ottoman rulers of the time). Loosening themselves from the grip of an oriental despotism resulted in the Greeks persuading themselves both that they were part of Europe and that this was the kind of struggle in which they had been engaged since antiquity. Part of the PR for the cause involved encouraging northern Europe in the conviction that Greece was the birthplace of European civilisation and that therefore Greece needed to be freed from a foreign – and Eastern – oppressor. In the persistence of early nineteenth-century lyrics in the Greek anthem we read traces of what we can consider the modern nation's originary logic. These lyrics (representing two of Solomos' original 148 stanzas), offer the world, in Greek and in English, an anthropomorphic spirit (nation deity) that can as well represent the classical democratic or the medieval orthodox ideal.[6] Setting aside the long running competition between two golden age myths (pagan Athens versus Orthodox Constantinople) for the hearts and minds of Greek nationalists, we can say that in the case of Greece, the nation-making logic of an ancient–modern continuity has never really been challenged. So, despite the almost two thousand year gap between antiquity and modernity, we may take Greece's case to be one of the least apparently paradoxical instances of a claim to unbroken tradition. What makes Greece's continuity myth so plausible (despite its obvious difficulties) is the fact that it is not only Greeks who believe in it. A myth may be sustaining and unproblematic, as in this case; but when there is competition between nations for a myth, such as that of Alexander the Great (as between Greece and the neighbouring former Yugoslav Republic of Macedonia), things may run less smoothly.

The more general point is that anthems, as social process, are atavistic, a throwback to the time (religious ages past) when music was a participatory activity in which collective identity was regularly and ritually asserted through unison in song. In singing an anthem with one's compatriots one feels, as per Anderson's first paradox, that one is attending to a long-established duty, a duty that has been passed down as a sacred trust. Although song and singing appear to be continuous and permanent aspects of human culture (and prohibitions by English Puritans or Afghan Taliban aberrant), the singing of anthems today presents itself, particularly to the outside listener, as the collective conjuring up of a meaning continuity the summoning of a spirit from and of the past.

Anderson's second paradox is that nations are particular instances of identity of which all persons are – at least notionally – possessed. That is to say, nation is a kind of universal difference: everyone's nationality is not the same as someone else's. Nations are imagined communities in the sense to which W.B. Yeats drew attention with his poem 'An Irish Airman Foresees His Death':

> I know that I shall meet my fate
> Somewhere among the clouds above;
> Those that I fight I do not hate,
> Those that I guard I do not love;
>
> (*Collected Poems*, 152)

The fate of the members of the armed forces is tied up with the fate of nation and this means it depends on the reification, as a political entity – a community – of persons who cannot be known to each other and who yet imagine that they are familiarly related. Nor can the enemy be known in the case-by-case sense. The military are the ultimate test for belief in the arbitrary and anonymous nature of national affiliation. In war survival often depends on the trust of unknown others who are on your side. If one doesn't have a king to believe in then faith is placed in a chain of command that ultimately vests authority in the abstraction that stands symbolically where the crown was. In this more or less world-typical case today, sovereignty lies in the anonymous collectivity we call the 'nation', feeling for which is most eloquently expressed by worship at the tomb of the unknown soldier.

Beyond the fact of the nation consisting of persons, there is nothing personal about nation. Everyone has unique nationality; dual nationals and the presence of refugees in and 'between' nations complicate this picture, but they are exceptions to prove the rule. Nations are different from each other, and yet, when we come to consider it, just as they all have borders, passports, coinage and armies, so the means of symbolisation of nations are remarkably uniform: flags are all rectangular (except for Nepal's); many national anthems might be mistaken for each other, both in terms of lyrics and music. Consider the rote quality of the lyrics in the national anthem of Grenada:

> Hail! Grenada, land of ours.
> We pledge ourselves to thee.
> Heads, hearts and hands in unity
> To reach our destiny.
> Ever conscious of God,
> Being proud of our heritage,
> May we with faith and courage

> Aspire, build, advance
> As one people, one family.
> God bless our nation.
>
> (Bristow, 238–239)

With the possible exception of avowedly atheist states, it is difficult to imagine citizens who would have trouble rendering this unconvincing devotion to their nation. These are portable lyrics and yet one presumes that a great proportion of the population of Grenada feels the special-ness of their identity and identification-in-common when they sing these words together. That this rote universalist sentiment can inspire particular peoples to feel particularly themselves is *prima facie* a mystery needing explanation.

Anderson's third paradox of the national is between the political power and the intellectual weakness of the abstraction. National-ism is – against the world's other -isms – conspicuously lacking in great thinkers (5). The most pernicious form thus far, fascism, makes the point abundantly clear. Herder and Hegel, even Voltaire, may be considered, each in their ways, proponents of nationalism, but for none of these was it their main philosophical game. As Anderson tells us – it is the Hobbeses, Tocquevilles, Marxes and Webers who are absent from the story of this ideology. Thus Anderson opines that it would be easier for everyone if nationalism were considered as a subject alongside kinship and religion, rather than fascism or liberalism (5). Nor is Grenada's the only anthem showing signs of less than impressive care in the composition of the lyrics.

Despite the paradoxes, nationalism, as Anderson has theorised it, is everywhere. The paradoxes go unnoticed precisely because the world today consists so overwhelmingly of nations, of national space. Michael Billig's 1995 work *Banal Nationalism* investigated the manner of nationalism's ubiquity:

> In so many little ways, the citizenry are reminded daily of their national place in a world of nations. However, this reminding is so familiar, so continual, that is not consciously registered as reminding. The metonymic image of banal nationalism is not a flag which is being consciously waved with fervent passion; it is the flag hanging unnoticed on a public building. (8)

Less noticeable even than the flag is the coin that circulates from purse to hand to cash register, carrying with it, along with the sign of monetary value, a carefully chosen symbol of nation.[7] Most of the machinery of nation is invisible in this sense of going unnoticed. Just as muzak constantly instils a melody (and concomitant sentiment) without drawing attention to itself, so the machinery of nation is mostly 'just there', providing the citizen with a set of unconscious investments, the knowledge of a 'tune' able to be cranked up for a practical purpose, such as a football match or a war. Paradoxically, it is vital to nation that its signs, which blare from time to time, be mainly buried in the everyday, and be thus – like a citizen army – always available to serve at short notice.

The seeming eternity of nations is had at the price of this kind of vigilance, the paradoxical vigilance of those who are not looking. The words in the anthem are lodged in the head, they can be sung for a need. As Billig writes: 'Nationalism, far from being an intermittent mood in established nations, is the endemic condition.' Nor, Billig suggests, should the banality of nation be taken as indicating that nations are harmless (6–7). In the case of anthems, the banality of this most essential text of nation is clearly shown when one assembles examples together. Then we see that, while there is certainly a wide affective range, anthems from countries around the world offer the reader similar sentiments, and similar clichés repeated. The repetition in the uniformity of these texts goes unnoticed precisely because the lyrics of anthems are not often presented together, except perhaps at international sporting events, where one might hear two or three anthems in quick succession (and often without lyrics). The magic of anthems works, I would argue, in the manner of a mass hallucination. These texts, taken together, reveal the gravity of Anderson's second paradox: peoples believe they are unique in asserting their national identity when what they are mostly asserting is the national basis-in-common of their identity. The magic that makes people unaware of such a paradox is in need of careful scrutiny.

Identity – and Other Key Terms

Nation and anthem are key terms in this study. It is no accident that these abstractions are, in their modern senses, historically coextensive; they are parts of the one phenomenon. National anthems are cultural expressions of nationalism or nation-ness, the quality-in-common of those geopolitical entities we call 'nation states'. This work is an attempt to define what an anthem is, and more particularly, to get to the essence of 'anthem quality' – the soul-stirring effect that certain combinations of music and lyrics achieve, most typically in the service of national affiliation. So anthem and anthem quality will be defined and re-defined from various perspectives through the chapters that follow. Other key terms in this study are 'affect', 'identity' and 'unison'. Let me briefly arrange these ideas. 'Affect' we can gloss as 'feeling': the affective range of an anthem would suggest the various emotions that song would engender or allow. 'Unison' is straightforward enough: the 'unisonant' are those who sing together to express a common identity; 'unisonance' is the abstraction of that expression.

'Identity' is a fraught term, and one that will, again, be approached from various angles throughout the book. Entailed here is the sense of *who I am* and of *who we are*. At stake in these sociocultural formations of self is a range of ethical issues, to do with spontaneous emotion, with fellow feeling and feelings towards others, inclusion and exclusion (refugees, the loss of nations), the manipulation of affect and sense of self by the state, questions of democracy and the imposition of ways of thinking. This book is, in essence, about an aspect of the manner in which a key form of identity has been generated in the modern world. I will close this chapter by considering in a little more detail how identity in the world today relates to the feelings of identification an anthem might evoke.

In a chapter, 'Identity and Meaning in the Network Society', in *The Power of Identity* (volume 2) of the three volume series *The Information Age*, Manuel Castells defines identity, as it refers to social actors, as 'the process of construction of meaning on the basis of a social attribute, or a related set of cultural attributes, that is given priority over other sources of meaning. For a given individual,' Castells writes, 'there may be a plurality of identities.' And for Castells, 'such a plurality is a source of stress and contradiction in both self-representation and social action' (6). Identity, in this sense, is a source of stress and contradiction because it has to be distinguished from norm-defined roles: 'Identities are sources of meaning [...] constructed through a process of individuation' (7). These sources of meaning, and their individuation, have a context, so the national part of one's plural identity will relate closely to that of a plurality of like-national subjects. To be born into a nation that already exists is to have had national others (fellow citizens) sacrifice for you already, much in the manner that Christ (in Christian thinking) has already died for sins humans are yet to commit. An identity of the national kind is prepared for those who will be national citizens and who, to become such, will require an apprenticeship in the symbols and rituals of the nation-in-particular. The symbolic apprenticeship will enable them to realise that national aspect of the identity into which they are born. None of this is to suggest that there is anything static or permanent about the formation of identity, national or otherwise; but for the purposes of the national aspect of identity it will be important that individuals see themselves as participating in an order, in certain respects, unchanging.

To historicise the nation-making past (and so the Zeitgeist that brought the national aspect of identity to the fore in European thinking), one notes that the late nineteenth-century's golden age of anthem making coincides with the high-tide mark of European imperial expansion and the carrying of capitalist modes of production and exchange into some of the planet's most remote places. It also corresponds to the first golden age of children's literature, the age of the fairy tale – that genre, one might say, in which apparently timeless and placeless values were lauded as exemplary of golden ages past (ones typically medieval, hierarchic, patriarchal).

Compared with feudal society, nineteenth-century Europe was a place of great social mobility, as well as being a place of unprecedented physical movement and communication. The identity demands on European subjects of this time were complex and rapidly shifting, perhaps not compared with our own times but certainly when compared with preceding ages. One may see, in this light, the making normative of national symbols (and for example, of anthems) as a means of anchoring the identity of individuals in common traditions and values that might otherwise have been slipping away. Yes, nation, in the modern sense, was something new, and the long shadow it cast was the state. But for the most part, nations came from somewhere, they had the ethno-symbolic roots Anthony D. Smith is keen to emphasise (2008 *passim*). So nationalism (and anthem singing) may be seen as a kind of state insurance against the vicissitudes of class conflict, separatist terrors and erosion of the traditional orders the state itself was, by sleight of hand, superseding. Those subjects now becoming citizens had had in the past limited needs to be reminded *en masse* of who they were and of what their responsibilities were. The state had had limited powers to do the reminding but now memory needed to be jogged and now the technology existed to do this. Nor is it fanciful to see the idea of collective 'memory' (as represented in a state machinery, as per Anderson's first paradox) as an ideological trick: in the guise of 'reminding' people who they were, states were insisting to their citizens who they had become and what they had to do. The more abstract, anonymous and bureaucratic the state became in relation to its citizens, the more necessary it would be to 'remind' them of who they were and what they had to do. It might be a little pointless to seek for cause and effect between the modern state and its means of popular dissemination (phenomena by no means limited to propaganda) because perhaps the link is definitional. Certainly, it was alongside the bureaucratic anonymous state that the technology came into being to spread the word to citizens of who they are . So we can see the general abstraction 'nation' as the signifier of self-in-the-collective-sense that floated into the modern anonymous position occupied for the feudal mind by, on the one hand, the crown, and on the other, the *heimat* (or native sod, place of belonging).

State power now needed to remind citizens of what modernity had made of their traditions and of what the tussle of past and present had made of them. Now that there was such a thing as the masses (as opposed to the peasants or townsfolk of a particular place), an affective machinery would be needed to standardise feelings of the national kind. What better means than having people sing together, as they always had, but now on a grander and much more uniform scale. In a nation like England, increasingly at the forefront of Europe's world-dominating imperialism, this kind of thing had been taking place since the seventeenth century, with the most important of all Ur-anthems, 'God Save the King'.

To give perspective to the emotional arsenal available to states, it will be fair to say that nation has no more essential affective mechanism than the anthem.There are no cultural artefacts capable of generating consistently more powerful feelings among large populations. Nation and anthem are each equally artefacts of modernity, but in most cases they come from somewhere. Traditions may be invented or embellished for them, as Hobsbawm and Ranger and others have convincingly shown (1992 *passim*), but the affect national songs evoke is not typically *ex-nihilo*; the nation and anthem in general have historic/contextual bases, without which it is difficult to see how the nexus between them could be as heartfelt as it commonly is.

Do ages succeed each other in the manner of Kuhn's paradigm-shifting scientific revolutions or do they coalesce (pile up, like the cities that were Rome) in the way Freud suggested for the unconscious in 'Civilization and its Discontents' (768–769)? The golden age of nations was the golden age of children's literature and the fairy tale; unsurprisingly it was the golden age of anthem making as well. And importantly it was the golden age of European world empire – because in the late nineteenth century nations at home could be empires at large. Nation and empire: the cases of Belgium and Germany show that both ideas could be borrowed and quickly put to impressive effect, and at the same time.

The anthems of that golden age (many of them treated in later chapters of this book) were, for the subjects who first sang them, harking back to traditions (real or imagined). Those traditions of a golden age or a national ideal were evoked through a rhetoric purposed to engage the attention of the masses on a particular image set. Focussing on a common imagery through a common rhetoric (increasingly delivered through universal schooling) would allow citizens to share common memories of who they were, had become, had to be. The opening of the US national anthem, 'The Star Spangled Banner', is merely the most obvious example of that kind of rhetoric: 'O say can you see …'

If anthems were peddling tradition to the relatively new national subjects of the nineteenth century, today, though one might, with the passage of time, regard them as even more atavistic, their survival imbues them with real tradition and continuity, a feeling that there is a trans-historical 'we' because this is the song *we* sang a hundred years ago. So, with time, the invented tradition gains plausibility, much in the manner that the high street shop ('established 1983') seems less ridiculous in 2013 than it did in 1984.

In the age of the internet and 'free trade', plurality of identities has proliferated so that it is not simply a case of mobility complicating a sense of who we are. Identity has many parts and aspects as defined by language, ethnicity, gender, sexuality, class, occupation, politics and hobbies, among others; nor is it uncommon in the modern West for each of these to present as 'complicated' (in Facebook parlance) for individuals. In terms of media demands and presence, the contemporary Western white-collar subject communicates in the course of a day through e-mail, Facebook, text message, telephone and in person, even occasionally by writing on paper. These different modes of relating (typically for quite different purposes) make us different characters.

Castells has written that 'the age of globalisation is also the age of national resurgence' and that this historical trend has been surprising to some because it had seemed, in the decades leading up to the fall of the Berlin Wall, that nationalism was doomed: globalisation, universal culture (Disney, Hollywood, Murdoch) and the kind of critique offered by scholars like Gellner, Hobsbawm and Anderson, seemed like nails in the coffin of the weak doctrine that was holding off an inevitably more cosmopolitan world (30). If, in the twenty-first century, nationalism seems to be back with a vengeance, then one may read this as corrective reaction to the formidable threats posed to national belonging by the various identity complications listed just above. One notes also that if, as per Gellner's 1983 thesis, we accept that nation, up until that time, had been, whatever its folk pretensions, ultimately a state-sanctioned invention of high culture (57), then we will have to admit that in the twenty-first century, it is by and large from global elites that cosmopolitan pressures are brought to bear on national ideas and identities; conversely it is local and popular feeling that defends nations against such threats.

When the self is as divided as it is today, how can societies or communities cohere? Very many of the contemporary demands on the world's internet-connected subjects (at the time of writing, more than one-third of the global population) are of a cosmopolitan (apparently post-national) nature. How do nation states defend themselves from this ongoing erosion of the authority in defining identity they had been able to take for granted throughout the twentieth century?

If we consider nation to be that abstraction which, among all others, today inspires the most potent feelings of identity and identification with the interests of other humans, then we should acknowledge there is something godlike in its properties: it is ubiquitous (at least within a territory), it is an anonymous possession-in-common sustained by collective faith (prime ministers are temporary, the nation goes on), it is mainly unnoticed (a banal fact of existence) and its power over us is invisible in the manner of a religious mystery – which is in fact what Benedict Anderson and others have suggested belief in nation is akin to (Anderson, 1991, 11–12).

Identity-in-common is what the act of unison implies: we sing together to assert ourselves as being who we together are. The singing of anthems is ambiguously involved in the production, confirmation and reproduction of identities-in-common of the national kind. The singing of anthems affirms to subjects singing and listening that identity of the national kind has primacy among the various ontological demands felt today by subjects who are also citizens of a nation. The fact that national feeling remains strong today, against the multifarious identity demands on the modern subject, may suggest not only the widespread perception of a need to maintain a unified identity in the face of threats to that possibility; it may also suggest the efficacy of the kind of symbolic/rhetorical strategy that anthem singing represents.

The study of nationalism must inform our understanding of how a text of the kind, 'national anthem', has meaning. Perhaps though the value of a study such as this is that, given anthems are the artefacts of nation *par excellence*, they have much of a practical nature to tell us about the operation of national feeling. And so national anthems may help to explain the nature of nations, and national affiliation, and nationalism and of identity in the national sense.

Notes

1. For example in Eric Hobsbawm's distinction between civic and ethno-linguistic nationalisms (1990, chapters 3 and 6), Anthony D. Smith's distinction between territorial and ethnic nationalism (1999, 190).
2. Use of which the OED dates back to 1340.
3. Derived from Karl Bühler's Organon Model, Jakobson's classification has had huge influence, and has been developed, through various structuralisms, down to the present day where its echoes can be read, for instance in the systemic functional grammar of M.A.K. Halliday.
4. The OED gives us a number of definitions of nationalism, the earliest example dating to 1836.
5. The homepage of the Greek president gives Rudyard Kipling's 1918 translation:

   We knew thee of old,
   Oh, divinely restored,

By the lights of thine eyes,
And the light of thy Sword,

From the graves of our slain,
Shall thy valour prevail.
As we greet thee again –
Hail, Liberty! Hail!

Throughout this book, citations of national anthems, in particular, are from four main sources – from two encyclopedic works – Bristow's and Xing Hang's anthem collections, from Wikipedia and from official government websites.

6. In Solomos' original the Christian cross was a persistent motif.
7. Note the interest of modern poets in banal nationalism, as for instance evidenced in 'the circular nature of money' in Howard Nemerov's poem, 'Money' (McLatchy, 126).

Chapter 2

The Official Poem of the People

anthems, their contexts and their common characteristics

Od's life! must one swear to the Truth of a Song?

(Matthew Prior, 'A Better Answer')

The lyrics of national anthems are among the best-known poems in the world today, and they are poems with official sanction, usually of a government authority, of a parliament or of a constitution.[1] As artefacts, anthems are symbolic shadows of nations, a kind of proof-in-writing of a social abstraction's reality; as events, anthems are the bringing-to-life of the abstract reality of nations. By means of unison they make a community of strangers. National songs that crave or lose official status are dangerously akin to nations-in-waiting or nations past their use-by date. Diachronically, the songs of a particular nation are like next or last slides in a slide-show, there in a series, because the nation, though synoptically framed through continuity as identical with itself, is in fact always something different than what it was – becoming new so as to survive, so as to keep its sacred traditions alive. The manner in which anthem lyrics reify a national imagery (for instance landscapes or scenery evocative of the homeland) is key to the way in which anthems aid in the process of making national communities of those who are otherwise strangers. This facility of anthems – to make general the praise of place as a personal possession – has a long and highly esteemed history in many poetry traditions. Consider an example relevant to one kind of anthem, the tableau that presents the national scene, or what Anthony D. Smith would call an 'ethnoscape' (1999, 149–160). Lyric poetry in praise of one's home dates, in the West, to the classical forms found in the eclogue or the bucolic, forms in which Virgil's models have pre-eminence. The phenomenon of praised place is as ancient in Chinese poetry. In either case, what is lauded, for the benefit of the reader, is a here-and-now scene or alternatively a place remembered as dear to the persona – a place that, though unknown to the bulk of readers, will yet be read in their hearts also as home. In anthem lyrics, the loved place in particular is generalised into a form available for praise in common and in unison by all citizens of a defined national territory. Nationalists did not invent the idea of a generalised (often idyllic) landscape, able to be loved by a reader as if it were his/her own. One may read Hesiod's 'Work and Days' as instructions for the Greek-speaking inhabitants of any place; his history of ages is certainly intended to be universal as are his husbandry tips. Shakespeare is full of praise for England as a place that is a kingdom; perhaps the most conspicuous example of such an encomium is in John of Gaunt's speech in Richard II: 'This royal throne of kings, this scepter'd isle […] other Eden […] fortress built by Nature for herself […] this blessed plot, this earth, this realm, this England'

(II, I, Shakespeare, 388). What states have done in sanctioning anthems as official is to make generic for a particular people its praise of the nation as place-in-common.

And who are these people (better to say, who is 'this people') who join in organised unison to adopt the self-symbolising strategy of anthem singing? Rhetorically, it will be safe to assume their identity with the nation-as-entity: folk, for instance, of the sceptred isle whose self-conception comes to entail that they live in the fortress Nature built for herself. Nation and people are joined in an associative circle where the name of the nation and the name of the people may be used interchangeably. The synecdoche or metonymy entails an anthropomorphism that we recognise with the use of gendered pronouns standing for the nation. 'France will do this', 'Paris will do this', 'the French will react by...' France may be a 'she', the French people cannot be; we cannot imagine the English are all women, but we can imagine them to be represented by the female figure of Britannia. In other words, the idea of a collective abstraction, something like a nation, is rhetorically necessary to the social entity engaged in the process of unison; states may not require anthropomorphic representation but *international* relations demand that peoples be imagined in terms of such avatars. The terms of the metonymy are self-enjoining and mutually confirming so that the official poem tells the people who they are. There are good reasons to read all of this as tautology: the kind of tautology that reifies social relations, thus diminishing the likelihood of their being called into question.

Social scientists of many different stripes have an interest in bringing to consciousness the manner in which social relations are hypostasised as natural, eternal or necessary. Then why are anthems so little discussed, so neglected as cultural phenomena? Why are they under-theorised? An easy answer to these questions is that anthems are often (if not typically) among the world's worst surviving poems. Working from Pierre Bourdieu's theory of cultural capital we could say that anthems draw attention to a contradiction between the two types of cultural capital that they embody. On the one hand an anthem has high-art pretensions as demonstrated by the use of orchestras (by preference the best in the land); on the other hand anthems embody cultural capital (we can call it 'national cultural capital') of a necessarily populist type. Not uncommonly, national orchestras are, for nationalistic purposes, pressed into service to play music that, for the musicians' and for the orchestras' usual audiences, would be deemed of dubious aesthetic quality.

The Musical Aspect of Anthems

'Mellow and inspiring music': at the end of the movie – where the subtitles would be if words were spoken – these words appear on the screen. They seem an apt beginning at a definition of 'anthem quality'. These words capture the religious-historical origins of anthem quality in music and they account for the amorphousness of anthem quality as an idea. How much can we glean from these epithets, 'mellow' and 'inspiring'? At the least, a little reflection (of the kind that comes from the labelling) shows that there is a lowest common denominator in the imagined good listener here and that a function is being served, much in the manner of muzak in a mall; whereas muzak is calming, this movie-end music should be moving. What muzak and anthem quality have in common is that neither is really working properly on its (half-)listening subject if it draws attention to itself. What is incongruous about the caption, 'mellow and inspiring music', is that it does draw our attention to intentions and effects that work, at least largely, because they are unconscious (if not subliminal). Reflecting on such music at such a moment might have the effect of breaking the spell for some text participants, who would then critically reframe what they hear as 'enervating and jingoistic music, purposed to lull me into not noticing that my emotions are being manipulated'.

To avow an admiration of anthem quality in music is to admit that one's critical filters are switched off; one's mind is in belief, rather than doubt, mode. Because a sense of who we are is invested in the way we listen to this kind of music, people have strong feelings about, or arising from it, and what it evokes. Those who hear anthem quality music are naturally divided into believers and non-believers; it *works* for them or it does not. One can of course love the anthem of a nation not one's own without becoming, through the process of listening, a traitor to one's country. One can easily believe in the nation but not believe that a particular song provides it with the appropriate anthem quality. One might feel sorry for a certain group of foreigners on such a score: feel sad that such nice people should have to sing such a crappy song. Thinking about the question will not help to make it work. Or one might say that anthem quality is *about* feeling, rather than thinking; thinking about it will break the spell.

This book is not a work of musicology or music aesthetics; its subject is the lyrics of national anthems; still, one acknowledges from the outset that the immediate context of those lyrics is their accompanying music. Anthems are, like songs more generally, texts made equally of word and of music. From a musicological point the most immediate context of the music constituting the anthem will be those words that fit with it and perhaps provide the listener with a sense-in-language of the music's import – what it is about and how the listener might react to it. And of course, the lyrics, for musician and musicologist alike, are what give the citizen-listener a word-defined role to play in relation to the anthem. The listener can use his/her voice to be a part of the unison. In which of these art forms (words accompanied with music, music to which words fit) does the emotional effect of an anthem most essentially lie? How easy is it to understand – indeed to apprehend, or appreciate, at any level – an anthem as dual text, as text *equally* of words and of music?[2]

Many, if not most of us, have music running in our heads unbidden much of the time. Perhaps less physical than tinnitus, this music may nevertheless powerfully affect our conscious (and unconscious) thinking and our sense of self. Where does this sound come from? In his 1973 study, *How Musical is Man?,* John Blacking writes: 'Music is a product of the behaviour of human groups, whether formal or informal: it is humanly organised sound' (10). From this assertion, one may draw the conclusion that music is something collective in nature, which, for the long ages of human existence prior to sound recording (indeed prior to musical notation), existed only in the moment of performance. Music was in this sense the paradigm of cultural expression that is fleeting. This property of music, and its putative affinity for the soul's meaning depths, was something that fascinated the Romantic poets; in Chapter 6 I will investigate how poets' ideas of music helped to shape the affective experience that has come down to us as anthem quality. Music may have been evanescent but it could still stick in the individual's head, as a 'haunting melody' Whether it stuck in the heads of the ancients more or less than the 'earworms' of today, is a moot point. Certainly the contemporary phenomenon does seem to be associated with mass culture and is perhaps an example of what Richard Dawkins theorised as the *meme* (or contagious idea) in his 1976 book, *The Selfish Gene*.[3]

In his 1962 work, *Primitive Song*, C.M. Bowra links the origins of song to prayer: 'song comes into existence when a rite based on rhythmical movement calls for something more explicit to make its purpose plain, and this need is satisfied by appropriating words from the art of prayer' (32). Surely it is at least as likely that song antedates prayer, that singing to oneself or to one's companion(s) would be an older phenomenon than addressing a deity through song? For Bowra, like Blacking, song is communal activity: 'the voice of a common consciousness, of what a whole society or a representative part of it feels on certain occasions' (33). Foregoing speculation as to which, of prayer or song, is older, the anthem, in both the national and the pre-national sense, fits perfectly with the idea (however unfalsifiable) of song as descended from prayer. Later in this chapter I will outline a little of what is known of the religious lineage of anthems.

***

Why are anthems sung, not spoken? The origins of lyric poetry are with music and so perhaps the more sensible speculation is that it would be odd if anthems had become unhinged from the melodies and rhythms that bring their words to life and make them memorable. The problem here is that so many forms of lyric poetry have been divorced from music in just this way. Little of the world's serious poetry today is set to music; conversely, popular songs today are typically (but by no means exclusively) what would have to be regarded as poor words set to poor music. The same could frankly be said of many *libretti*. Frequently, in popular song, both words and music are simple, in the sense of lacking challenge for the reader/listener. In terms of analysis, the disciplinary separation of music from poetry means that where these art forms are joined, one will tend to be seen as a framing structure for the other, or perhaps in the terms Derrida has theorised from Kant's notion of the 'parergon' (Derrida, 78–79) – an inessential or decorative exteriority that brushes up against what, in the case of anthems, would be taken to be the emotive content of the work. The subject of this interdisciplinary study is the lyrics of national anthems. It is my hope that this book will interest musicologists and others to join forces in helping to understand a type of text with which the citizens of nations worldwide are preoccupied and psychologically/spiritually invested. In anthems, music and words bind the personal with the political in such a way as to embody sense of self and face shown to others. Where the personal and the political meet, we may have recourse to Raymond Williams' 'structures of feeling', instanced when it is discovered through analysis that things 'taken to be private, idiosyncratic and even isolating' are in fact 'emergent, connecting and dominant characteristics' (132). What was taken to be personal turns out to be the basis on which a collective identity is unconsciously determined through views and assumptions in common, and through the common affect these imply.

While certain poems, stirring in the patriotic or some related sense, might be considered (by analogy) to be possessed of anthem quality, in the twenty-first century, anthem lyrics require music in order to function as anthems. There are a number of anthems with no lyrics (Spain's 'Marcha Real' and Beethoven's 'Ode to Joy' [as Europe's anthem] being conspicuous examples), but there are no official national anthems recited or chanted as such en masse, without music. This is not to say that anthem quality cannot be recognised in words alone. Dorothea Mackellar's (1908) 'My Country' (9–11) would be one of many good examples of a nationalist poem with anthem quality; in the case of Blake's 'Jerusalem' ('And did those feet in ancient time' [514]), we can safely assume that Hubert Parry set Blake's poem to music in 1916, precisely because of its anthem quality.

Why then is music essential to anthems and to anthem quality? One could regard this nexus as a fact of nature (a biological/neurological given) with cultural implications: the kind of music that happens to stir the soul fits with the poetic expression of love of home, and home may be generalised to include the 'homeland' or 'nation' in the modern sense. This would leave us with a question as to how a particular piece or type of music stirs the soul (and whether all souls would be stirred, and if not, which, to what end and under which circumstances). A brief excursion into the territory of music aesthetics will be necessary to establish some parameters for speculation as to the nature of the power of the music that accompanies anthem lyrics and to delimit what can be understood of this.

In his essay on 'Value', in the *Routledge Companion to Philosophy and Music,* Alan H. Goldman spells out the parameters of what he considers to be a mystery entailed in understanding music:

> When one truly describes music as sequences of sounds or tones, it immediately seems mysterious how it could have the value for us that it does. Pure instrumental music does not (or need not) represent anything or inform us about anything. It does not teach us about ordinary life or the objects that occupy us within it. Unlike painting and literature, it is an essentially abstract art, lacking referential content and any direct relation to the world of ordinary objects.
>
> (Gracyk and Kania, 155)

From an intentional point of view, of all symbolic systems music is perhaps uniquely suited to the task of developing affect-in-common of the kind nations harness in order to unite a citizenry for peaceful and for warlike purposes alike. This force for fellow feeling, I would argue, has nothing to do with a putative representational power of music; on the contrary it is because such a power is apparently lacking that music is able to serve as a vehicle for the kind of amorphous sentiment that nations, like religions, require of their faithful adherents. As Roger Scruton writes in his volume, *Aesthetics of Music,* 'thoughts about a subject are never essential to the understanding of music' (138). The titling of classical music (aside from opera) is by and large like the titling of an abstract painting: a means of giving an audience a representational way into understanding a work, which in and of itself may offer no such clue. That understanding might be ironic or offhand, it might *suggest* a tangential 'look again/think again' approach to a topic or an idea or it might seem very direct. A representational power may be lacking in music, but Stephen Davies argues in his *Themes in the Philosophy of Music*, 'music does refer beyond itself, in that it is expressive of emotions' (122). Still, the idea of a representational power in music in-and-of-itself is difficult for many to resist and might perhaps be likened to the need some people feel to 'see things' (i.e. real-world objects) in paintings that are avowedly abstract/non-representational or indeed in nature. Along these lines one might think 'The Flight of the Bumble Bee' could not but represent what its title suggests; even in this extreme case, the acceptance of the representation depends on suggestion and force of habit. These apparently idiosyncratic phenomena of personality are things we might associate contextually with Raymond Williams' 'structures of feeling' (1977, 128–135 passim).

To explain how these work on the social scale it will be useful to have recourse to the theory of *habitus*, as developed from Aristotle by Marcel Mauss and Pierre Bourdieu. For Mauss, habitus encompassed embodied aspects of culture, discernible in the practices of individuals and in society (including nations) (73). Those embodied aspects of culture include such things as habits, skills, styles of dressing or walking or dining, tastes: in short the whole gambit of characteristics defining a person or a social group in such a way as to go without saying, viz. personal/social character-defining embodiments that operate on an unconscious level. In *Distinction* Bourdieu defines habitus as enabling 'an intelligible and necessary relation to be established between practices and a situation, the meaning of which is produced by the habitus through categories of perception and appreciation that are themselves produced by an observable social condition' (101). And Bourdieu writes of a question that he says is strangely ignored by economists: 'of the economic conditions of the production of the dispositions demanded by the economy' (101). For Bourdieu, habitus is cultural capital's embodied state; it consists in a person's character and ways of thinking (his/her habits in that sense). Anthem singing, the visible swelling of the breast with pride, the humming of tunes stuck in one's head, the seeing or not seeing of things in putatively abstract paintings – each of these might be taken as an example of habitus, each is evidence of how we came to where we are and of the place we occupy (disposition/position) in relation to cultural capital.

Because music does not depict in the way a work of literature or other-than-abstract painting might, it is able to be put in the service of any *plausible* image or idea or sentiment. In semiotic terms, music is a 'floating signifier' that carries a content supplied, potentially, by whoever (or whatever other system of meaning) has control of it. The idea of such control is notoriously problematic in the case of music: it is difficult for a state to manage, citizen by citizen, which tunes will stick in which heads; it is difficult to determine which associations that national subject will individually have with a particular fragment of tune or with a phrase. If language is difficult to legislate on account of its naturalness (its refusal to simply sit still and mean what is meant), then why would music be more obedient to political whims? Still, we know from advertising and the mass media more generally that opinion and feeling are manipulable on a grand scale by word, music and image, within and beyond national borders. In the case of anthems, the fellow feeling (and its intentional shaping) is usually within borders. The affect anthems conjure is typically powerful to the initiate and weak for the outsider (and, as we will see, in some cases, inscrutable). But it is precisely this kind of social control that state authorities attempt to exercise when they decide on anthems, rewrite their lyrics and create and manage events for the dissemination of popular feeling. The fact that words, music and visual images are, for all their unruliness, available as tools for the moulding of sentiment does suggest that each has an independent semantic power as a means through which feeling can be evoked. It seems unlikely that unaccompanied music would persist in advertising if it were merely decorative and had no independent effects on its listener.

Music may not represent in the way language does, but two important caveats to this claim have already been provided. We can frame these by way of two related questions: how does musical 'suggestion' work and how can a particular image, idea or sentiment be *plausibly associated* with a particular piece of music? A third question arising from these would relate to the common lay-notion of music as a 'universal language': does music have at its disposal a means of generating emotions that any listener would feel?

Let us take for example the Israeli anthem. The Western listener will find it entirely plausible that Israel's anthem, 'Hatikvah', should be in a minor key and that this fact should sit ironically with a title usually translated as 'The Hope'.[4] The plausibility of such an unusual arrangement for an anthem (the use of sad music to cultivate national feeling) has to do with what is generally known of the historic circumstances of the Jewish people as these relate to the founding of the State of Israel. Reflection reveals this apparently fundamental manner of evocation of emotion from such a basic binary as major/minor = happy/sad is culturally determined by the history of Western music, now a world-canonic tradition. There is ample evidence to suggest that both in the ancient world and in modern other-than-Western music (for instance African and Asian), this binary and its apparently fixed affective connotation set need not apply. It seems likely the minor third, as a less stable interval than the major, came over time to be heard as an acceptable dissonance, with a specific range of connotation in Western music, classical and popular. There is no evidence of the naturalness of this perceptual arrangement. And so it is easy to imagine ancient and modern listeners who, fully informed of the Holocaust and its relation to the creation of Israel, would not be able to decipher musical meaning or feeling by listening to an arrangement of 'Hatikvah'.

Philosophers agree that music expresses emotions and that it (sometimes) refers beyond itself (Davies, 2003 122). David Kania writes,

> we find music an art steeped with meaning, and yet, unlike drama, pure instrumental music has no obvious semantic content. This quickly raises the question of why we should find

> music so valuable. Central to many philosophers' thinking on these subjects has been music's apparent ability to express emotions while remaining an abstract art in some sense.
>
> (Zalta)

Is it the case that any given piece of music only expresses emotions by referring beyond itself, at least in the immediate sense of obeying structural or other patterns of meaning present in the musical tradition? In other words, is it the case that a given piece of music is only allowed to make meaning by referring, in some way, to what has already been meant musically? As to the sense in which music is an abstract art: it would appear that the difficulties in the way of music's possibility of representing anything are matched by a converse implausibility of music in particular not referring, at least to other music. What makes sense *in* a context will, in perhaps mainly unconscious ways, also make sense *of* a context.

Anthems undoubtedly express emotions and they also elicit emotions. Individuals may find themselves in tears on hearing their own (or another's) anthem; crowds may be moved by circumstance to sing. Composers, we must imagine, have felt themselves overwhelmed with national feeling when composing the words or the music of a national anthem. Nor have such outpourings always been shared by others, there having been many more efforts to create national songs than there have been official adoptions of such texts.

I have perhaps suggested some doubts as to the efficacy of labelling anything musical 'pure'. Anthems are not in the 'pure music' category that music aestheticians typically use to test assertions about the nature of musical meaning. That is to say, anthems are normatively combinations of words and music, and where there are words there is always meaning of the kind we find in language and, because words come from somewhere, there is always reference beyond the text itself. Words and music fit together in song by means of long-established formal practices; rhythm is essential to both poetry and music, and in song these parallel arts of rhythm conflate. Apart from this similarity, a like 'musicality' in the arrangement of words and tones, there is the inter-referentiality of the text that is words and also music. Inter-referentiality allows music to connote words and words to connote music, whenever the other half of the text happens, for whatever reason, not to be there.

The fact that the connotative power of the parts, when isolated, suggests that of the whole, might be considered a proof that neither words nor music can be considered a decorative addition or fancy frame, in the case of a song which 'works' (for instance affectively *on* a listener). When anthem quality is working its magic (when the proper feelings are expressed and elicited), then the inter-referentiality appears to have a synergistic effect. It is the music and a meaning avowed in words that fit together to give the unisonant powerful feelings of a national kind. This observation still begs a question as to the relationship between pure music and feeling. How is it that 'pure' music (let us say, music without any association with lyrics) can generate feelings among its listeners? If music lacks representational power, then does it elicit emotions from its listeners through what can be called the 'making of meaning'? Do listeners (at least 'good' listeners) 'understand' what music means? If it were possible to affirm this in a manner that definitely assigned meaning, perhaps on a genre-by-genre basis, then this might suggest the efficacy of particular types of music, for instance, patriotic purposes. To turn then to the plausibility of analogies between language (in the literal sense of human speech) and music: the obvious affinity is the capacity for emotional expressiveness. But for Stephen Davies, music neither is, nor can be properly compared with a language; it does however have meaning and that meaning can be understood. Davies writes, 'to understand a musical utterance is not to know whether that utterance is true or false. We do not regard musical utterances as subject to truth-conditions or as meeting standards of assertive correctness or incorrectness of use. In respect of its meaning, music cannot usefully be compared to a language' (125).

Interestingly, though the idea will be contradicted by the banality of many anthem lyrics, Davies' idea of a 'musical utterance' would *prima facie* appear to be a useful condition of poetic meaning (especially in Modernism and later) – to understand a poem is pointedly not to know whether it is true or false. Much of the language in cumming's *oeuvre* cannot (clause by clause or sentence by sentence) be understood in terms of being subject to truth-conditions or as meeting standards of assertive correctness or incorrectness of use, but it will surely be a narrow kind of pedantry to, on that basis, declare that it is not language. Along the lines of Keats' 'negative capability' (and of Bakhtin's (194–210) and Kristeva's (83) notions of ambivalent 'yes-and-no' logic in poetry), one may claim without much controversy that aesthetic production of every kind depends on the generation of meaning that is open to interpretation (therefore aesthetically valuable) because it is not interested in meeting standards of assertive correctness. Poetic meaning, we may say, entails knowing and not knowing as a simultaneous aesthetic event.

Let us, for argument's sake, say that the expression and eliciting of feeling in/from anthems is the result of a kind of meaning: a kind of meaning that, like that of poetry, has an openness and an ambivalence about it, inaccessible to truth-conditions or standards of assertive correctness. Then, far from claiming that poetry's openness or facility for generating ambivalence was an obstacle to its expressing 'truths of the heart/soul variety', one might easily claim that this was a special power possessed in common by music and poetry. Let us take a look from the other side of the glass. Far from having to accept one of two extreme cases, that the emotional force of an anthem lies in either the words or in the music (and that the other part is a parergon to the real vehicle of meaning), we can now suggest that the synergy of lyrics and music, and their affective efficacy, has to do with what we could call the musical quality of poetic meaning (and/or perhaps the poetic quality of musical meaning).

Can music be 'pure' if either its semantic or emotional content is culturally determined? I do not think that this matters for our present purposes. From the point of view of understanding the nexus or synergy of lyrics and music, the key point is that music, in and of itself, instance by instance, can have the power to elicit feeling from a listener and from those who participate in making it. This will mean that certain kinds of music are, either or both, generated by composers (and sanctioned by state authorities) because of the feeling that is in them (because of their affective meaning) or because they are more serviceable than others for the practical purpose of making a people feel a certain way.

Now, beyond the question of cultural specificity we tackle by way of the minor key in 'Hatikvah', we can ask if music, within the framework of a general (as opposed to particular) cultural milieu, is able to generate particular kinds of feeling in the absence of specific reference. The evidence for this is circumstantial and more compelling in some cases than in others. What we call a 'march' has a sense of going forward at a regular rhythm, and in fact the habitus of soldiers marching and of the music with which they march is closely related, marching bands and particularly percussion accompaniment to marches dating in the West from ancient times. Marches and the music and instruments accompanying them have evolved together and, in the last several centuries, achieved a high-art status (Mozart, Beethoven, Mahler, Sousa) with clear military/ceremonial functions. These characteristics made the march an ideal genre for nations in the modern sense, nations being political entities that saw themselves as striding very decidedly into the new era ('going forward') and needing the validation of a high cultural tradition. Beyond this clear match of political metaphor, habitus, avowed function and an emphasis on an insistent rhythm, we might entertain various expectations of other kinds of music. Music that is more in the manner of a prayer (or to accompany one) we will expect to have a sombre aspect ('God Save the King'); music presenting a national landscape or ethnoscape (say, Smetana's) to inspire awe for the sublimity of nature (as evoked within national borders). It is not hard to imagine operatic music allowing the national story to unfold in the manner of a *libretto* (for instance in the case of Brazil's anthem) for a fanfare to wordlessly introduce some grand personage or avatar in the place of one (in the case of some Middle Eastern nations). None of these latter examples of generic meaning in music has the undeniable fit of a march with the act of marching, yet each is convincing in its way and has been helpful in considering the generic classification of anthems, as dealt with in the next chapter.

***

My aim in this excursion has not been to come to any definitive conclusions with regard to the semantic properties and possibilities of music free of the connotations of lyrics, rather to suggest that puzzles along these lines will remain even after any analysis of the words that go with the music of a national anthem. Music is important to us; it has emotional power over us, it can be deployed to exercise emotional power. The manner of operation of that power remains in important respects mysterious. When the devotees of a nation sing an anthem they are, like co-religionists, participating in a genuine mystery as to the manner in which musical and linguistic meaning empowers, and exercises power over, them.

The planting of earworms or contagious ideas of any kind naturally entails repetition, or what is sometimes referred to as a 'dinning it into the skull' of the listener. Repetition of the dinning variety is relevant to the national anthem, which, to follow Walter Benjamin's construct, is an artefact of an age of mechanical reproduction. While all music is in principle repeatable, prior to notation and sound recording, evolution of a musical text from performance to performance would have been unavoidable. Along the lines of what is known of the oral epic we may assume that the survival of a particular song (whether or not named as such) would have been because it was able to maintain the interest of audiences from one context to another. Notated music should be able to be repeated with some accuracy, notwithstanding versions, renditions, rubato; nevertheless, music evolves with performance and it survives (perhaps to become canonic or classic) on the basis of how well it 'travels'. We do not hear the works of Mozart as his contemporary listeners would have, nor perhaps would Mozart's contemporaries understand what we understand when we listen to a modern performance of Mozart's work.

Against this social conception of music, there is a Platonist idea of music in which works exist for all time and may have only been 'discovered' rather than created by a composer (Peter Kivy, 35–38). There is an interesting match between this way of seeing music and national thinking in general. It is of course great works, not pop songs, that are to be thought of as having always been meant to be. However risible in certain instances, anthems in general have the pretension of being serious music; they demand to be taken seriously, and often legal sanction is enlisted to ensure the seriousness of the unisonant.[5] Parodies, to be discussed in Chapter 4, seriously undermine such pretensions. The important point is that the eternity of a piece of music is somewhat akin to the eternity of a nation. The Platonist affinity (if I may call it that) is fortuitous for the cause of nation in general and it makes the anthem the ideal servant in that cause. So while music in particular lacks meaning in the sense that words, clauses and sentences convey meaning, on the grand scale (if convincing, i.e. if able to be taken seriously) music in general conveys a paradoxical sense of the permanence of the moment. The paradox is that the most evanescent of art forms has had the most persuasive hold on the idea of eternity. And this, I would argue, is the particular meaning that nations borrow from music. Music immortalises; it gives the good subject the feeling that the entity with which the music is concerned will outlast things of the moment passing. As we have seen with Yugoslavia and the Soviet Union, and with Hitler's Third Reich, neither nations nor states are eternal. Nor, as we will see in each of these cases, are their anthems. Nor are the reigns of monarchs; though, as we will see in the case of 'God Save the King/Queen' (as the case may be), the claim has been rhetorically important to the ideal of state and governance presented by an anthem.[6] That 'long to reign over us' call is mild compared with the many hyperbolic claims to eternity we find in anthems in various parts of the world. In Lebanon's case: 'May God preserve her till the end of time', 'Her name is glory since time began'; and the glory and immortality are in this case represented by the cedar that is the symbol of Lebanon (Bristow, 323).

Alan H. Goldman concludes the essay, from which I quoted earlier, with the observation that,

> The musical medium is not only other-worldly, but is also immanent, evanescent, ephemeral, transparent. We hear musical tones as wholly present to us, but only for the fleeting moments in which they occur. The feeling of transparency, the fact that our contact with this art appears to be unmediated by physical objects, indicates the purest meeting of minds possible within the confines of the physical world. Indeed, as already

> noted, the meeting appears to take place in a wholly different, ideal world. The musical object is constantly disappearing as it appears, leaving the creative force behind it more fully exposed. Music then represents the purest kind of Hegelian overcoming of matter by mind, the purest expression of the creative human spirit. Its peculiar value lies not only in its providing us models of perfect order that we seem to cooperate in creating while listening to them, but also in the purity of its revelation of the creative mind itself.
> (163–164)

The soul is stirred by many means, but among these, music has a key place. 'All art', Walter Pater wrote, 'constantly aspires to the condition of music'. The reason for this, for Pater, was that it was art's constant effort to obliterate the distinction between matter and form (64). Prior to the advent of abstraction in painting, unburdened with the necessity of representing anything, music uniquely possessed a power to just be itself and so to stand outside of the diurnal, and equally the calendrical, flow of time – thus to be the audible 'image of eternity' Plato had put in motion. Mechanical reproduction may have robbed music of some of its aura, still it is the conflation of the abstract and the affective in melodic and rhythmic form that renders both mysterious and effective the power of music. Music is emotionally effective *because* the conflation is mysterious and even arbitrary. How can music *represent* anything to its listener? And yet music – *the* invisible and vanishing art, brings listeners to where its experience can be shared. Nothing *but* affect is given, this is what must be shared. It is just this ineffable power of the musical experience that provides those succumbing to it with a quasi-religious experience. As Roger Scruton writes, 'if all art aspires to the condition of music it is because music achieves the greatest possible distance from the explicit statement, while still inviting us to "enter into" its expressive content' (*Aesthetics of Music*, 364). It is because of the affinity of musical forms for experiences deemed sacred and mystical, that down through the ages, music has indispensably accompanied religion. It is because of the pseudo-religious investment of nations that anthems have become one of their indispensable signs. The affective/representational effects of a song are however less ineffable than those of music without words. In the case of song, it is through words – or the trace of words – that a specific imagery may be associatively tied to a tune.

The Religious Origins of Anthem Quality

Anthems today are one of the core series-in-common defining nation. The other most obvious inter-national series is the flags of the world. Like the flag, the anthem is closely associated with the idea of nation. Anthems are indispensable to nationhood. By metaphorical extension, 'anthem' or 'anthem quality' is applied popularly to evoke any kind of musically inspired fellow feeling, analogous to that which a national tune inspires among those who share a nationality. A song on the radio with 'anthem quality' is one promoted (or perhaps mocked) on the basis of its presumed capacity to generate an identifiably collective affect: it can stir a group of people, defined in whatever manner, to a celebratory feeling of solidarity with each other. Examples would include Helen Reddy's 1971 'I am Woman', Queen's 1977 'We are the Champions' and USA for Africa's 1985 'We are the World'. In each of these cases a 'feel good' cosmopolitan identification is achieved through the same solemn catchiness required of a *national* anthem. There is a moral and proselytic seriousness to the lyrics of 'I am Woman' and 'We are the World', in each case matched with suitably serious melodic and rhythmic progression. Perhaps neither is quite as solemn as we would expect of an established nation's established anthem. These songs were anthems *of their time*; in other words, their pretensions to eternity were somewhat more limited than is generally the case with national anthems, which, in serving present purposes, need to have worked for generations passed away and for generations yet to come. It is interesting that the least morally engaged of these songs, 'We are the Champions', seems to have been the most enduring, perhaps because its message is so portable, perhaps because it suits the Zeitgeist. Pop and rock anthems need to be more up-to-date than the national kind. They may serve specialised interests; take for instance songs of Lou Reed, such as 'Walk on the Wild Side' or 'Perfect Day' (both from the 1972 album *Transformer*), that may be considered 'gay anthems'. But while nationally oriented pop music easily takes on the anthem mantle, more generally the term, in relation to pop or rock music, has come to mean a canonised or even a memorable text of its genre: any song well-enough remembered that those nostalgic for the days of its popularity might, at a later date, wish to sing along. Paradoxically, the definitional range of anthem quality has broadened so as to allow a wide variety of narrow interests to be represented by what might be captioned, 'mellow and inspiring music'.

A note though, before we go further with the definition of anthems and 'anthem quality'. We should remind ourselves that this book is in English. Anthems as a phenomenon are commonly considered in the English language (as originals or as translations) and with regard to English language models. However, before briefly considering the etymological journey of the word 'anthem', it will do well to consider that in many languages, it is a cognate of the English word 'hymn' that is used to indicate the singular song of national devotion that a nation in particular officially possesses. In this case, the English reader sees very clearly the link with the earlier forms of religious devotion. The 'something like a nation' rhetorically necessary to the process of unison organised on a national scale pre-existed the modern political state in the form of local, kingdom, empire or worldwide religious communities – in what we might think of as the idea of a congregation, as instanced in but abstracted beyond any particular physical gathering of the unisonant.

In terms of English language usage, 'anthem' comes in the first place from collective affective investment in song with a religious purpose. In the fourteenth edition of the *Encyclopaedia Britannica* (issued from the 1920s to the 1950s) the entry for anthems is as follows:

> Derived from the Greek through the Saxon *antefn*, a word which originally had the same meaning as antiphony. It is now, however, generally restricted to a form of church music, particularly in the service of the Church of England, in which it is appointed by the rubrics to follow the third collect at both morning and evening prayer, 'in choirs and

> places where they sing.' It is just as usual in this place to have an ordinary hymn as an anthem, which is a more elaborate composition than the congregational hymns.
>
> (Volume 2, 25)

The *Grove Dictionary of Music and Musicians* dates the term 'anthem' in its religious sense back to the eleventh century, although the detailed discussion thereafter commences in the fourteenth century (Sadie, 454).

There is in the fourteenth edition of *Britannica* also an entry for 'National Anthems', which carries no definition but rather a list beginning: 'In *Europe* the chief national anthems are: [...]' (Volume 16, 134). In the OED today the first two entries for anthem likewise account for the older religious context. We have to turn to a third definition to read of a usage made 'loosely in poetry', a 'song of praise or gladness', an example of which is given as the British Royal or National anthem, which is 'technically a hymn'.

These definitions demonstrate *anthem* as evidence of Benedict Anderson's contention that religious senses of identity were borrowed into the secular realm for the purposes of nation. Just as the old meaning of *nation* persists in modern usages and serves to illustrate Anderson's first paradox of objective modernity belied by subjective claims to antiquity, so the old (and popularly forgotten) meaning of anthem helps to sanctify the nation so praised by its pious citizenry.

The religious origins of the word 'anthem' are much narrower than most anthem singers today would suspect. They relate specifically to the Church of England service; they are songs (from scripture or liturgy) appointed to accompany the gathering of prayers known as a 'collect'. Anthems, in this original English sense evolved from the sixteenth century on and are distinct from (and more elaborate than) sung psalms and hymns. Originally homophonic, they became more complex over the centuries and as they attracted the interest of serious composers (from Purcell to Ralph Vaughan Williams). It is not that this practice is unique in the Anglican Church, rather the use of the word 'anthem' is a uniquely Anglican term for prior or analogous practices known as the 'votive antiphon' or the 'motet', for instance in the Catholic and in the Lutheran Churches. The musical form that has developed from the practice is however essentially English in its development. The political connection is something we may credit to the Church-State nexus in English affairs, following the Reformation.[7] Anthems were written (for instance by Purcell) for use at court (the Chapel Royal), and came to play a conspicuous part in coronation services.

Just as the religious term for a particular kind of singing in a particular context has expanded to include celebrations of national feeling and solidarity, so national sentiment has allowed, by analogy, other forms of sung identification-in-common to be gathered under the rubric 'anthem'. But the genealogy of the term is not gratuitous; more than simple solidarity has been borrowed from one context to the next. Where there is anthem quality there is an implied obligation for members included in a particular group to have the anthem make them feel good about that inclusion. That feel-good core of anthem quality has a self-righteousness about it. That self-righteousness is achieved through a process of sanctification, the making sacred of that with which we identify, that which the anthem celebrates. The sacredness of national anthems today is demonstrated by the respect they demand or which is demanded on their behalf. US citizens are accustomed to the flag-waving banality of their national identification: the flag is always there. If the hand is over the heart when the anthem is sung, this is not the result of any legal obligation. In Thailand, by contrast, the national anthem is played all over the country at fixed times in the morning and the evening; it may interrupt television programming; whenever it is played citizens are expected to stand in respectful silence. In the Philippines, there has in recent years been much contention over the appropriate ways of singing the national anthem and concerning who has the right to decide what proper respect for that symbol would consist in. Kazakhstan has a 2006 law 'obliging everyone to stand and press the palm of their right hand to the left side of their chest when the national anthem is performed in public' (as reported by Radio Free Europe, 2006). In Russia, a 2001 decree stipulates:

> During official performances of the State anthem of Russia, those present are to listen to it standing, men without headgear. In the event that the performance of the anthem is accompanied by the raising of the State flag of Russia, those present are to turn to face the flag. Any performance or use of the anthem in violation of this law, and also disrespect toward the anthem will be subject to prosecution in accordance with the legislation of the Russian Federation.
>
> (Daughtry, 46)

Worldwide, though, such prescriptive protocols are rare. Where they do occur they might be taken as conspicuously flouting Renan's 'daily plebiscite' through which the nation perpetually reconfirms its existence. One might hazard that in most of the world, the strength of national identification is such that citizens do not need to be told how national symbols, including their anthems, are to be respected. What we see in the borrowing of sung sentiment, from the national to the sectional interest, is that anthem quality offers those who can harness it something much more powerful than official sanction. The belief and collective sense-of-self a citizenry embodies when they join in unison to sing themselves together is a powerful force, a 'plebiscite' force that overrides political divisions of the moment. In democracies, politicians seeking election challenge this power at their peril.

How has the definition of anthem travelled over time? To speak of anthem in the sense of implying the fellow feeling of co-religionists is today to apply a metaphor analogous to that which football songs borrow when they are considered to possess anthem quality. The core meaning of anthem today is as indicated by the collocation, 'national anthem'. Today, it is by analogy with national sentiment, considered in the light of musically stirred affective investment, that we are able to conceive a hymn as having 'anthem quality'. I think we can take this as lexicographic evidence for Anderson's contention that the realm of the sacred has passed, in the age of nation, from the church to the state.

If we think of rock anthems as falling short of the solemnity demanded of their national prototypes, then we should consider how profane national anthems appear from the religious point of view. A national anthem effectively makes a man-made political abstraction the object of a genre intended for the glory of God (whom good atheists would naturally describe as a man-made political abstraction). Whichever way one looks at it, the making national of the anthem genre is a squaring of the circle.

Common Themes and Characteristics of Anthems Today

While this present study has no case-by-case evaluative ambitions, it nevertheless has been admitted that many of the lyrics of the world's anthems are bad poems. Imagine singing the first stanza of Burkina Faso's 'Hymn of Victory'[8]:

> Against the humiliating bondage of a thousand years
> Rapacity came from afar to subjugate them for a hundred years.
> Against the cynical malice in the shape
> Of neocolonialism and its petty local servants.
> Many gave in and certain others resisted.
> But the frustrations, the successes, the sweat, the blood
> Have fortified our courageous people
> And fertilized its heroic struggle.
>
> (Bristow, 101)

The solemnity anthems demand is often at odds with the awkwardness of forced rhymes, solecisms and unwarranted hyperbole. Surveying anthems as a worldwide phenomenon of modernity, one is tempted to see them as proof positive of Anderson's third paradox – the intellectual weakness of the national idea. The official place and/or popularity of these songs has to do with having achieved, or been granted, anthem status; lines of dubious quality are frequently overlooked by those called on to sing them on the basis of a guaranteed canonic position and/or place in the hearts of the unisonant. Words frequently, ritually repeated fall easily into cliché, and cliché is susceptible of parody. These issues are discussed in Chapter 4, where we consider the automatisation of affect in anthems. Certainly anthems have been interestingly parodied, but they are protected somewhat from the descent into bathos by the sombre feelings and the religious awe they are typically intended (by authors, custom and government authorities) to inspire. A little literal content analysis shows the critical reader readily how anthems make their appeal and what anthems purport to be about. 'Heart' is a conspicuous term-in-common of anthem lyrics worldwide. Along with 'soul',[9] 'God',[10] 'blood'[11] and 'die' or 'death',[12] 'heart'[13] is one of the key abstract preoccupations of anthems from a wide range of cultures. This little list illustrates the fact that anthem lyrics tend to an interest in life-and-death matters. Anthems have deep and meaningful pretensions. This makes sense in terms of the powerful feeling anthems generate, but sits paradoxically with their banality, their clichéd predictability and the routine nature of anthem singing. There are good reasons why anthems should interest themselves in life and death. The nations they represent are typically invested in having citizens prepared to die for them, and anthems are a key symbolic means by which the life of nations is asserted, maintained and sometimes challenged.

The most commonly occurring word in anthems worldwide is 'our'. This apparently trivial fact suggests that anthems are not merely about identity, they are also about possession. They are about being possessed as well as possessing; as in the lines of Robert Frost's poem, 'The Gift Outright', a poem about the nature and entailments of US citizenship:

> The land was ours before we were the land's.
> She was our land more than a hundred years
> Before we were her people. She was ours
> In Massachusetts, in Virginia,
> But we were England's, still colonials,
> Possessing what we still were unpossessed by,
> Possessed by what we now no more possessed.
>
> (Frost, 316)

What makes a place yours? What decides that you belong to a place? This is – as Frost's poem shows it be – a complex issue. One could gloss those last two lines above as follows: *We owned land to which we did not yet belong, with which we were yet to identify. We were identified with a country we didn't own or belong to anymore.* The use of 'possessed' at the beginning of the last line here has some of the flavour of supernatural possession. In other words, the identity in *us* (let's say, Englishness) was something we no longer had any control over (we didn't own any land in England; we'd never been there, didn't know England): our Englishness was a kind of possession that would have to be exorcised. What would exorcise it? The gradual and lagging realisation of where and who we were; the gradual and lagging realisation of where we belonged and what we *were* a part of. 'The Gift Outright' is then a poem about how identities are arrived at (or given) rather than chosen. And yet the realisation that the poem itself represents, in claiming a shift in identity, does constitute a kind of choice. Identities may claim those 'possessed' by them, and yet poetry does have a role in preferring a certain world over another. Frost's poem does precisely what the lyrics of national anthems typically do not do: it makes us think about the nature of identity, about what-goes-without-saying about who we are in the national sense.

The analysis of anthems draws attention to all sorts of dualities, ambiguities, ambivalences that the singing of anthems would generally tend to obscure. An important dual aspect of anthems (to which Chapter 3 of this book is largely devoted) concerns their status as fixed written documents of nation and their status as speech acts, often freely entered into by the citizens of a nation. Anthems are both official recorded forms and the collective (if not entirely spontaneous) speech of citizens. In this sense, anthems are much like the prayers in a prayer book. They are written down, so already known; but they are also what individuals (together or alone) say to God (and whether or not there is a God to listen). The analogy with prayer is not gratuitous; as we have seen, anthem and prayer have an affinity by way of religious observance. Beyond relationship of citizen to and of state to deity, it will be useful to adumbrate the range of interests we see expressed in the lyrics of anthems.

Anthems are norm-setting texts, texts of conformity. So it should be unsurprising that many of them urge obedience to various forms of established authority. In Mauritania's national anthem:

> Be a helper for God and censure what is forbidden,
> And turn with the law which he wants you to follow,
> Hold no one to be useful or harmful, except for Him,
> And walk the path of the chosen one, and die while you are on it!
>
> (Bristow, 364)

These lyrics, Koranic in tone, draw together a number of common characteristics: righteousness, the desirability of sacrifice for the national good and fatalism, among others. God is, as mentioned earlier, an important interest in anthems, whether they are addressed to Him, as in prayer, or whether, as in the case of Mauritania, it is God's path that is being laid out prescriptively for the unisonant. Anthems speak of rights to territory as God-given (Chile), of nation as gift from God (Georgia), of destiny as written by the hand of God (Mexico). There is also the idea of God as umpire among nations, the idea of a 'God of nations' (Gabon, New Zealand).

Duty of the national kind often points in the direction of death, and in fact the death (or blood) of citizens (and especially citizen soldiers) is a kind of sacrament in the life of the nation. The nation is inherited from the dead; when we who now sing are gone, it will be bequeathed to the as-yet-unborn. So anthems may tutor the citizen in a nonchalance in the face of death, as in the case of Congo's anthem: 'And if we have to die / What does it really matter?' (Bristow, 153). In Cuba's anthem, we are presented with the paradox: 'to die for the country is to live' (Bristow, 163). We may be assured that in many cases the association with death is not mere rhetorical flourish: Israel's national anthem 'Hatikvah' was, prior to the creation of that state, reportedly sung by Jews in the Holocaust at the entrance of the Auschwitz-Birkenau gas chamber. In Cuba's case, the words 'morir por la Patria es vivir' are what the song's author, Perucho Figueredo, is reported to have shouted at his Spanish firing squad after their order to fire had been given; this was only two years after he had composed the song.

Fatalism is common in anthems. In Honduras' anthem: 'We shall march, oh fatherland, to our death; / Our death will be honoured' (Bristow, 260). Hungary's anthem reveals a nation that, Christlike, sees itself as having already paid the price for any sins it might commit in the future (Bristow, 263). Perhaps the most fatalistic (and cosmic) of all anthems is Iceland's, which ends with the lines: 'Iceland's thousand years, Iceland's thousand years, / One small flower of eternity, with a quivering tear, / That prays to its God and dies' (Bristow, 266).

A sense of suffering as foundational is common, especially in the anthems of postcolonial countries. This has given rise to some of the strangest metaphors we find among anthem lyrics, as in Columbia's anthem, which asks us to imagine good germinating in furrows of pain (Bristow, 141).

Most bloodthirsty of the best-known anthems is France's 'The Marseillaise' (to lines in which Columbia's furrows of pain probably allude) that will be discussed in the next chapter. Alongside the many professions of the necessity of violence, there is the problem of peace as discussed in El Salvador's anthem, clearly the hymn of a people tired of being at war with itself. The spirit of reconciliation is powerfully there in multilingual anthems, like those of Canada and New Zealand, and most recently in the case of South Africa's anthem, which combines lyrics from the former apartheid era anthem, 'Die Stem' or 'The Call of South Africa' and the former ANC revolutionary anthem, 'Nkosi Sikelel' iAfrika' (originally a Xhosa methodist hymn), sung in five languages (Xhosa, Zulu, Sesotho, Afrikaans, English) so that the official complete lyrics[14] are now:

Nkosi sikelel' iAfrika
Maluphakanyisw' uphondo lwayo,
Yizwa imithandazo yethu,
Nkosi sikelela, thina lusapho lwayo.

Morena boloka setjhaba sa heso,
O fedise dintwa le matshwenyeho,
O se boloke, O se boloke setjhaba sa heso,
Setjhaba sa South Afrika – South Afrika.

Uit die blou van onse hemel,
Uit die diepte van ons see,
Oor ons ewige gebergtes,
Waar die kranse antwoord gee,

Sounds the call to come together,
And united we shall stand,
Let us live and strive for freedom,
In South Africa our land.

(*The Presidency, Republic of South Africa*)

The Kingdom of Yugoslavia (between the World Wars) provides an earlier example of composite lyrics from several songs mirroring a new nation comprising older entities, the entities in that case being the peoples of Serbia, Croatia and Slovenia. Many anthems play a role in explaining the symbols of the nation and especially the flag. 'The Star Spangled Banner' is a conspicuous example with which I will deal in the next chapter. Consider for the present the anthem of Honduras:

> Your flag is a splendor of sky
> Crossed with a band of snow;
> And there can be seen, in its sacred depths,
> Five pale blue stars.
> In your emblem, which a rough sea
> With its wild waves protects,
> Behind the bare summit of a volcano,
> A star brightly shines.
>
> (Bristow, 260)

Samoa's anthem, addressed to the nation, discloses that 'your banner is your crown' (Bristow, 475).

Anthem is often the means of articulating a circle of symbols that confirm each other in establishing the nation's meaning for the citizen, and so the nature of an identity-in-common. We see this in Albania's 'Hymn to the Flag':

> The flag which in battle unites us
> Found us all ready for the oath,
> One mind, one aim, until our land
> Becomes free from the enemy.
>
> (Bristow, 13)

And Albania's national hymn presents another common characteristic of anthems: the mention of vague generalised enemies or others to guard against, a colourful instance of which we find in Gabon's anthem: 'And banish the sorcerers, those perfidious deceivers/ Who sowed poison and spread fear' (Bristow, 222). Some anthems, by contrast, keep very specific grudges alive. Take the third stanza of Poland's 'Dambrowski's Mazurka' for example: 'As Czarniecki Poznan town regains, / Fighting with the Swede, / To free our fatherland from chains, / We shall return by sea' (Bristow, 446). The other-to-be-resisted need not even be human in form. Various abstractions (neocolonialism, for instance) demand resistance, and in the case of Niger's anthem, it is the battle with nature that is foregrounded.

> We confront ferocious and treacherous animals
> Often scarcely armed,
> Seeking to live in dignity,
> Not slaying with a lust to kill.
> In the steppe where all feel thirst,

Brilliant. In the burning desert,
Let us march tirelessly forward
As magnanimous and vigilant masters.

(Bristow, 408)

Here, nation is something to be sung from the wilderness/jungle; nation building is a collective effort at protection from other-than-human forces. Senegal's anthem likewise celebrates 'the tamer of the bush' (Bristow, 493).

There are anthems focussed more on the 'I' than the 'we' (e.g. Estonia's), but these are unusual. Some anthems are quite inscrutable to those lacking knowledge of their story. One such would be Holland's anthem 'William of Nassau', dating to 1572, and so arguably the oldest of the world's anthems:

William of Nassau,
Of a Dutch and ancient line,
I dedicate undying
Faith to this land of mine.
A prince I am, undaunted,
Of Orange, ever free,
To the king of Spain I've granted
A lifelong loyalty.

(Xing Hang, 455)

Without some historical background, no one would be able to make sense of these words; the same might be said of Portugal's and a number of other anthems. This need for an induction into the story of the anthem points to an important characteristic function of official national songs: that the learning of them (and what they are about) serves as an initiation for the child into the national culture. The Dutch child who understands how the lyrics of 'William of Nassau' represent him/her has become party to a secret few other-than-Dutch people will understand. In the manner of secrets, anthems exclude as they include, show one face to citizens and another to the world. Against the grain, perhaps, there are also cosmopolitan anthems, as for instance in Europe's use of 'Ode to Joy' (Beethoven's music suggesting Schiller's words, even if the words are not there), Slovenia's 'A Toast', and of course 'The Internationale' (all texts with which I will deal in Chapter 6).

In a spirit of conciliation, there are those anthems that, like Grenada's, could be anyone's, or, conversely, could have come from anywhere. The first stanza of 'Hail the Name of Ghana', written by a government committee in 1957, has most of the bases covered. One can imagine key points of agreed ethos being ticked off, line by line, as the verses were composed.

God bless our homeland Ghana,
And make our nation great and strong,

Bold to defend for ever
The cause of freedom and of right;
Fill our hearts with true humility.
Make us cherish fearless honesty,
And help us to resist oppressors' rule
With all our will and might for evermore.
(repeat previous two lines)
Hail to thy name, O Ghana,
To thee we make our solemn vow:
Steadfast to build together.

(Bristow, 229)

'God Save the King/Queen' is the paradigm of the portable hymn, in this case – the monarchist devotional hymn. The spirit of pan-Slavism gave the second Yugoslavia (Tito's) an anthem composed by a Slovakian, to the tune of a Polish march. Pan-Africanism is evident in many African anthems (for instance, those of Mali and Mozambique). And the original Bolivarism has provided Paraguay (among others) with an anthem almost any Latin American nation might find serviceable.

For three centuries a reign oppressed
The unhappy peoples of America,
But one day, their anger aroused, they said:
'An end to this!' and broke the reign.
Our forefathers, fighting magnificently,
Displayed their immortal glory.
And when the august diadem was shattered,
They raised the triumphal cap of liberty

(Bristow, 434)

Anderson's first paradox (modern nations' claims to antique authority) is well represented in anthems worldwide. We have already seen Greece's example; Bulgaria and Egypt would be other obvious ones. Many anthems make hyperbolic claims. In Peru's: 'And let the sun rather deny its light / Than that we should fail the solemn vow / Which our country raised to God' (Bristow, 439). Typical of the hyperbole we find in national anthems is the claim that logically could be true of one country but cannot be true of all, as in Lesotho's 'land of our fathers, you are the most beautiful country of all' (Bristow, 325).

There is much self-description in anthems – telling ourselves who to be. This is especially prevalent in postcolonial anthems. The citizens of Congo are an ardent people (Bristow, 149); those of Costa Rica are simple farmhands, but valiant and virile (Bristow, 158). And there are particularising, as well as universalising, anthems; so, for instance, Brazil's anthem pays attention to the size of the country, Russia's likewise to extent (from southern seas to the North Pole), China's to the size of the population. Cambodians sing of temples in forests. And in the second (English-language) stanza of 'O Canada', we read: 'Where pines and maples grow, Great prairies spread and lordly rivers flow' (Bristow, 116). As in the case of Canada's 'true north', Swedish and Norwegian anthems give emphasis to northern-ness as a national characteristic. Anthems may typically draw attention away from the ethical dilemmas of nation-making, but there are some strongly reflexive texts among the world's anthems. Consider Moldova's 'Our Tongue', a lyric that unites nation and language as the one cause: 'Our tongue is made of songs', 'Our tongue is more than holy', 'Resurrect now this our language, / Rusted through the years that have passed' (Bristow, 375).

There are oddities among the lyrics of the world's anthems. Consider for instance the pledge of Ecuadorans, who 'greet the homeland a thousand times', thus demonstrating a friendly commitment to their compatriots. Consider the near-inscrutable last lines of the Mauritanian anthem: 'And just in case a disputant calls you to dispute about their claims, / Do not then, dispute on them, except by way of an external dispute' (Bristow, 364). But perhaps we might gloss this as: 'avoid internal dissension'? Many anthems carry in their lyrics poignant ironies that the good national subject will not notice. The disappearing island nation of Nauru (hollowed long since by phosphate sales, and now threatened by rising sea levels and refugees who had hoped to settle in Australia) provides a nice example: 'Nauru forevermore', the citizens console each other in their anthem (Bristow, 394).

Aberrations aside, from the popular thematics outlined above we can make some generalisations about the function of national anthems on the world scale. At its simplest, most innocent, an anthem is a poem of love of place; more specifically it is the love of a place shared by people who, though mainly unknown to each other, are members of the one polity. They imagine the different scenes that comprise the territory within the borders of the nation as a unified ethnoscape. The national scene may be conspicuous for the variety it offers, as in the case of Russia:

> From the southern seas to the polar region
> Spread our forests and fields.
> You are unique in the world, inimitable,
> Native land protected by God!
>
> (Xing Hang, 530)

What is important for national purposes is that – as in the case of Woody Guthrie's 'This Land is Your Land's' 'From the redwood forests to the Gulf Stream waters', the discontinuities of landscape should be unique to the nation in question. There are grand claims of borders within which everything worthy of admiration is contained. Often there is boasting involved, claims are naturally competitive, as one would expect of songs played for competing teams.

At their most sinister, anthems administer the anaesthesia that allows dark deeds to be forgotten and, in some cases, committed afresh. As we have seen, the lyrics of anthems are dual in nature in several senses. These texts are written and spoken, official and popular (rote and yet spontaneously available), they aspire to both high and low audiences (they are arranged orchestrally, but you are encouraged to sing along); they are inward and outward looking (letting us know who we are, presenting a face to the world); perhaps most importantly, they have a conscious and an unconscious aspect – they invoke memory but, to function, they require a certain amount of forgetting. The study of anthems likewise suggests the utility of a dualistic approach. Ferdinand de Saussure's dichotomies are of immediate use. In terms of meaning, anthems have arbitrary and motivated aspects: they perform functions for historical reasons but they come, with acceptance, to behave as conventional signs. The official/popular duality suggests the plausibility of considering anthems as both *langue* and *parole:* canonic texts sanctified in fixed form, the spontaneous speech-in-common of a populace. Bakhtin's dichotomies are also serviceable in the study of anthems: for instance between the official and unofficial, epic and novelistic, monologic and dialogic. Anthems may not be generically epic; however, they cast the origins of a state in an epic, as opposed to a novelistic, light. Unison is a monologic act of course, but that anthems are monologic, rather than dialogic or polyphonic as texts, is illustrated neatly by comparison with the song 'America' in Bernstein and Sondheim's (1957) *West Side Story*. Theirs is an argument-in-song that, line by line, celebrates and denigrates two places and identities (arguably national) – those of the mainland United States and Puerto Rico. Rosalia sings:

> Puerto Rico,
> You lovely island …
> Island of tropical breezes.
> Always the pineapples growing,
> Always the coffee blossoms blowing. …

Anita responds:

> Puerto Rico …
> You ugly island …
> Island of tropic diseases.
> Always the hurricanes blowing,
> Always the population growing …
> And the money owing,
> And the babies crying,
> And the bullets flying.
> I like the island Manhattan.
> Smoke on your pipe and put that in!

What relationship is there between the official and the spontaneous in anthems and at the events where anthems are enacted? Official status is what, perhaps ironically, makes an anthem the poem of the people. An anthem is the people's poem because it has the sanction of the state. But the nation, we will remember, in Renan's scheme of things, continues to exist only as a result of an unrecorded everyday agreement; the nation continues, that is to say, because at however banal a level, its imagined community goes on being believed in. Saussure's synchronic/diachronic dichotomy is pertinent here. It is tempting to see anthems purely as synchronic ornaments of nation. With the interesting sometime-exception of an Afghanistan (under the Taliban music was forbidden so there could be no anthem), all nations have them; they each should have one only. Historically though, the choice of an anthem (as considered in Chapter 5) is often the result of long (and sometimes bitter) struggle, telling us much about forces contending for both national hegemony and national identifications-in-common. So it is the process of arriving at anthems and the sense in which current anthems may be regarded as unstable that tells us most about the nature of the unisonance presented at a particular time by a particular anthem. To view anthems simply in the synchronic sense of being a unique universal attribute of nation is to fail to engage the contradiction resolved in Anderson's first paradox. Nations justify their existence through appeal to authority; that authority is essentially ancestral. Duties to nation are, like religious duties, analogous to filial obligations. The obedience and sacrifice nations demand of us are akin to those that parents may have traditionally demanded on the strength of a claim that children owe their existence to them. The native in her native land may as easily contend with her citizenship: 'I never asked to be born here'. This kind of retort, which might bring Renan's plebiscite to consciousness, is very seldom uttered, except by those anathema of nation, the refugees, now numbering some fifteen million worldwide (according to the UNHCR).

On the Deadliness of Nations

In *Imagined Communities* Anderson writes of the *unisonance* of strangers in the anthem, as sung experience of simultaneity:

> Take national anthems, for example, sung on national holidays. No matter how banal the words and mediocre the tunes, there is in the singing an experience of simultaneity. At precisely such moments people wholly unknown to each other utter the same verses to the same melody. The image: unisonance. Singing the Marseillaise, Waltzing Matilda, and Indonesia Raya provide occasions for unisonality, for the echoed physical realization of the imagined community.
>
> (145)

Musical communion of the religious, national or any other kind involves a necessarily abstract imaginative connection between the communing participants. This applies equally in the passive experience of a concert as in the active experience of the choir. Clearly in the latter case the embodiment of the musical sentiment is personalised, individuated through the bodying forth of the singer and thus probably intensified for that individual. There is a daunting responsibility in being among the chosen who are to deliver the song. It is a responsibility to an audience, but perhaps more importantly to one's colleagues in unison. This is as true of plainsong or the chanting of 'aum' in the meditation class as it is of a choir. The bigger the chorus the smaller – the less important – this one voice: the voice of the individual. The greater the unisonance joined, the less the individual's responsibility for that unisonance; the greater the feeling of communion, the less feeling there is of being an individual.

Anthems are in this sense an expression of the principle 'safety in numbers'. Anderson continues: 'How selfless this unisonance feels! If we are aware that others are singing these songs precisely when and as we are, we have no idea who they may be, or even where, out of earshot, they are singing. Nothing connects us but imagined sound' (145).

Singing anthems with compatriots one avows a disinvestment in the personal. One sings for the greater – and not merely for one's own – good. Anthem singing is in this sense self-absolving. It provides the individual singing with a pseudo-religious moment of purity, a moment in which his or her motivations are notionally subsumed in those of a higher collectivity, one for which blood sacrifice would be exemplary. The individual's moment *in* the anthem is humbling *in that* it allows him or her meditative pause to consider the sacrifice made by others on her behalf.

There is safety in numbers and there is safety on the level playing field. Some sing more sweetly than others, some more loudly, but unisonance is a leveller. In unison, one's voice is a part of a greater whole. There is an ideal average voice in the embodiment of anthems. It is the voice of the state's ideal soldier/servant, that *sine qua non* who does his/her duty by drawing no attention his/her way. Anthems, in this fashion, suit equally well a democratic or a subservient temperament or, as in the case of 'God Save the King/Queen', the feeling that there is a level on which an entire citizenry can be loyal *as a man* to the monarch metonymically serving their collective interest. In the singing of an anthem individuality is subsumed in notional equality of the religious sort. Christian, Muslim, Buddhist: all these religionists are sinners, all have to be saved. Equality of humans in the face of the divine is borrowed from the realm of the sacred for the purpose of sanctifying the profane. Note that in this process a cosmopolitan equality – one that would for instance combat racism – is borrowed for more parochial purposes, purposes that might for instance promote racism. The difference Anderson points out between religious and national devotion, in his essay 'The Goodness of Nations', is that while one might declare one's national adherence in a formula such as, 'My country, right or wrong', for the adherents of a religion, their faith 'could not conceivably be wrong' (196). This observation is enough to show, I think, that national devotion is a faith borrowed from another sphere.

***

How seriously should anthem business be taken? Let us return briefly to the commonly occurring theme of death in national anthems. Death is frequently enjoined as a desirable outcome for citizens in the circle of abstractions anthems sanctify. Consider these lyrics in Haiti's anthem:

> For flag on high, for Native land
> 'Tis fine to die, 'tis fine to die.
> Our traditions demand
> Be ready, heart and hand,
> 'Tis fine to die, 'tis fine to die
> For flag on high, for native land.
>
> (Bristow, 254)

Haiti's is one of numerous examples extolling the virtue being *pro patria mori*. People do not die in the name of car accidents or cancer; they do die for human rights and to save the environment and – along these lines – more people die in the name of nation today than for any other 'cause'. This goes unnoticed perhaps because it has been going on for so long. Nation has, in this sense, replaced empire and religion as the world's deadliest belief-inspiring abstraction. Communities of co-religionists under God-appointed rulers have been superseded by nations (democratic or otherwise) along republican (or constitutional monarchic) lines. For the purposes of ritual unison, the anthem that was a co-religionist's song of praise for God has been replaced by the compatriot's song of praise for the state to which s/he is devoted. When did the change take place? Will and Ariel Durant write, in the seventh volume of their *Story of Civilization, The Age of Reason Begins* (dealing with the period 1550–1650) that in this period the basic developments were 'the rise of murderous nationalisms and the decline of murderous theologies' (2). The religious tone of the national sacrifice expected is clearly demonstrated in texts like the Bolivian National Anthem, 'Canción Patriotica':

> We have kept the lofty name of our country
> In glorious splendor.
> And on its altars we once more swear
> To die rather than live as slaves.
>
> (Xing Hang, 73)

The British national anthem, 'God Save the King/Queen' demonstrates the link between two forms of mass devotion; here the hymn, addressed to God, purports to be for the benefit of the monarch who rules by a putative divine right (one that, as we will see, if asserted by the refrain, is undermined by the stanzas of the song). 'The Marseillaise', as mentioned, is the deadliest, the bloodiest of the well-known anthems. I will deal with both of these songs in the next chapter.

As one would expect with religion, there is a deal of piety and a pile of faggots ready to light for the blasphemer. It is for this reason that much of what purports to be serious scholarship or objective reportage on the subject of anthems turns out to be something we might better describe as fan literature (a literature, one should add, of great interest for the student of anthems, and constituting an object of study in its own right). Take for example Xing Hang's account of North Korea's anthem in his *Encyclopedia of National Anthems*:

> The Democratic People's Republic of Korea (DPRK) has all along used the 'Patriotic Song', its national anthem, which was created in Juche 36 (1947), for half a century. The song is the symbol of solemnity, noble feelings, national pride, and honor. It is a source of the patriotism and optimistic emotion of the Korean people. The song was created thanks to the Great Leader Comrade Kim Il Sung. Just after Korea's liberation from the Japanese colonial rule he gave creators a direction for the creation of the national anthem and gave concrete guidance as regards the conception of words, content, appearance, and depiction of the song. The song written by Pak Se Yong and composed by Kim Won Gyun under his guidance reflected the ideas and emotions of the people of a new Korea. The song that was played on the day when the DPRK was founded with due ceremony on 9 September 1948 has served as the national anthem of socialist Korea for 50 years. The Koreans like to sing the song very much. In Korea where the song is sung as the first item of the radio program at dawn the leader, the party, the army and the people move as one in response to the song. The Korean people are working hard to exalt the dignity and honor of the country and build a prosperous country, singing the song. The great achievements and praiseworthy deeds that can be witnessed in their everyday life are based on the idea of the song. In Korea, led by the Dear Leader Comrade Kim Jong Il, who is attaching importance to the Juche character and the national character, the song will remain the eternal national anthem of Kim Il Sung's Korea.
>
> (339–340)

This is surely a case of 'send the press release – we will print it as ours!' There is nothing at all bellicose in the lyrics of North Korea's anthem:

> Let morning shine on the silver and gold of this land.
> Three thousand leagues packed with natural wealth
> My beautiful fatherland.
> The glory of a wise people
> Brought up in a culture brilliant
> With a history five millennia long.
> Let us devote our bodies and minds
> To supporting this Korea forever.
>
> (Xing Hang, 340)

The music might be described as slow, simple, majestic. The illustration should serve to show that, for all the mundane fitting-the-series quality of this hymn, its accompanying propaganda and the state it sanctifies ('this' Korea) are parts of a package justifying the existence and actions of a nation state, and this symbolic package has real meaning and real consequences for the citizens and neighbours of North Korea.

Are anthems then part of the solution or part of the problem? When one considers, in the study of anthems, what is hyperbolic and what is hidden of national culture and memory, one is left with the kind of question one might well ask of the role of sport in national life – do these phenomena foster a spirit of violent confrontation or are they a sublimation of that kind of spirit, even an inoculation against it?

Singing to Say Who We Are

Anthems – as acts of unison – amount to *singing to say who we are*, and this saying who we are is normatively national. Anthems are hopefully heartfelt; that is to say they *work* if they generate (or reflect) national sentiment, strong feeling for one's country. The fact that singing to say who we are is today focussed on nation indicates that nation, however problematic or unconvincing it may be for certain people at certain times, remains the core identity-forming abstraction sung in the world today. In the twenty-first century, multinational capital and empire (in several senses) may be seen as the emergent dominating forces that determine the identification of persons worldwide. Following the work of Castells and others, identity in the twenty-first century may be thought of in terms of a multi-dimensional simultaneity of networked belongings and obligations. Among these, national identification, made official in a national anthem, may feel a little nineteenth century, and in fact it is a link for the individual in a chain that anchors belonging to the era when the assertion of an identity as national (rather than imperial or religious) was an assertion of modernity and of humanity. It is because of this stabilising virtue, and harking after of an ideal embodying progress and at least suggesting democracy, participation in national anthems remains by far the most plausible means of singing a collective identity in the world today. Corporate jingles aspiring to that kind of affect-making feel like pale imitations to most listeners, who, if they catch themselves joining in, may well feel that they have been tricked. The (US) Kraft corporation boasts on its website that the 'Vegemite song' is Australia's 'second unofficial' national anthem (2011). The lyrics of the 'Vegemite song' (for those who do not know) are as follows[15]:

> We're happy little Vegemites
> As bright as bright can be.
> We all enjoy our Vegemite
> For breakfast, lunch, and tea.
> Our mummies say we're growing stronger
> Every single week,
> Because we love our Vegemite

We all adore our Vegemite
It puts a rose in every cheek.

It may be true that more Australians know these lyrics than those of 'Advance Australia Fair', and certainly Vegemite television advertising from the fifties was interested in reciprocally inculcating citizenship and national values through the building of product loyalty. If that song stirs what we can call 'national sentiment' then this is something I would attribute to the self-parodic nature of Australian self-conception. Australians will generally remind each other that it has been a long time (1935) since Vegemite was Australian owned. If singing the Vegemite song gives adult Australians patriotic feelings then these are of an ironic nature, suggesting, while still indulging, cynicism about the nature of national identification. Worldwide though, few allow themselves to feel that they have been tricked into feeling the kinds of national goosebumps their own anthem produces. The anthems of other nations, however attractive, however identified with their interests we may be, seem nevertheless alien. Anthems and flags, one might hypothesise, are in this sense key symbolic means of promoting illusions of sovereignty among those who are dominated by foreign powers or alliances.

My tentative hypothesis is that national anthems have such a power of identification over citizens because of their homogenising dynamic; in an age where lives are shaped by evermore many and varied identity-forming forces, national identification is a means of dispelling conflicting tugs on the heartstrings. Rich and poor, old and young, left and right, despite it all, we are … (fill in the blank). Today, what stirs the soul most in the way of song is national identification or its more tribal analogies, such as the following of a football team or a recognition of oneself as belonging to a proud minority. This train of thought suggests we should possibly ask whether nation is the deadly abstraction here, or is the culprit rather the fervour for an including/excluding identity-in-common, such as anthem singing promotes? As suggested just above, we can equally argue that this same sentiment employed for peaceful, for instance sporting, purposes, makes the world a more peaceful place.

Without wishing to psychologise the unisonant, reading Oliver Sacks' *Musicophilia* one is struck time and again how the individual (music- and speech-related) pathology aptly describes a general societal condition we would not typically think of in terms of disease. Sacks, for instance, records musical hallucinations involving, what I would describe as, music of anthem quality (87, 91), leading one to wonder whether anthems might be considered in the light of mass musical hallucinations, hallucinations of whom or what the subjects singing assume themselves to be.[16] Music, in the canonic/popular (if not anthemic) mode, is, in particular in cases of dementia, able to rouse emotion in patients otherwise catatonic, is able to evoke a sense of self that seems otherwise lost (385). Why do nations, and why do humans more generally, need something like anthems? Sacks writes, rhythm (in the musical sense) 'binds together the individual nervous systems of a human community' (269).

All needs are exploitable, and in the case of anthems, we see that music, affect and identity are able to be exploited for the purpose of fostering identifications-in-common of national subjects. Corporate tunes and lyrics seem frivolous and lack the self-important solemnity of the anthem. Does the seriousness of an anthem come from being official; or do anthems become official because they are the most serious contenders for the post? What can be said for certain is that there is plenty of anthem quality in unofficial texts worldwide and that there are many official anthems that are unconvincing because they lack what most of the world's citizens would consider anthem quality. Anthems may be the official poems of a people, but official sanction is not sufficient to persuade a people that a song (or any other symbol) is truly theirs. In this light one might argue that anthems are, of their nature, a force for democracy: a people has to be convinced that these are the words and this is the tune for them. It would be nice to think that anthems provided some such guarantee of well-meaning sincerity, but many examples show that peoples are unconvinced or insincere and/or that they are manipulable by the right kinds of persuasion.

Anthems, as we have seen, are, despite their common features and homogenising effects, yet varied in the specificity of sentiment deployed and in the nature of identification produced and reproduced in particular national contexts. Beyond the question of definition, we need then to consider how anthems function and what functions they fulfil. In order to do this it might be helpful if we were able to classify them; this is a task I undertake in the next chapter, with close reference to a small group of well-known anthems.

Notes

1. One notes that in situations where no one anthem has official sanction, there may effectively be several *de facto* anthems. The most famous instance of this is in the case of the United States prior to the legislating of sole anthem status for 'The Star Spangled Banner'.
2. Brave, if tentative, attempts have been made to understand the nexus, for instance in the recent quantitative work of Nichols et al., in a 2009 paper, 'Relationships between Lyrics and Melody in Popular Music'. Efforts have been made to understand the relationship between musical and linguistic processing of song text by listeners, but the jury would appear to be out on the question of whether the processing of music and lyrics happens concertedly or independently in different parts of the brain (Schön et al., 2005; Sammler et al., 2010).
3. An early example is given in Mark Twain's 1876 story, 'A Literary Nightmare', in which a narrator, and his clergyman acquaintance, and that gentleman's entire flock, are infected with some 'jingling rhymes' that they cannot get out of their heads (*The Queenslander*).
4. Another anthem with this name is the Esperantist's hymn, 'La Espero'.
5. Kazakhstan, Russia and the Philippines are notable examples of nations with legislated protocols for observance in the case of anthem performances.
6. These are, in some cases, carefully spelled out. Take the first stanza of Cambodia's national anthem, for example:

   Heaven protects our king
   And gives him happiness and glory
   To reign over our souls and our destinies

The one being, heir of the sovereign builders
Guiding the proud old kingdom

(Bristow, 109)

7. Not that Henry VIII invented a self-sanctifying state–church nexus. There is a long history of state and religion intertwining. Consider the Athenian worship of Athena: god of the place but also a generally available god, of great potency, and whom one would be well advised to have on one's team. Roger Scruton speculates that though 'it is doubtful that there was such a thing as a national anthem before the eighteenth century … maybe the Spartans had such a thing, since they were in the habit of assembling to sing the patriotic ode of Tyrtaeus before going into battle' (2009, 111).
8. In the original, French text:

Centre la ferule humiliante il y a deja mille ans.
La rapacite venue de loin les asservir il y a cent ans.
Centre la cynique malice metamorphosee
En neocolonialisme et ses petits servants locaux
Beaucoup flancherent et certains resisterent
Mais les echecs, les succes, la sueur, le sang
Ont fortifie notre peuple courageux
Et fertilise sa lutte heroique.

(Bristow, 101)

9. 'Soul' (either of the nation or of the individual citizen or both) features in the anthems of Azerbaijan, Belgium, Burkina Faso, Cambodia, Republic of China, Congo, Denmark, Dominica, Guatemala, Haiti, Iran, Israel, Kuwait, Moldova, Niger, Philippines, St Lucia, Sao Tome and Principe, Ukraine, Uruguay.
10. 'God' is in the anthems of Antigua and Barbuda, Bahamas, Belize, Botswana, Brunei, Burundi, Canada, Chad, Comoros, Croatia, Dominica, Ecuador, Estonia, Fiji, Gambia, Ghana, Grenada, Guyana, Haiti, Hungary, Iceland, Italy, Kenya, Kiribati, South Korea, Latvia, Lesotho, Liberia, Libya, Lichtenstein, Madagascar, Malawi, Marshall Islands, Mauritius, Mexico, Morocco, Holland, New Zealand, United Kingdom, Nigeria, Norway, Papua New Guinea, Peru, Russia, St Kitts and Nevis, St Vincent and the Grenadines, Samoa, Saudi Arabia, Seychelles, Slovenia, Solomon Islands, Sudan, Switzerland, Tanzania, Togo, Tonga, Trinidad and Tobago, Turkey, Tuvalu, Uganda, the United States, Vanuatu, Vatican City, Zambia, Zimbabwe. Nations, by and large, are not atheist, at least in their efforts at symbolic legitimisation.
11. 'Blood' gets a mention in the anthems of Algeria, Azerbaijan, Belgium, Belize, Benin, Burkina Faso, Cameroon, China, Colombia, Comoros, Denmark, Djibouti, Ecuador, El Salvador, Finland, France, Guinea-Bissau, Hungary, Italy, Mexico, Morocco, Namibia, Nicaragua, Niger, Palestine, Thailand, Tunis, Turkey, the United States, Vietnam. In one version of Ferenc Kolcsey's lyrics for Hungary's anthem, we find a sea of blood beneath a sea of flame (Xing Hang, 285). In Mexico's anthem we meet waves of blood (Xing Hang, 418).

12. 'Death' appears in the anthems of Armenia, Brazil, Burkina Faso, Cuba, Denmark, Dominican Republic, Estonia, Guatemala, Honduras, Romania, Paraguay, Senegal, Sudan, Surinam, Togo, Tunisia. The verb 'to die' is found in the anthems of Algeria, Angola, Argentina, Armenia, Bolivia, Colombia, Congo, Cuba, Guatemala, Guinea, Haiti, Honduras, Italy, Mali, Monaco, Philippines, Romania, Tunis, Turkey, Uruguay, Uzbekistan. The 'grave' appears in the anthems of the United States, Cyprus, Denmark, Greece; the 'tomb' in the anthems of Uruguay, Chile, Hungary and Mexico.
13. 'Heart' is in the anthems of Australia, Azerbaijan, Bangladesh, Barbados, Belgium, Brazil, Burkina Faso, Burundi, Canada, China, Republic of China, Congo, Croatia, Denmark, Dominica, Egypt, Gabon, Germany, Ghana, Grenada, Guatemala, Haiti, India, Israel, Italy, Kenya, Kiribati, South Korea, Kyrgystan, Laos, Lebanon, Liberia, Lithuania, Luxembourg, Madagascar, Malawi, Morocco, New Zealand, Niger, Nigeria, Philippines, Qatar, Romania, St Vincent and the Grenadines, Sao Tome and Principe, Senegal, Sierra Leone, Togo, Turkey, Uzbekistan, United Kingdom, Yemen.
14. In English the complete lyrics are as follows:

    Lord, bless Africa,
    May her spirit rise high up.
    Hear thou our prayers,
    Lord bless us, your family.

    Descend, O Spirit,
    Save our nation.
    End all wars and strife,
    Bless South Africa, South Africa.

    Ringing out from our blue heavens,
    From our deep seas breaking round;
    Over everlasting mountains
    Where the echoing crags resound.

    Sounds the call to come together,
    And united we shall stand.
    Let us live and strive for freedom
    In South Africa our land!

    (Xing Hang, 580)

15. I offer no attribution here because I have written them from memory.
16. 'The vast majority of musical hallucinations take the form of popular songs or theme music (and, in an earlier generation, hymns and patriotic songs), even in professional musicians or very sophisticated listeners' (87).

Chapter 3

The Classification of Anthems

genre and speech act

And say, 'The thing I hum appears to be
The rhythm of this celestial pantomime.'

(Wallace Stevens, 243)

As part of the *sine qua non* of nationhood, anthem participates in a self-justifying circular logic: nations have anthems because they are nations. Anthem, arms, flag, constitution: these are all aspects of the easily attained equal footing on which *inter*national events depend. Each of these signs of nation participates in codes of imaginary devices that, if fanciful, are not to be taken less seriously for that. Unicorns are par for the course. Origins and meanings are allowed to be obscure. Origins may also be apocryphal and even invented on the basis of some grain of past truth (as in Hobsbawn and Ranger's *The Invention of Tradition*, 1–15 *passim*). The apparent level-playing field for symbolism (all nations have flags, anthems, votes in international fora) however belies the real – if unpalatable – power relations in the world. A moment's reflection on the reality of those power relations (and the idea of sovereignty) suggests that national symbolism distorts the truth of global relationships. To recognise the associative chains in which these symbols are enjoined is to recognise the largely arbitrary and tautological nature of national identification. There is a playing field on which the nations of the world cooperate or are pitted against each other. The one vote per country set-up of the United Nations General Assembly does not provide us with an accurate picture of that field. On the other hand, were General Assembly votes weighted for national potency (however measured), the field would be much less level. However unrealistic a worldview it betrays, the idea of a level-playing field looms large in the *national* rhetoric of *inter*national affairs today, particularly as related to such issues as 'free' trade or 'universal' human rights. What is at stake here is the appeal to legitimacy, which Franz Fanon made a theme in grounding the idea of nation in his 1961 work, *The Wretched of the Earth*.

The signs of nation participate in a dynamic nexus between, on the one hand, official and unofficial culture and on the other hand, between real and imaginary schemata of power and identity. Awareness of a worldwide reluctance to consider the tautological nature of identity-in-common throws such schemata and the culture of nation usefully into question.

In this chapter I consider the classification of anthems from the points of view of speech act and genre. As examples of genre I discuss three of the world's great Ur-anthems: 'God Save the King/Queen', 'The Marseillaise' and 'The Star Spangled Banner'.

I do not write with any convinced belief that generic classification will be an essential means of understanding anthems and their relationship to each other. It merely seems that there are different kinds of song that serve the function of national anthem and so some kind of classification will be a helpful starting point. The classifications I use in this chapter have already been suggested, in outline, in the last chapter (march, prayer, tableau, opera, fanfare). They are musical in origin, conventional in nature and based on some perhaps unargued assumptions about relationships between lyric sub-genres and musical forms. I would like from the outset to undermine the impression of any recounted (or proposed) orthodoxy by offering some other possible lines of classification prior to, for the sake of convenience, setting up a provisional classification system. And I begin with this caveat: It is plausible that any sustained attempt to systematically file all of the world's anthems (words and music) would fail, simply because in so many cases, words or music or both are confused as to genre or because the two are ill matched. One can imagine an international conference or a number of journals devoted precisely to testing the question of genre in anthems. It would be fun to see how many sets of lyrics and musical scores could be arbitrarily swapped among the world's anthems. Perhaps though that ironic distancing of the subject at hand is not something we would wish to see imposed on our own anthems? It would be a fiery meeting of participant observers; the parties attending would likely have serious battles of judgement with themselves and each other, not simply because of unavoidable national pride, but because of the canonising virtue of what had been long since dinned into their separate skulls. One can assert as much objective distance from the text as one likes, it is difficult to see things long since official as not fitting. Still, if a doubt as to the fit of words and scores were somehow sustained then I would suggest the advisability of attempting a generic classification of lyrics, and of music, separately. Where would one look to classify lyrics in such a case? Matching rhetoric with political systems (nation type) would be one way to go. A number of suggested schemata of nationalism theorists could be helpful for this purpose, for instance Hobsbawm and Trevor-Roper's distinctions between what Smith summarises as civic (political and democratic) nationalism of the 1830–1870 period as opposed to the later empire-disintegrative secondary nationalisms, with ethnic, linguistic and cultural bases, that dominated the period from the Franco-Prussian till the Great War (Smith, 1999, 204). Adoption of these latter kinds of rhetoric would be reflected in the official anthem texts of post-Versailles, post-Trianon Europe. To these we would add the more recent postcolonial texts of the type, which though typically based on earlier models, emerge in the decolonising post-1945 world. Various dyadic means of classification may be of use in arranging the world's anthems: forward-looking as opposed to nostalgic, inward- or outward-focussed, songs of liberation as opposed to songs expressing loyalty to a tradition – e.g. 'God Save the King/Queen' versus 'The Star Spangled Banner'. Another useful schema might be the one Smith developed to account for the components of national myths: myths of location and migration, of ancestry, of heroic ages, of decay and of renewal (1999, 62–67). Or again, we might turn to three types of identity: legitimising identity, resistance identity and project identity, which Manuel Castells has outlined in *The Power of Identity* (5–12).

Given the fatalistic obsession of many anthems, it might be useful to look at them in terms of the tragic/comic divide. Joseph Meeker's 1972 book *The Comedy of Survival: Studies in Literary Ecology* casts an interesting light on this most fundamental of genre contrasts. Tragedy for Meeker is based on the 'now absurd assumption' that 'the universe cares about the lives of human beings'; this Meeker sets against 'the comic imperative of preserving life' (167). Meeker observes that the tragic view of man has rarely been achieved, whereas comedy is nearly universal. Comedy grows from the biological circumstances of life and has no room for the moralism that dominates tragic modes of action (157–158). For Meeker, 'warfare is the basic metaphor of tragedy [...] Comic strategy, on the other hand, sees life as a game' (168). One might wish to claim on this reading that anthems are normatively comic texts, or lyrics with comic intent, because they are declarations of an intention to survive. Comedy's triumphs are quiet ones, the pyrrhic-equivalent perhaps, of the defeats of those who have survived, for instance, beyond the war they had talked (or sung) themselves into believing in. True, anthems are texts that, death-and-sacrifice obsessed as they are, take themselves rather seriously. The tragic view of man may have rarely been achieved but, in the lyrics of many anthems, the unknown soldier or national everyman is idealised in terms of ultimate sacrifice. Tragedy's magnificence is with all embracing death, that unequivocal resolution in everyone's democracy. But, firing-squad legends aside, those who sing anthems, along with their nation, tend to survive the singing. Anthems are frequently mocked and derided and/or parodied (even by avowed patriots) simply because it is difficult to maintain the tragic outlook for long. The tragic view of life is not merely dour, moralising; the longer it is presented, the less convincing it becomes. It is difficult to maintain tragic outlook in a song that has to be staged again and again by the singers who are the listeners and who, in these acts of performance, continually prove their survival. The text may be tragic, moralistic, fixed and proper; its performance context is however fluid, fidgety, distracted by what precedes or is to follow – the carnival moments of sport or victory or a few commemorative drinks. On the comedy/tragedy divide then, we may say that anthems express a powerful ambivalence, one that perhaps reflects more broadly-based doubts as to the entailments of national identities and national consciousness.

These are merely some first suggestions for an investigation that is beyond the scope of this current work. The assumptions as to genre with which I shall proceed here are, accordingly, perhaps more convenient than provisional.

One assumption I will defend to commence is that all texts – all acts of communication – serve functions (even if that function is, in an extreme example, to prove that art is functionless). Function and meaning are interestingly related; one gets to the nub of that relationship by asking a simple question – how does a text mean what it means? In the case of literary texts (a rubric anthem lyrics loosely fit) one would be wise not to attribute their function to any simple or unified intention. In her essay, 'Sociopolitical Control and the Structure of National Symbols: An Empirical Analysis of National Anthems', Karen Cerulo tells us that 'the function of national anthems is highly similar across nations. Ruling bodies use them as a tool for creating bonds and reinforcing goals among their citizens' (78). In general terms, we might accept Roger Scruton's idea that an anthem is a text that allows a population 'to rehearse its obedience and collective will to endure' (2009, 111).

Anthems perform a range of functions in the national interest, some of which are suggested by the topics and themes outlined in the last chapter. To focus directly on the idea, we can for instance say that an anthem like that of Azerbaijan has the function of self-blessing.

> May you become a flourishing garden
> We are ready to give our heart and soul for you.
> A thousand and one endearments are in my heart.
> To raise your banner
> And protect your honor
> All the youth are eager.
> Cherished land. Cherished land.
> Azerbaijan! Azerbaijan!
>
> (Xing Hang, 36)

Belgium's anthem, 'La Brabançonne' seems, from its lyrics, an act of desperate assertion:

> We swear with one cry – You will live!
> You will live! [...]
> And your invincible unity
> Will have as your immortal emblem –
> For King, Justice and Liberty
>
> (Bristow, 65)

'La Brabançonne' insists on the idea of 'unbreakable unity'. In a polity divided between French and Flemish populations, one can say the function of this anthem is to assert the coherence of the nation.

Portugal's anthem works hard to remind the citizen that there is a past (of world conquest) of which to be proud. As we saw in the cases of Burkina Faso and Paraguay, many postcolonial anthems insist on a seminal struggle against colonial domination and injustice, many picture for the unisonant the originary moment of nation as the event in which the people are liberated from the foreign (usually European) oppressor. In each case the anthem works to make citizens understand their situation in terms of a particular reading of the past.

The functionality of anthems is something observed not merely through legal or constitutional sanction, but through use in the daily life of a people. Unison exists in real time in instances such as singing before or after a sporting event, singing when we remember the dead, singing to mark a national occasion. The act of singing an anthem entails a circularity of address to selves and others: we welcome ourselves to the participatory event in which we understand or assume we are as the others are who sing what we sing, mean what we mean in so singing. *We* are singing *together*. So singing the anthem with others is a kind of agreeing with them, the kind that never need be stated as such. Singing the anthem – our anthem – with the others, we know we are as they are, and (concomitantly) we know we are not as others who do not sing (for instance those who lack the membership qualification that would entitle them to sing). The singing of anthems does not just happen to represent those singing as, for instance, an act of musical taste, rather it constitutes an avowed (if at times automatic) act of self-representation, one for which citizenship qualifications are required. In these senses, we may think of anthems as both a very particular genre of lyric and as a particular speech act.

***

As we have noted above, there are many angles from which the question of genre might be considered in the case of anthems; for the sake of convenience of classification however, the most obvious discernible categories of anthem would be:

- The marching song, such as 'The Marseillaise'[1]
- The self-congratulatory tableau (picture of the worthy nation), such as 'Advance Australia Fair' or 'The Star Spangled Banner'
- The prayer-song, entreating a deity, such as 'God Save the King/Queen'.

There are many anthems that blur these categories and there are a number of anthem types that will not quite fit into them. In the Middle East, a number of countries have short fanfare-style anthems (e.g. Kuwait, Bahrain), with sparse lyrics (or sometimes none). By contrast, in Latin America we meet the most musically complex and varied of anthems (El Salvador's is the most impressive example), arrangements that might be considered epic or operatic (influenced as they were by Italian opera). In Eastern Europe, there are anthems in which folk elements are discerned through the orchestral arrangement (e.g. Poland, Czech Republic, Croatia). In each of these cases, we can however generally still discern a march, tableau or prayer. For instance, fanfares tend to involve the soul and approach to the deity (Bahrain) and so might be thought of as hymns; the operatic epics in South America (e.g. Brazil, Uruguay) tend to provide tableaux (in the form of a series of historical scenes from the national story); and folk motifs are another means of achieving this effect (e.g. Croatia).

So, for the sake of convenience, we may provisionally say the march, the tableau and the prayer are the dominant sub-genres of anthem. In this chapter I will look, for different purposes in each case, at one example of each, namely 'The Marseillaise', 'The Star Spangled Banner' and 'God Save the King/Queen'. Analysis of the world's best-known anthem, 'God Save the King/Queen', immediately reveals the pitfalls inherent in pigeon-holing anthems in terms of sub-genre. Still, genre and speech-act theory may yet prove helpful in answering two key questions: What does an anthem mean for and about those who sing it, and how does it mean what it means?

Before we look at these particular songs and their generic/rhetorical qualities, let us briefly consider how the study of speech acts casts light on the functioning of national anthems.

Phatic Communion

An anthem – national or otherwise – is *inter alia* a self-welcoming gesture, and it is an identity-focussed instance of unison. It is a kind of *phatic communion*. This kind of communion paradoxically involves forgetting who we are and even forgetting what we are singing. 'Phatic communion' is a term devised by Bronislaw Malinowski, an anthropologist who, in the early twentieth century, studied the speech and customs of the Trobriand Islanders (cf. Jakobson's 'phatic function', as mentioned earlier). 'Phatic communion' refers to communication, the purpose of which is to keep the channel of communication open. For Englishmen this classically entails the discussion of the weather by strangers. Malinowski described this kind of communication as a means by which 'ties of union are created by the mere exchange of words' (in Ogden and Richards, 315). That communication which functions unconsciously to keep a community in communication with itself necessarily invests a common identity in likewise unconscious manner. An earnestness about the weather is, in a certain context of culture, a safe topic, one that allows strangers with something in common (e.g. nationality) to feel that they are on common ground. Phatic communion is a way of agreeing, in words, to be together without having to worry too much about negotiating that kind of meaning. Those in phatic communion, are, we might say, taking each other for granted and likewise hoping to be taken that way. It is the kind of strategy in communication that might unravel should a Gandalf enquire of a Bilbo Baggins just what he means by the expression 'good day'.

Singing our anthem, we switch – from doubt to belief, from dialogue to script, from manual to automatic. When someone says 'good day' to a speaker of the same language community, in general, neither party will be thinking either of the weather (whether or not it is a good day in that sense) nor of the immediate welfare and wellbeing of the partner in dialogue (as in *I really sincerely hope you have a good day by which I mean a day in which your happiness will be conspicuously in your thoughts*); the hope that things are well in these senses is in the expression certainly but it is in there on an automatic (or to be unkind, one might say, rote) basis. In anthems too, as in clichés of all kinds, an original meaning has been worn away by use, as in the famous example employed by both Nietzsche and Mallarmé, of the coin that no longer shows a king's head, but is now merely a token of value.[2] We will see below, for instance, that the worldwide reception of 'The Marseillaise' has little to do with either the content or the originating context of that song.

Agreeing in words how to be together could be a more or less explicit or inexplicit arrangement. If language is the structure ultimately determining how people can be together, then we could think of phatic communion as a particular instance of the ideological phenomenon French Marxist Louis Althusser named 'interpellation' or 'hailing' (174). Althusser's claim was that 'ideological state apparatuses' hail us into particular subject positions. It is not only state-sponsored institutions that adopt such a strategy. For instance a Disney film might hail all in its audience as well-off white people living in America with a love of large soft toys, hamburgers and carbonated high-calorie drinks. That is to say, the Disney text more or less assumes that you are someone like that, and so participating in that text you come to see yourself that way, even if you live hand-to-mouth in a slum or in the third world, making do with toys scavenged from a tip and a scaled-down hamburger, if any. The apparently passive couch potato goes to Walmart to purchase the soft toy s/he has learned to love. Monologic texts, such as books, films and songs on the radio, must make suppositions about their audiences. Marketing research helps their makers to arrive at appropriate assumptions about who the audience is and who these people think they are (or can be persuaded to think they are). Althusser's 'interpellation' helps account for the manner in which the state or like structure weaves a citizenry into a web of belief and self-identification. People do these things to themselves, and the state of which they are citizens does this hailing – reasonable or otherwise – on their behalf. In this sense, interpellation is just the kind of phatic communion a social structure of the order *nation* needs in order to have its citizens recognise themselves as such and form and reproduce an identity-in-common. Perhaps this account amounts to a description of activities needing to be undertaken under the unseen *aegis* of a collective will to endure?

An anthem is phatic communion on the grand scale: a people greets itself by means of words it has remembered well enough to forget to understand: a kind of collective 'rote' memory, in the service of self-hailing. And in this posture, demanding as anthems are of awe and *dignitas*, a people, like a dog at its dinner, does not wish to be disturbed. A people does not want its self-greeting, its self-recognition, to be beset by clever delvers under and over the truth. The Athenians did not appreciate this kind of behaviour on the part of Socrates; they gave him a cup of hemlock for his trouble.

Speech-Act Theory

A basic function-in-common of anthems is to normalise the content sung. We all sing the song together. Which song? We all know; we all know the words (or enough of them to mumble along inconspicuously). When more than one song might claim this function, there is a doubt needing to be resolved because a multiplicity of texts might threaten a notionally unified identity. The repeated act of singing creates a kind of numbness in the mind with regard to content and perhaps the specificity of function. A kind of anaesthetic is at work in anthems; they help us to forget certain things that we would appear to be in the act of remembering when we sing: things to do with who we are or who we are meant to be. The anaesthetic has an averaging effect (as per Anderson's second paradox) so that the main thing anthem singing asserts is nation-ness in general, rather than the specialness of a nationality in particular. Yet under the numb skin of the unisonant, serious commitments (vague and specific) are being made in the process of anthem singing: for instance, commitments to getting the job done, doing the decent thing, picturing ourselves, making sacrifices, dying, dying gladly. There are, likewise, serious pleas to God; vows are made, hyperboles are attested. Anthems typically proceed from an assumption that the nation sung is better than the rest, and this becomes a motive for spurious assertion. We saw just this kind of thing in North Korea's anthem: 'Three thousand leagues packed with natural wealth / …My beautiful fatherland. / The glory of a wise people' (Xing Hang, 340).

Anthems, as written texts, generally have *de facto* or *de jure* constitutional significance. From a juridical point of view, however blank or ambiguous the surface meanings they entail might be, they are also sung utterances-in-common of people – the what-we-sing-together in order to be the *we* of *our*selves when we sing. As suggested earlier, if this seems to be a tautological arrangement, then this is because, in the most fundamental sense, anthems are documents of tautology – along the lines of that silly song – 'we're here because we're here... – sung to the tune of 'Auld Lang Syne'[3] by soldiers marching to the trenches in the First World War. Anthems are spoken and written texts at once; like affidavits or prayers are recorded that they might be faithfully repeated, we take it that the enacted aspect should guarantee sincerity, that the recorded aspect should guarantee continuity and fidelity to past intentions. But the fixedness of anthems militates against the possibility of a sincere and spontaneous outpouring of common feeling, and the constant enacting of anthems in unison is what wears the face from the coin; it is the repeated remembering of the words that, in time, makes us forget their meaning.

Nevertheless, anthems have tremendous power and influence over a citizenry. This, I would argue, while largely unconscious in process, has to do with conflation of speech-act functions found in anthem lyrics, and are typically regardless of genre.

Speech-act theory is a sub-discipline of sociolinguistics, more or less established by John L. Austin with his famous (posthumously published) 1962 study *How to do Things with Words,* and further developed by John Searle. In a nutshell, Austin theorised a relationship between what he called 'locutionary', 'illocutionary' and 'perlocutionary' acts. For example, if someone says to you, 'there's a draft in here', meaning 'can you please shut the window', then their locutionary act is a statement about local atmospheric conditions, their illocutionary act is a request that you close the window and (if successful) their perlocutionary act will have been to cause you to close the window. For Austin, speech acts will be felicitous or not (i.e. they work as such or they do not) on the basis of whether, case by case, the right conditions apply for their proper functioning. It will, for instance, be infelicitous to sentence criminals (or anyone else) to gaol terms if you are not a judge with such powers.

In 1975, Searle developed a system for classifying illocutionary speech acts in his essay, 'A Taxonomy of Illocutionary Acts'. Searle's five main categories were as follows:

assertives commit a speaker to a proposition's truth
directives (as in requests and commands) are meant to cause the person hearing them to take some particular action
commissives (promises and oaths) commit a speaker to future action

expressives (e.g. congratulations, thanks) express a speaker's attitudes and feelings towards a proposition
declarations change the world, as in when a judge pronounces a defendant guilty.

The world-changing idea was first suggested by Austin when he theorised the 'performative' utterance. A performative, as in the 'I do' bride and groom pronounce at a wedding, effects ontological change. These words make an unmarried person a married person, and obviously it is not just the one person who is made married by this utterance, which only works when made as well, just before or after, by the other party. There is much contention and dissension in the field about these claims and classifications as outlined above, but this a rough picture of the territory.

Anthems can, I think, be called 'performatives': the singing of an anthem is an act that confirms the citizenship-in-common of those citizens who are singing together. The fact that the act is often performed accounts for the undermining of its sincerity conditions. Saying 'I love you' for the first time may be performative, but years later, perhaps that statement will at best be what Searle would call an assertive; at worst, it would be a rote and meaningless utterance, which might nevertheless have a range of illocutionary and perlocutionary effects, on which the reader is free to speculate. And of course it could be simply sarcasm. Is an anthem, sung down through generations, this kind of speech act? As speech act, anthems seem to float amorphously among all of the possibilities Searle has listed. Like the saying of 'I love you', they are assertives because when I sing the anthem I assert citizenship among other citizens and possibly to non-citizens (those who are not singing along). Anthems are directives addressed to me, the singer; I gird up my loins to do what the nation requires of me. Anthems are commissives because they imply commitment into the future. When I sing the anthem, I promise to do what I think is required of me as proper devotion to the nation; among such things, I promise to go on asserting citizenship, girding up loins; I promise to go on promising. Along the lines of earlier observations about tautology, this is one of the many mindloops in which the singing of anthems appears to be implicated. Anthems are expressives because when I sing the anthem (with sincerity) I show how I feel about the nation and my participation in it; I congratulate myself and my fellow citizens on our citizenship, on the greatness and the justness of our nation. And as we have seen, anthems are declarations; singing my anthem, I declare my loyalty – and so I assert a right I have to be a citizen; in so doing I reaffirm my citizenship, devotion to nation, patriotism. Singing an anthem for the first time may likewise be taken as indicating the adoption (or 'coming into') of a citizenship.

This account draws attention to an unremarked ambiguity characteristic of anthems: anthems place those who sing them in an interesting subject/object position. One singing an anthem is addresser and addressee at the same time. We can take the phatic communion analogy a step further with this observation; in anthems a people is talking to itself. The skeptic will say the same thing of prayer, but in the singular – that those who pray are in fact speaking to themselves; in the case of anthems (and even of the prayer type), the conclusion seems incontrovertible. God may well be listening; nevertheless, those who sing are minimally singing for each other's benefit. The act of singing makes each essential to the other.

In sum, in anthem singing a commitment to nation is greatly overdetermined by the range of speech acts in which the unisonant are simultaneously involved. When people sing anthems they are doing many things at once, and so they do not really know what they are doing. Now, one might argue, as M.A.K. Halliday would, that language in use is typically like this. In terms of Halliday's meta-functional theory of language, in the vast majority of utterances many kinds of meaning are being made at once (broadly, ideational, interpersonal and textual kinds of meaning are encoded in most speech acts). But I think the fact that in anthems we find the whole gamut, not of meta-functions, but of speech functions themselves, reflected, is quite surprising. Certainly, it would be difficult to imagine other-than-anthem-quality poetry having these kinds of effects. The point that so many kinds of meaning are happening in an anthem means, I think, that for the unisonant, the text that seems to be rote (in the sense of requiring no thought) is, at the same time, quite distracting. When one sings an anthem, committed as one is to many kinds of meaning, one has little opportunity to challenge any one mode of meaning. Too much thought would be required; if you started, where would you stop? My country right or wrong? To have citizenship of a nation of the sort that anthem singing asserts, commits to, expresses, declares is a normatively lifelong contract for which one never sees the fine print. One is in any case committed to it, by circumstance, from a time before one can read, speak or reason. (On this basis one might wish to consider the imposition of patriotic symbolic machinery on the young a kind of child abuse.[4]) Perhaps though, there are some caveats, some ways in which the unisonant might be hedging bets in their contract with the nation and/or its symbols? Apart from the possibility of spontaneous parody, this I would argue, is work that has to be done for the unisonant ahead of the instances of performance of the anthem; it is the work of authors and ultimately of the state, to get any bet-hedging into the picture.

'God Save the King/Queen'

Roger Scruton contends that the Spartans may have had something very similar to what we today call a national anthem because they got together to do some singing (not the kind of thing for which the Spartans are known to posterity) prior to battle (2009, 111). Spartans aside, the Netherlands and England are the serious contenders for the earliest persisting anthem that could be thought of as national. The melody of the Dutch song, 'William of Nassau' may date as far back as 1574. This song has international origins and it certainly has travelled (as a child Mozart thought he had composed the tune), but it has not had the currency or the effects 'God Save the King/Queen' has had on the world scale (Nettl, 90–95 *passim*). As suggested in the last chapter, a little historical exegesis is required to make sense of the lyrics at all. 'God Save the King/Queen' is the undoubted Ur-anthem of the prayer type. This hymn, apparently addressed to God, purports to be for the benefit of the monarch who rules by a putative divine right. An examination of the lyrics reveals, below the surface, other more complex intentions on the part of the unisonant.

Percy Scholes' 1942 work *'God Save the King': Its History and Romance* claims the earliest known performance of the song was at Drury Lane Theatre on the 28th September, 1745.[5] While a traditional attribution of the song to John Bull (1563–1628) may be dubious, there is little doubt the song played an important role during the Jacobite crisis of the 1740s when the Hannoverian ascendancy and succession were under threat. The complete official words are currently as follows:

God save our gracious Queen,
Long live our noble Queen,
God save the Queen:
Send her victorious,
Happy and glorious,
Long to reign over us:
God save the Queen.

O Lord, our God, arise,
Scatter her enemies,
And make them fall.
Confound their politics,
Frustrate their knavish tricks,
On Thee our hopes we fix,
God save us all.

Thy choicest gifts in store,
On her be pleased to pour;
Long may she reign:
May she defend our laws,
And ever give us cause
To sing with heart and voice
God save the Queen.

(Bristow, 576–577)

Though its origins will likely remain shrouded in mystery, the song's pan-European popularity is well attested. Words with this tune have at various times provided a national anthem for Prussia (and then Germany), Lichtenstein, Denmark, Norway, Sweden, Switzerland and of course many parts of the British Empire and later Commonwealth. Generally the words have had a monarchist sentiment to them, the great exception being in the case of the United States, where the 1831 words of Samuel Francis Smith to the hymn, 'America', are conspicuously about country rather than king. In the first of its many stanzas:

My country, 'tis of thee,
Sweet land of liberty,
Of thee I sing;
Land where my fathers died,
Land of the pilgrims' pride,
From ev'ry mountainside
Let freedom ring!

('My Country 'Tis of Thee', 2012)

In America too, the tune has been of great importance, Smith's song serving as *de facto* national anthem for the United States prior to the twentieth-century acceptance of 'The Star Spangled Banner' as official anthem. 'God Save the King/Queen' has influenced the composition of prayer-like anthems everywhere and it has had notable influences on some of the world's most famous composers. The tune has even been touted as a cleansing cure for earworms (Chatterjee). Whatever the provenance of the tune or its sentiment, by the end of the nineteenth century this song (in its various forms) would have evoked loyal sentiment among Americans and in your average western European monarchic subject.

In each case I think we can say that what was expressed was loyalty to a status quo and the instruments – however symbolic or actual – through which power and order maintained themselves. The title of the song – and its most repeated line in each case – indicates a desire to continue indefinitely what common knowledge of the human condition tells us must end, that is, to make eternal the temporal reign of the individual monarch. That making eternal depends on the making impersonal of monarchic power; this in turn points away from the promotion of tyranny and towards a constitutional arrangement. It is the job description, rather than the monarch in particular, being promoted in this one-song-fits-all formula. So it's not 'God save a king in particular', it's 'God save the king thing by letting the present one reign, victoriously and graciously and so on'.

It might at first seem odd that the nineteenth-century rise of nations in the modern sense should be accompanied by the rise and spread of a song that appears to express a pre-national kind of sentiment, which seems to be promoting the absolutism of an earlier era. But it is in this sense 'God save the King/Queen' perfectly fits Benedict Anderson's first paradox of the national: the objective modernity of nations at odds with the subjective claims to unbroken tradition that characterise the sentiments of nationalists. In the case of 'God save the King/Queen' it is the simple expedient of omitting the monarch's name that allows the song to express an eternal order.

How is it 'the king thing' survives in the world of modern nations? Much has been made of the discontinuity between monarchic and republican government, but by and large constitutional monarchies function with the benefit of long-lived symbols and with few of the drawbacks of absolute authority. 'The king thing' is useful today as metonymic abstraction because nation stands in relation to disparate individuals just where a king stood. Keeping the king, the crown and the sceptre (the whole range of authorising metonymy) available for the purposes of the state simply reduces the symbolic burden borne by a particular nation, in the course of representing itself. What is entailed in the case of a constitutional monarchy is an associative circle: by this means the investments of authority slip away beyond reproach through the expedient of being always other. Authority is in every case elsewhere derived and so the danger of the state's power coming to seem mutable is minimised.

In the case of 'God Save the King/Queen', Protestant insistence on a direct and personal relationship with the deity demonstrates the kind of association that commoners are not privileged to have with the monarch. The monarch in these lyrics does not so much represent God's temporal authority as a kind of geometrical necessity in a social contract (perhaps yet to be written), which God allows among men. The monarch merely enjoys the empowered position between God and man: as head of the Church of England, s/he is of and yet apart from the flock. Enacting the bidding of a parliament, s/he can directly represent the will of the people in a way that God cannot be made to do. Hence the long list of epithets; we are constantly, if indirectly (the song addresses God, never the monarch), telling the sovereign how to be: gracious, noble, happy, glorious, long of reign. Note how these qualities feed off each other. Equanimity is required in remaining happy and glorious for a long time. This feat requires grace and nobility of spirit.

Much history has gone into these lyrics. In the second stanza, we read traces of various plots and pretenders to the throne: 'Scatter her enemies, / And make them fall. / Confound their politics, / Frustrate their knavish tricks...'. In the third stanza, we understand that the monarchy this song envisages is very much post-Cromwell: constitutional and contingent on good behaviour: 'May s/he defend our laws, /And ever give us cause...'. If the monarch wants to go on having faithful subjects, singing 'God save him/her'; then whoever that incumbent may be had better provide sovereign service.[6] It is as though the citizenry were collectively saying 'don't even think about having more than symbolic power; we've had this experience in the past and we won't accept it again'. The loyal subjects deliver the message indirectly, which seems polite, through a conversation with God that is meant to be overheard by the only person in the kingdom who is not entitled to sing because s/he is not one of them. Or rather we might say that the sovereign's citizenship is analogous with Christ's humanity (i.e. part of a dual nature: one of us and not one of us).

Christ's justice (of the eternal kind) is the unmentioned backdrop in all of these proceedings. 'God Save the King' – from mortal peril or from threats to the immortal soul's journey to grace with God? The good monarch after a long reign doing good would get to be with God. Perhaps a monarch has a better than average opportunity to do good and get God's reward, but in this song the people subject to the monarch are shown to be privileged with as close a relationship to God as that possessed by the head of their church. The people, advising God, in relation to their sovereign, deliver the incumbent a tacit warning to remember that his/her soul is as imperilled as theirs, needs saving as their souls do. We all know that power corrupts and power is what the king is always close to, so the king needs saving principally from himself.

The warning delivered harmlessly to the symbol of the state is – by association – a warning to its apparatus in general and to those who exercise its powers: the state should ever give cause for the people's prayerful support. Of 'God Save the King/Queen' we can say that when the whole of the text is sung with an effort at awareness, the effect is to collectively assert the contingent nature of the monarchy in Britain: to demonstrate that the comfort and security of the person occupying the throne are dependent on a notional pact between God and man, a pact in which the individual voices of men are recognised as such and mediated only by their collectivity and not by the monarch as a person. As a hymn 'God Save the King/Queen' adopts a standard locutionary strategy of prayer: that of making strong suggestions to God with regard to a third party. What everyone sings in 'God Save the King/Queen' is a shorthand formula justifying the interdependence of civil society and constitutional monarchy.

This logic is taken an interesting step further in the lyrics of 'God Defend New Zealand', where in the third stanza, after a familiar sounding, 'Put our enemies to flight', we read the curious verse, 'Let our cause be just and right' (Xing Hang, 458). It seems that the doubts the British public have entertained as to state and monarchic power are doubts the people of New Zealand might have about themselves. Perhaps what this indicates is a closer identification between the polity and the people? Or is it merely that the young country may be sure of its rhetoric but less sure of itself?

'God Save the King/Queen' helps us to think through the relationship between an anthem and its evolving contexts: the context from which it comes, the context in which it is later received. Texts surviving from age to age face this question: how is the original consciousness of a first maker, first audience, first context mediated in the lack of consciousness that carries the text to next generations, down to the present day and on from there? If the breath returns to those words that were someone else's, then consciousness of those words has transcended itself in the process. This is the way worn words become unchallengeable. This is the process of 'reification': the fashioning of the real from signs. What can be more impressive than lapidary letters, monumentally imposed? Words passed from heart to heart last because they are loved.

In 'God Save the King/Queen' we recognise an inverse proportion characteristic of anthems between fervour and the ability to actually mean anything by the expression of it. Praying for God to help the monarch to live up to the work of being a kind of symbolic glue ultimately provides a means for a people to express faith in itself without, as it were, getting too close to itself. The necessary rhetorical distance is provided by way of metonymy. There may be something archaic about this adaptation of the feudal and absolute worldview to the evolving relativism of the democratic parliament-governed state; but hundreds of years of singing wears that accommodation into a general expression of loyalty, one that obviates, for

Britons at least, the need to discuss the accommodation or the meaning of loyalty. Would it be fair to say that there is something British about this; or rather that it is this kind of rhetorical arrangement in the identity mechanism that makes the British who they are?

And what of those around the world whose sense of self is shaped by the British symbolic forms of an identity-in-common? Consider the role of 'God Save the King' in Norman Lindsay's 1918 illustrated children's novel, *The Magic Pudding*. In this text, where the Puddin' may be read as Australia – or the Australian – it is also cornucopia personified as badly-behaved child. This is not the Dickensian image of the Oliver Twist type of child asking for more; this recalcitrant child Albert *is* the more. Once stolen, the Puddin' is discovered through the demand of loyalty placed on (the native) miscreants by the rendition of 'God Save the King'; thieves are powerless against this expression of authority. They must remove their headgear, and when they do so the world can see that it was under their hats they were hiding the magic pudding. Authority bid them reveal what convention had allowed them to conceal. 'God Save the King' has an automatic effect, it invokes the *sine qua non* of national loyalty: when you hear this tune you must remove your headgear.[7] By means of this automatic, arbitrary and apparently permanent expression of loyalty, the character cum object in contention is revealed. 'Rightful' possession of the Puddin' will be restored to those who, by virtue of their gift of the gab, are able to subvert the legal process to serve their own interests. One cannot help but feel an affinity here with the pragmatic logic with regard to rights expressed in 'God Save the King'. In Lindsay's tale for children, through the automatised expression of loyalty, as expressed in the national anthem, the character cum object in contention is revealed. The recognition in either case is that – whatever duties of respect we may owe to them – symbols serve practical, if not pragmatic, purposes.

'God Save the King/Queen' may be the Ur-text and paradigm model of the national prayer song; it nevertheless should be regarded as a disingenuous speech act, the kind of prayer one makes with fingers crossed behind one's back.

O Say can You See...?

Let us return to the idea of anthem as phatic communion on the grand scale: a people greeting itself by means of rote words it has remembered well enough to forget to understand. That memory is archetypically of some originary moment or primal scene. Best example of that archetype, representative of the tableau style of national song, is in the US anthem, 'The Star Spangled Banner':

Oh, say can you see, by the dawn's early light,
What so proudly we hailed at the twilight's last gleaming?
Whose broad stripes and bright stars, through the perilous fight,
O'er the ramparts we watched, were so gallantly streaming?
And the rockets' red glare, the bombs bursting in air,

Gave proof through the night that our flag was still there.
O say, does that star-spangled banner yet wave
O'er the land of the free and the home of the brave?

On the shore dimly seen throughout the mists of the deep
Where the foe's haughty host in dread silence reposes
What is that which the breeze o'er the towering steep
As it fitfully blows, half conceals, half discloses?
Now it catches the gleam of the morning's first beam
In full glory reflected now shines on the stream.
Tis the Star-Spangled Banner, Oh long may it wave
O'er the land of the free and the home of the brave.

And where is that band who so hauntingly swore
That the havoc of war and the battle's confusion
A home and country, shall leave us no more?
Their blood was washed out their foul foot steps pollution
No refuge could save the hireling and slave
From the terror of flight or the gloom of the grave.
And the Star-Spangled Banner in triumph doth wave
O'er the land of the free and the home of the brave.

Oh thus be it e'er when free men shall stand
Between their lov'd homes and war's desolation!
Blest with vict'ry and peace, may the heav'n rescued land
Praise the Pow'r that has made and presrv'd us a nation
And conquer we must when our cause is just
And this be our motto: 'In God is our trust.'
And the Star-Spangled Banner in triumph shall wave
O'er the land of the free and the home of the brave.

(Bristow, 578–580)

The original star-spangled banner was a thirty by forty-two foot US flag flown during the 1812 war between Britain and the United States. Note the circular and mutually justifying relationship among these namesake artefacts of nation. The song commemorated this particular flag and a particular occasion on which it was seen to be flown. The flag is now famous – revered as a relic – because it inspired the song. The song involves its listening/singing participant in a train of thought that proceeds from a single event or rather non-event. During the 1814 British bombardment of Fort McHenry, near Baltimore, Francis Scott Key, composer of the words of the anthem, was briefly detained by the British and, in this circumstance unable to aid in the defence of his country, had time to pen a poem about what he could see from his ship, which was under British guard. His song commemorates the fact that, after the smoke cleared on the morning after, the big flag was still flying. The fact that the big flag was still flying meant that the defence had been successful. The success of the song suggests that Keys' time was not wasted either. Note though that Congress did not make 'The Star Spangled Banner' the national anthem until 1931.

There is symbolic training for the child patriot in getting to the bottom of all of this.[8] That is because, for the child, all of these highly motivated and tightly connected evocations of American nation – history, song, flag – present themselves as arbitrary and abstract. What do stars and stripes have to do with America? What does a song have to do with a flag? What do these old-fashioned words have to do with my identity now? There is a quasi-religious initiation involved in satisfying oneself with answers to these questions. The child – or the migrant – who contents herself that she sees what Francis Scott Key saw, has had the national epiphany. She has witnessed the glorious originary martial moment of the American nation: the tableau of battle, in which truth and right are revealed just as soon as the smoke clears. What you need to envision for the purposes of this epiphany is the scene of self-defence, in which the symbols of nation persist (and even multiply) under fire. 'The Star Spangled Banner' involves its unisonants in an act of witness, taking place in circumstances of danger. It is in this sense that the expression of nation presents as a kind of valour (cf. 'With courage let us all combine / To Advance Australia Fair'). When you sing 'The Star Spangled Banner' with fellow Americans you pay homage to the valour of those who risked all for the abstractions defining their nation and yours, the historical continuity in which you are enjoined. In order to achieve this – to rekindle the national epiphany – one follows ritual instructions for the imagination, which one has already memorised: 'O say can you see…'

The American flag is a characteristic symbol of modernity – of nation in the modern sense, as well as of one particular nation – and it is also a symbol of post-modernity. Consider the iconic raising of the Stars and Stripes, Iwa Jima 1945. Consider the bugle-supported horse-back flag bearer of the United States cavalry in the classic western. Consider the US flag on the back of a tank in Iraq in 2003. Consider the burning ('desecration') of the US flag by disgruntled 'nationalists', 'separatists' and 'insurgents' of various shades the world over.

As Michael Billig frequently points out (e.g. 39–43 *passim*) the US flag, when it is at home, is mainly banal, mainly unwaved and mainly unnoticed. It is also mainly in peaceful circumstances. It is the other-than-banal wavings of the stars and stripes that maintain for people around the world the association with bombs bursting in air. Without the benefit of the mainly banal 'flaggings' of US nationhood, most of the world's people have no choice but to read differently what they read from the outside. Pictures of the flag in the corner of the classroom need be neither banal nor benign to them.

For Americans, the brilliance of the 'Star Spangled Banner' is in the effectiveness of the closed loop in which the symbols of nation confirm each other: the song points to the flag that represents the originary moment that contains the nation's permanent moral stance (witness of the brave defence of freedom). Evocation of that scene points forward into the story today involving the song's participant – the witness of the flag.

Affective participation in this song and the symbolic loop in which it is entailed is by no means restricted to Americans. This is because of America's pre-eminence as nation. The United States was *the* nation that became itself just at the moment when nation in the modern sense came into being. It is in that sense typical and original. French nationhood had older and distinctive regional, linguistic and political traditions on which to graft itself; France was a kingdom become a republic. That is despite the fact that the French 'nation' borrowed traditions (especially Roman Republican ones) as other nations have done. But in the case of the United States, in terms of the doctrine to be later named *terra nullius* (land belonging to no one), *nation* was written over the territory of a previous non-polity. The nation, coming into existence apparently *ex-nihilo*, relies on traditions from elsewhere to authorise its foundation. This situation exemplifies the modernity of nations. The *American* moment of national origin one might say *is* the moment of nation in the modern sense. The US is in this sense the oldest member of the club of nations. Neither the oldest nor the most typical of anthems, 'The Star Spangled Banner' is yet the bearer of a core meaning of anthem quality. Fourteen of the world's national anthems are in praise (to a greater or lesser degree) of a national flag.[9] In the case of countries as diverse as Honduras, Albania and the Philippines, we may go so far as to call the anthem the song of the flag, so central is this symbol as focus of national devotions. Many more anthems are in praise of an originary martial tableau as national keepsake, something equally shown in a march composed two decades before 'The Star Spangled Banner', Rouget de Lisle's 'La Marseillaise'. Other national anthems need to be understood in relation to these defining texts, which, along with 'God Save the King/Queen', set what we might call the Hollywood-standard for the sacredness of what is sung together (especially in the English-speaking world today) concerning nations and our belonging to them.

Muzak Interlude

In the case of 'Star Spangled Banner', the history of this one song's long journey from composition to acceptance as *the* national anthem, reflects a tension between the unique and the archetypal, a tension reflecting the United States' historical position among nations. As has already been seen in the case of 'America' (or 'My Country 'Tis of Thee', set to the tune of 'God Save the King/Queen'), other songs are able to provide US citizens with the right stuff in terms of patriotic sentiment. 'America the Beautiful' and 'God Bless America' are equally serviceable, and it is no doubt because of the popularity and impeccable character of these songs that Congress took so long to give 'The Star Spangled Banner' the official and permanent laurel. As national devotions are to one country, so to avoid the prospect of division as to the nature of national sentiment, it seems to be universally accepted that each country should have only one official national anthem. In a country like the United States, where the banal flagging of nation is very frequent, any tune with a national function becomes – like Christmas carols in December – a kind of citizens' muzak.

Are songs (are tunes, are lyrics) ever unique? Are they for instance ever – strictly speaking – thought of for a first time? How original and how distinct can they be? One of the attractive things about the Francis Scott Keys story is that it makes the origins of the song of the origins of the nation distinctive. The story of the song is in itself a cause for patriotic pride. How could the British have suspected that by detaining Keys they were ensuring the symbolic efficacy of their enemy far into the future? Compare what is known of the origins of 'The Star Spangled Banner' with the fog surrounding those of 'God Save the King/Queen'. The tune to 'The Star Spangled Banner' is much older than Keys' words, is English in origin, pre-revolutionary[10]; and yet Americans were happy, for a very long part of their postcolonial history, to have the tune of the British national anthem express their patriotic republican sentiment. But perhaps there was a subversive pleasure to be had in the substitution of republican for monarchic lyrics? Was it a case of the Americans telling the English that they could not own the patriotic sentiment that the tune of 'God Save the King' universally expressed? Or was it the case, as per Robert Frost's poem, that the American people were 'possessed by what (they) now no more possessed'? I think we can say that this question should be answered differently in 1831, when Samuel Francis Smith penned the lyrics, 'My Country 'Tis of Thee', and in 1931, when Congress finally decided that the tune of 'God Save the King' could not be the music for the US national anthem.

Much more mysterious than the obscurity of origins is the fact anthems survive and continue to generate national feeling over long stretches of time. It is mysterious because what is sung in an anthem is typically of another era, often one with which those singing have little or no connection. It is mysterious because the heavy demand on nostalgia-in-common made by anthems generally would not be accepted by listeners of other-than-avowedly-nostalgic songs. Should we accept then that anthems are a sub-genre of nostalgic songs and that this would explain why we tolerate a lack of the otherwise personal-generational connection typically demanded of popular music? This would not explain why citizens who otherwise have not the slightest interest in nostalgic music are nevertheless devotees of the national anthem. They are devotees of the anthem because of what the anthem represents. And the words and the music represent, above all, the moral imperative of patriotism, as delivered by a circle of hollow and mutually confirming signs. The music of the anthem represents the nation, as we established in the last chapter, through abstract and arbitrary rather than representational means. So humming along, singing along, skipping along to the national song – these are typically signs of national devotion rather than musical taste. The music of the anthem is a shell filled with national meaning. Once the filling of the shell has been effected, the music becomes, along with the flag, the most potent sign of nation. Much verbiage is required to get these extra-verbal signs into operation, but once accepted they carry the emotional weight of patriotic feeling. Their efficacy lies in the fact, I would argue, that their power, being conventional (having become arbitrary), is difficult to challenge by verbal means.

Consider the pop song designed to tug the heartstrings; consider the overplayed hit song. By and large these are one and the same. There is a kind of short-duration canonicity that operates in the case of this type of popular culture. Step back from the frame and it is as if one were watching a Malthusian population catastrophe. Played weekly, then daily, then hourly, the song climbs the charts, finally falls away, its customers sated and then over-sated. Cultural capital is invested in the pop song as it rises through the charts, becoming canonical (Have you heard that song? Do you recognise the tune everyone is humming?); cultural capital vanishes from the song to the extent that it is overplayed, becomes *passé*. (Not that damned song again!) The pop song burns itself out by being for a while too much in the popular consciousness; it becomes too affectively demanding. The listener rebels, is no longer prepared to have her heart strings tugged again as they were before.

The canonicity of anthems – and of national songs more generally – is of a different order. Once established, their popularity is lasting, even if not made official. There is something in the nexus of nation and song that allows the anthem to get around the usual rules that apply to the popularity and longevity of songs. I shall deal with this apparent contradiction in the next chapter. The coincidence of the popular and the official (and quasi-official) is not a paradox in its own right; rather there is in this nexus a powerful form of authority, which can be expressed in the reversible formula: *the popular is made official; the official is made popular.* That kind of mesmeric mindloop is the glue needed to make nation stick to its citizens. One can see the emotional potential of a situation or a people as actually justifying forms of authority. As Catherine Lutz writes in her essay 'Engendered Emotion', 'because emotion is constructed as relatively chaotic, irrational and antisocial, its existence vindicates authority and legitimates the need for control' (in Harré and Parrott, 166). Once officially popular and popularly official, the song of another epoch can maintain its homeostatic nation-hailing function through repetition and through the repetition of associations.

Music – as abstract affect-bearing form – relies on association to carry emotional investment. Music evokes and invokes. Where the lyrics are there, the listener is guided in seeing and feeling and in the specific identifications indicated, *in lieu of* action, for the duration of the song at least,. 'Oh say can you see…?' 'Avant, les enfants de la patrie…', 'Britons never, never, never, shall be slaves'. Where the lyrics *were* there, but are no longer heard or properly remembered, they may have more force than they did when they were susceptible of scrutiny. Patriotism is – as affect in general – keen to avoid an argument, and so patriotism profits by ineffable and unarguable associations. Still, anthem lyrics are, for the most part, not entirely evanescent. They can be and are recalled for a need. The recollection of lyrics for the purposes of singing does not however imply a critique or even mindfulness of their content. There are stages to – and degrees of – automatisation.

Contrast on this score the associative principles of jazz of the Miles Davis–Bill Evans era with the principle of muzak (product of a slightly earlier period, but peaking in popularity in the fifties and sixties). In the Miles Davis–Bill Evans kind of jazz a tune is buried in another, in order that the allusion-savvy listener will have the pleasure of excavating it. This is music for listening into. Muzak by contrast is notoriously anaesthetic, a soothing emotional wallpaper that gets you ready for a flight or a filling. It is purposed to prevent listening, although it might well facilitate an unaware humming along. Muzak lives in a declivity below the threshold of consciousness. Anthems are similarly anaesthetic, paradoxically stirring. They stir the soul by liberally applying chloroform to the mind. Anthems are the muzak of nation, but importantly, they are a participatory muzak.

A key difference between the national anthem and the overplayed pop song – even the song loaded with anthem quality – should be that although cynics are everywhere, there should ideally be no social stratum for whom the investments of the national anthem do not apply. Nation is inclusive in this sense, in the sense that religious community was in earlier ages, in the sense that a pop song may only aspire to be. Do all songs then aspire to the condition of anthems? The difference between an anthem and a pop song with anthem quality, for argument's sake, let's say a song with national application, is that the anthem has already been chosen. And in having been officialised (or quasi-officialised) it borrows the unarguable and eternal quality of the nation it represents. In this thought-loop we see that while anthem purports to represent nation, in fact it is the qualities of the nation, arbitrarily assigned to the anthem, which lend that song an at least notionally unchallengeable permanence, a sense of having always already been the anthem. Anthems, unless challenged for their position, are only to be compared with other anthems and only in those international situations where the anthems of different countries are played together.

As we have seen through some glancing reference to speech-act theory, an effective national anthem is simultaneously performing an impressive range of functions. It is troublesome to propose a classification system for the anthem phenomenon, not only for this reason, but because of the ways in which anthems are all things to so many different manner of people, and because, in different national situations, anthems serve a range of national interests (compare Portugal's national anthem with those of the nations it colonised). As we have seen in the case of the US, there are all sorts of patriotic songs that fill the bill, but that cannot be *the* anthem. There are ways around the difficulty: 'Rule Britannia' may be considered a British imperial hymn, rather than a national anthem; 'Waltzing Matilda' may be called a national song, rather than an anthem for Australia. The demand for a unique anthem per country may seem arbitrary, but it performs important functions in terms of inward unity and outward brand consistency. It might be observed that up until 1931, having a number of patriotic songs at its disposal served the US well, because they were songs that harmonised with each other: a single set, so to speak. On the world scale this would be unusual, although one notes (for instance in the case of South Africa) the distance certain countries will travel to harmonise their anthem options in the spirit of reconciliation.

The study of songs that almost serve the purposes of an anthem is interesting in the way a *near*-hagiography might be: why were certain (pious or not-so-pious) souls begun on the path to canonisation but unable to stay the course? (That action being mostly posthumous, one notes.) Saints are as numerous as virtue is undiluted; anthems by contrast are, as noted, notionally unique. Anthems are though miraculous in beatific manner: they allow powerful affect to be automatised and sacralised, available for use over long periods of time and among vast populations of citizens who must always remain strangers to each other. There must be something magical about songs which fit that bill. Or else there is something magical about making them fit it. Conversely there is something disappointing about songs enlisted in this service but that fail to produce the affective goods.

In the last chapter I canvassed the idea that one's own anthem has more emotional meaning for a citizen than do the anthems of other countries. This may, in principle be true, but it is an idea long since challenged by the Hollywood movie industry.[11]

'Here's looking at you, kid.'

Saintliness is apposite in the case of anthems because these songs are only able to effect the self-centring of an identity-in-common through some kind of hypostasisation. It is evocation of the blood of martyrs, or some close equivalent, that allows us to think of and to sing of ourselves like this, as collectively sacred or chosen, when we would never see ourselves individually as such. The anthem is a collective absolution for what would otherwise be hubris and it makes avatars of all who participate in nation worship.

Still there is the wallpaper–muzak mystery. How can wallpaper be participatory? Part of the answer is that the effect of anthems is not limited to participation. The similarity of anthems and the identity of their operational modes is such that it would be unsurprising to find ourselves moved in certain circumstances by the anthems of other states, provided they are familiar enough and that they have the right sorts of familiar associations, that they sufficiently remind us of ourselves or of an image we would like to have of ourselves (or perhaps of something about our ourselves we have collectively repressed).

Symbolising uniqueness is a key to participation in the *inter*national series entailed in national sentiment. National sentiment *feels to* appeal to the unilateral good of a unique identity. National sentiment only has appeal through series in which (though the mythology dismisses the idea) there is temporal progression as well as synchronicity. For most of the world's citizens, anthem quality would not work without a consciousness of others' anthems elsewhere, songs that we ourselves can only sing when we are pretentiously indulging an identity to which we have no authentic claim ourselves. To be stirred – as an Australian – by 'The Star Spangled Banner' or 'Rule Britannia', by 'The Marseillaise' or by 'Hatikvah' – is an experience of this order, an apparently vicarious experience of national sentiment. Why is it so much harder for an average (white) Australian to be stirred by 'Indonesia Raya', by 'Kimi Gayo' or by China's 'The March of the Volunteers'? This I would argue is – among other reasons of cultural capital – because these expressions of national sentiment are cognate with, rather than anterior to (or enabling of), Australian feeling.

Are there any nations able to exercise patriotic affect independent of the series in which the nation participates? Surely, as original nation in the modern sense, and as pre-eminent national exemplar in the world today, America need not refer beyond its own geography for the purposes of its self-evocation? Perhaps it need not today, but as we have seen with the music to both Samuel Francis Smith's 'America' and 'The Star Spangled Banner', this was not the case for Americans of previous generations.

Consider, against the near-synchronicity of anthems played at sporting events, the competitive 'anthems scene' in Rick's bar in Warner Bros' 1942 film *Casablanca*. We can see that scene as a kind of teaching text for Americans; it teaches them about the nature of national sentiment, about how that kind of expression situates Americans in the world. The marauding Germans in Rick's Cafe Americain have begun singing 'Die Wacht am Rhein' ('The Watch on the Rhine'), a song calculated to test the patience of the downtrodden French:

Lieb Faterland, magst ruhig sein,
Lieb Faterland, magst ruhig sein,
Test steht und treu die Wacht, Die Wacht am Rhein.

Dear land of ours, no fear be thine,
Dear land of ours, no fear be thine,
The watch stands true, the watch on the Rhine.

('Die Wacht am Rhein', 2012)

This is a song appropriate to the Nazi role purported in the film's story: the Germans are in Casablanca, not as an occupying force, but to observe. And the Germans are just getting into the sing-along mood when that maverick freedom fighter, Victor Laszlo (the Czech [?] with the Hungarian name), has the band – with Rick's nod – strike up 'The Marseillaise' for the benefit of the local patriots (French imperialists if we give things a moment's thought).

Allons enfants de la Patrie, Le jour de gloire est arrivé
Contre nous de la tyrannie, L'étendard sanglant est levé
L'étendard sanglant est levé, Entendez-vous dans nos campagnes
Mugir ces féroces soldats? Ils viennent jusques dans vos bras.
Egorger vos fils, vos compagnes.

Arise, children of the Fatherland,
The day of glory has come.
Against us the blood-stained banner
Of tyranny is raised,
Hear, in the fields, the roar of her fierce soldiers.
They come right into our arms
To slaughter our sons and our consorts.

Patriots, to arms!
Form your batallions,
Let's march, let's march!
May the tyrant's foul blood water our furrows!

(Bristow, 216–218)

The Germans had been a rabble of drunken soldiers singing, now scenes around the bar show various Francophone individuals intoning the lyrics that speak for liberty. In considering the originality of this idea, it is worth noting that Jean Renoir had juxtaposed the same two songs in his film, *La Grande Illusion*, in 1937. In Renoir's film, the international credentials of the 'The Marseillaise' are established when the singing is initiated by a British prisoner-of-war in drag.[12] Back in *Casablanca*'s cinema space, the world audience of mainly Americans (or of American-identified movie goers) finds its allegiance in the anthem of one country (France), that song representing liberty, while another kind of song – not properly an anthem, is associated with *la tyrannie* and blood spilt and to be spilt in opposition to it.

Put aside the colonial issue for the moment. The well-behaved reader of *Casablanca* does not devote thought to the relationship between imperialism and fascism, for instance along the lines of Aime Cesaire's (1955) dictum that fascism was the 'crowning barbarism' (174). What Cesaire meant was that fascism was a final – and implosive step – in the history of European imperialism. Why did Europeans object so strenuously to fascisms when they had got along more or less comfortably with imperialism for so long? Simply because fascism was directed mainly at other Europeans. And in *Casablanca* the characters are, in various shades, white people.

To historicise: what is at stake in *Casablanca* for the 1942 audience is America's participation in the world and in the war against the Axis powers. Americans need to be convinced that Europe has relevance to them. French freedom is useful as asserting an already-established link there, one already symbolised for Americans in the form of France's (1886) cooperative gift to America: the Statue of Liberty. The plot of *Casablanca* justifies American reticence, but it also justifies America's quiet altruism in entering the war. In a world gone mad, the US, like Rick's Cafe Americain, prospers, but how long can this go on before the tides of war drag Americans down too? The best way to persuade Americans of their need to participate in the war is through proving the validity, to them, of someone else's affect. The American position this way remains cool headed, objective, self-renovating and self-sufficient – a set of epithets that well describe how the US emerged from the war. This is more or less the image the US would present three years after the war's end in the rhetoric of the Marshall Plan.

In the anthems scene of *Casablanca* we see a kind of unilateralism at work. World sentiment is manufactured from the mill of nation, so that Germany means tyranny and France stands for freedom. The must-miss irony here is that the German lyrics are relatively benign, the words of the 'The Marseillaise' among the bloodiest of all anthems. The connections are between tunes and uniforms, nations and longstanding animosities. They are now arbitrary connections of the kind that cannot be disturbed by the actual meaning of actual words. Who is doing the manufacturing? Whose unilateral sentiment are we offered? The Americans are barely there at all. The laconic Rick ('I stick my neck out for no one') is a very unwilling patriot – even anti-fascist – if he is one at all. Perhaps he is a reformed anti-fascist. He will not find the faith again but he retains his distaste for Nazis, his soft spot for a Victor Laszlo. Rick is in Casablanca to escape from a world that was demanding on him in various ways, including the patriotic ones. We do not know precisely why he cannot go back to America, but this fact makes him no less American. The land of the free is the home of those brave enough to test the bounds of freedom. You can read Rick as the miscast outlaw turned saloon owner in a place so far West, it is East, in a place so old it is new to Americans.

The coy moralising of the story leads us to accept that sacrifice for nation (even someone else's, even unknown) and right of the most abstract kind (the struggle for freedom) overtake personal interest, personal feeling, but in a pragmatic way and just for the moment. The story is delivered with that 'round up the usual suspects' cynicism, but the cynicism does not kill off the value of nation in the story. The continued existence of nations *appears* to be in question in *Casablanca*. The national status of place (Casablanca) and person (Rick) is certainly in question, but ultimately these things are presented to us as fixed: Rick is an American, Casablanca is (should remain) a French possession. It is through such means the apparent disinterest of Americans is (disingenuously) invested in a kind of European-ness, the European-ness of the people who gave us the Statue of Liberty. So the Americans do care after all. They are slow to anger, and would not the world be a better place if we were all like that?

How well do anthems travel? How global does national sentiment need to be? How global can it be? In *Casablanca* the international scene of nation is such that somebody else's anthem, rendered by somebody else again, can swell any Hollywood acculturated breast – with rancour or pride – and seemingly on command, as if that breast were someone else's. It is the illusion of unique identity – of affect setting *us* apart – that allows the anthem singer to sing herself into world patterns of identification, of the kind implied by the series, nation.

To briefly historicise the songs in the film, 'The Marseillaise' was originally titled 'Chant de guerre pour l'Armée du Rhin' ('War Song for the Rhine Army'), so it would be fair to say that German lands were, from the outset, in the sights of this song. 'The Marseillaise' was written by Claude Joseph Rouget de Lisle in 1792 and became the national anthem of the First Republic in 1795. It was volunteer soldiers from Marseille who first sang the song, hence the name. As a republican song, it was discarded by Napoleon and by Napoleon III. The song is revolutionary, certainly, and has been a model for and source of allusions for many other anthems, probably the most notable of which is the communist anthem, 'The Internationale' (to be discussed in Chapter 6). 'The Marseillaise' is also the paradigm of the warlike march anthem: a little like the Maori *haka* (which we may perhaps equate with the Spartan's 'Ode of Tyrtaeus', sung before battle), it was surely designed to cower an enemy. In its original context, it was written to repel foreign forces, led by the Duke of Brunswick, which threatened the revolution and the young republic.

It is easy for the average wartime and post-war Hollywood movie-savvy citizen of the world to think simply of Germans as aggressors and French as fighters for freedom, but 'The Marseillaise' covers quite a span of history, and one cannot help but feel that the dis-unified Germans of the Napoleonic Wars would not have thought kindly of this tune.

'The Watch on the Rhine' ('Die Wacht am Rhein') is a German patriotic song originating from the period of the Rhine Crisis of 1840. Post-Napoleonic, but well pre-unification, it is a call to unity in response to French aggression, in particular, the policy of then French Prime Minister, Adolphe Tiers, to annexe the left (still German-speaking) bank of the Rhine and so assert the river as a 'natural' border between France and Germany. Tiers was not the first French leader to think this way; the idea goes back to Louis XIV and of course Napoleon succeeded in conquering quite a bit more besides. 'The Watch on the Rhine' underwent various revisions and additions, especially through the twentieth century, becoming more aggressive as time and conflict went on. It never became the German National Anthem, although it enjoyed quasi-anthem status, especially from Bismarck's time on.

Both of these songs have some claim to be defensive in function (to encourage defence of the homeland), but there is no doubt that 'The Marseillaise' is the more bloodthirsty of the two. For cinematic purposes though, world audiences have been given the opposite impression. 'The Watch on the Rhine' seems like an aggressors' song; 'The Marseillaise' is the underdog's. Of course, this is the relative position of the Germans and the French both in the movie (and in Renoir's film), and at the time of the movie's making. So as a feel-good-about-what-we-have-to-do wartime propaganda piece, this all seems entirely justified.

The songs bear the affect the viewing context provides for them; the songs become tokens of a particular affective image: the heroic fight against fascism. The most nationally affecting moment of *Casablanca* reminds us that Germans are bloodthirsty brutes and that the French are freedom fighters. Not that anyone, of the general world audience, is going to remember much of 'The Watch on the Rhine'; it is this meaning of 'The Marseillaise' all remember. 'The Marseillaise' stands for liberty, or more specifically, it evokes, for the listener and for the unisonant, the arduous struggle to throw off tyranny. *Casablanca* did not invent this connotative reduction; nor did Renoir. The Anglo-American idea of France and France's national anthem as bulwarks against German aggression was well established by this time. But *Casablanca* has had deep effects on the anthem-psyche of the world's cinema going subjects. One might go further and say the cinema has characterised the languages involved this way (French is the language of love, German the language of war); the world is still recovering from Hitler and the world recovers only slowly from such stereotyping.

***

In this chapter I have focussed on, respectively, a song to march to, a song to stand prayerfully by, a song for the mind's eye. Looking across these sub-genres, we can see some blurring of borders and we can see that the march, the prayer and the tableau have more in common as speech act than difference in the particularity of their functions. Still, the common functional quality of anthems and the relation of citizens to them are highly paradoxical; and this paradoxical aspect of anthems will be the subject of the next chapter.

Notes

1. Other examples of marching songs include Ireland's 'The Soldier's Song', and the old Slovenian anthem, 'Forward, Flag of Glory'.
2. The much quoted passage from Nietzsche, as follows:

> What therefore is truth? A mobile army of metaphors, metonymies, anthropomorphisms: in short a sum of human relations which became poetically and rhetorically intensified, metamorphosed, adorned and after long usage seem to a nation fixed, canonic and binding; truths are illusions of which one has forgotten that they are illusions; worn out metaphors which have become powerless to affect the senses; coins which have their obverse effaced and now are no longer of account as coins but merely as metal.
>
> (180)

Mallarmé writes more generally of language as a worn coin passed silently from hand to hand (368).

3. Former anthem of the Maldives.
4. Much in the manner that Richard Dawkins has argued for the imposition of religious doctrine on children, in *The God Delusion* (315).
5. Interest in historicising the song dates to pre-Victorian times, as in Richard Clark's 1822 *An account of the national anthem entitled 'God Save the King'*.
6. This rhetorical point was etched into the minds of Australians on 11th November, 1975, when the deposed prime minister, Gough Whitlam, declared on the steps of Canberra's parliament house, 'Well may we say "God save the queen", because nothing will save the governor general'.
7. It is interesting to note that the lifting dynamics of the song were naturally reversed for the monarch. Percy Scholes tells us that Queen Victoria was presented at her first Jubilee, in 1887, 'with a bustle fitted with an ingenious automatic apparatus so designed that every time she sat down the tune ["God Save the Queen"] should issue from it' (39–40).
8. As delivered to the child-citizen in numerous flag and/or anthem primers for American children, for instance, in Nancy Harris's *The National Anthem,* in the Patriotic Symbols Series by Heinemann-Raintree; in Elaine Landau's *The National Anthem*, in Scholastic's True Book Series.
9. Those of Nicaragua, Pakistan, Palestine, the Philippines, Sao Tome, Saudi Arabia, Honduras, Albania, Haiti, Seychelles, Turkey, Vietnam and Zimbabwe.
10. The melody is John Stafford Smith's 1760s composition, 'To Anacreon in Heaven'.
11. And of course not only by Hollywood's movie industry. John Schlesinger's 1963 British 'New Wave' Film *Billy Liar* (Vic Films) provides, in its closing scene, a fine example, with anthem music the viewer must associate with the protagonist's imagined nation, Ambrosia.
12. Further after the event an interesting comparison, in terms of Hollywood-generated anthem quality, can be made with the gentle anti-Anschluss song, 'Edelweiss' in Rodgers and Hammerstein's (1959) musical, *The Sound of Music:* a song which has been mistaken for the Austrian national anthem.

Chapter 4

Anthem Quality: Its Paradoxes and Parodies

the uniformity of differences and the automatisation of strong affect

Shall our blood fail? Or shall it come to be
The blood of paradise? And shall the earth
Seem all the paradise that we shall know?

(Wallace Stevens, 68)

The performance of an anthem – national or otherwise – is an identity-focussed instance of unison. When people sing anthems together they should strongly feel the distinct specialness of their identity-in-common. If they do not get that kind of fellow feeling from the event then the act of unison has not really worked. Benedict Anderson's first paradox of the national is demonstrated by the religious origins of both the word 'anthem' (and its synonyms/cognates) and of the musical forms from which anthems as we know them arose. The paradox of objective modernity contradicted by a claim to tradition is however itself undermined by a real continuity. To the extent that Christianising duty was, by the eighteenth century, evaporating as motive force (or excuse) for European expansionism, religious spirit can be seen – as per Anderson's thesis – as having been replaced by patriotism. Anderson shows that the apprehension of time in the era of the modern nation is markedly different from that which had previously applied when notionally world-extensive religious communities (e.g. Hebraic; Islamic – Sunni, Shi'a; Christian – Orthodox, Catholic, Protestant) had been key in the shaping of identities. But Anderson has also demonstrated an epochal continuity in the emphasis on sacrificial deaths, fundamental to the sacred in both the religious and the national community (1991, 9–46 *passim*). The town centred on the church centred on the image of the crucifixion gives way to the town centred on the cenotaph commemorating the sacrifice of its former citizens. Church and cenotaph coexist and there is a continuity between the two in the Christian cross, signifying death on the stone or timber Roll of Honour. The symbol of Christ's sacrifice becomes more stylised in the drift from the purely religious to the religiously authorised national observance. Jesus Christ was the exemplary everyman, and so is the unknown soldier, who having died the exemplary death, is now with Christ. In the Christian or post-Christian world it is Christ's ultimate sacrifice that models the sacrifice of named individuals on behalf of the nation not needing to be named; the nation best represented by the individual, who, through self-sacrifice, is no longer able to be named.

The singing of anthems is deeply implicated in the circular motion enjoining the reverenced anonymity of the subject worshipping the state as apotheosis of the state-worshipping subject. Anthem *quality* is, as claimed in Chapter 1, the soul-stirring effect of a tune and the lyrics it carries or connotes. A particular kind of tune (and a tune in particular) carries the affective investment of a people; it is the means by which they recognise themselves among themselves. It is, as noted, a kind of self-welcoming gesture. Anthem quality is both a tautological and a paradoxical phenomenon.

In Chapter 2, I noted a number of dual aspects of anthems (written/spoken, official/unofficial, inward/outward looking, conscious/unconscious) and the efficacy of the Saussurean dichotomies (arbitrary/motivated, synchronic/diachronic) and the Bakhtinian dichotomies (epic/novelistic, monologic/dialogic) in approaching the anthem phenomenon. Already a number of paradoxes have been observed. The eternity of nations is had at the price of the paradoxical vigilance of those who are – in the here-and-now – not looking. The unconsciousness of the devotion and the vigilance of national interests are paradoxical in anthems. Anthems have a quasi-legal declarative aspect to them; they are an effort to mean something tangible and important, but as we have seen through our brief excursion in speech-act theory in Chapter 3, anthems mean too many things at once for the unisonant to be fully aware of what it is they are meaning. There may be a lot happening functionally in anthems and anthems do have deep and meaningful pretensions; yet they are generally shallow in expression. The operation of memory is *prima facie* paradoxical in the case of anthems. Unisonance is selfless and so we have to forget ourselves to remember who we are. A paradoxical consequence of the inward and outward orientation of anthems is that they include by excluding; that is to say, the process of making a particular identity special for those who possess it entails emphasising that the national quality of that particular identity is not possessed by others. Universalising unisonance of the 'We are the world' kind is interesting to consider in this light. The self-excluding outsiders of this sentiment would be those cynics who cannot stomach the saccharine. In Chapter 6, I will consider this kind of wilful self-exclusion in relation to the cosmopolitan hymn. Later in this chapter I will discuss the self-exclusion of anthem parodists.

In rhetoric, a paradox is a resolved contradiction: sense made against the odds or where it does not appear to be sensible. A paradox is, in other words, a way past what seemed an impasse in thought. Mechanically, one might say, a contradiction is something broken, a paradox is something fixed. How are things broken and how are they fixed in the cultural determination of identity? To pose and to answer such a question takes us out of the realm of the purely rational. Outside of the immediate circle of identification, one will find unconvincing many of the 'fixes' sought and found for problems anthems cure and cause. *We* do not believe that *their* country is the best; for a start, it contradicts what we know of ours (ours is the best) – and so their hyperbole will seem just that to us. Still, as long as the unisonant feel they can go on singing, the world of bystanders will for the most part stand in polite silence, if not awe. What of places or instances in which contradictions are not resolved? Where there is a reluctance to agree that a paradox is working we often find a motive for parody. The unison not working is what we witness when a country cannot agree on its anthem or when the people cannot agree to sing what the government wants them to sing; we shall see some instances of this in the next chapter.

In this chapter I draw attention to two key paradoxes of anthem quality: these are the *uniformity of differences* and the *automatisation of strong affect.*

The Uniformity of Differences

Nations celebrate the distinctiveness of their signs but nationhood need not be conspicuous; in general, participation in the series indicated by and for nation is of much more importance, both to state power and to the forms of identification on which it depends, than is the expression of uniqueness. In the serious world of sincere nations and nationalists, uniformity of differences is revealed in the fact that the overwhelming majority of the world's national anthems are written and arranged according to the rules of Western poetics and musical forms. Every member of the series 'nation' must have a national anthem; as a consequence, though anthems are notionally intended to express uniqueness (and so the differences between nations), reflection reveals that they serve largely to illustrate the consistency of national investments across international borders.

In 'Sociopolitical Control and the Structure of National Symbols: An Empirical Analysis of National Anthems', Karen Cerulo excludes nine anthems from her world survey (of 154) anthems, on the basis that these do not employ the Western 12-tone diatonic scales. The countries excluded are Bangladesh, Central African Empire, India, Japan, Senegal, Sudan, Swaziland, Thailand and Tibet (96). The rest of the world's anthems, that is to say, are composed in conformity with the rules of Western tonal music as these have evolved over the centuries coextensive with Europe's world imperial domination.

Accepting in a general way Cerulo's contention and her list of exceptions, there are still some caveats to mention with regard to the putative Western-ness of forms dominating in anthems worldwide today. It may well be that what we now accept to be a world hegemonic form in music is more mixed in origin than it first appears. The pentatonic scale, which so much pop music depends on today, does seem to be a very ancient and worldwide phenomenon. It may be that the diatonic scale is neither intrinsically nor exclusively Western (or say Hindu-Greek or Sumerian) in origin. Witness the 45,000 year old 'Neanderthal Flute' discovered in Slovenia in 1995 (Divje Babe Flute). Perhaps the tuning-by-ear advantages of a diatonic scale are such as to have ensured the world spread of such a system prior to the West's imperial expansion from the sixteenth century. Such cautions aside, just as one cannot imagine philosophy on the world scale today without reference to Socrates and Kant, so it would be difficult to think of the world canonic norms of music today without the norms exemplified and transmitted by Bach and Mozart and Beethoven, by the European conditions that enabled them and that their music subsequently fostered. The defining features of Western music as it relates to national anthems are, firstly, harmony based on the triad as a harmonic unit and the system of harmony known as 'tonal harmony', which was in its heyday in the nineteenth century; and secondly, the strophic song form in which melody and harmonic pattern both follow the strophic form of the text. Whether or not a particular scale or mode might be blamed for the imposition of world-norms on anthem music, certainly we can say that particular music event settings, such as those associated with church choral traditions and military bands, have imposed an essential Western form on anthem aspirations everywhere.

Cerulo makes the weak claim that anthems vary musically from nation to nation (79); recognising that nations do not all have the one anthem, one could hardly disagree. The point is however that the variation is uniform, predictable within a narrow range. Or, as Alex Marshall wrote in a 2008 *Guardian* piece on national anthems played at the Beijing Olympics, 'The [...] big disappointment with the majority of anthems is that no matter which country they come from, they sound like they were written by a band leader from the Royal Navy. There are no cha-cha-cha rhythms in Cuba's anthem, no highlife guitars in Ghana's' (http://www.guardian.co.uk/music/2008/aug/11/olympics2008).

Paul Nettl's 1952 study *National Anthems* – stridently universalist in tone – makes no effort to fudge the fact, writing of the development of anthems worldwide along entirely Eurocentric lines. Describing the psychological character of national styles in music, Nettl contrasts the idealism of the German with the rationalism of the Frenchman, German heaviness with Italian lightness, folk with art music, the influence on rhythm of Slavic as opposed to Germanic languages, religious versus expansionary styles, imperial versus republican styles. Nettl considers the ancient origins of persistent tunes, the means by which these are assimilated to the 'musical character' of a particular nation, the role of dance music, the contrast between the hymn and the march (2–33 *passim*). 'People of a more feminine orientation in their cultures dance with short steps and use correspondingly narrower intervals' (31). Until Nettl contrasts 'the savage Caribbean melody to the highly civilised *passacaglias* of a Lully and a Gluck' (28), one might have been under the impression that song and music were entirely European inventions and developments.

In the same post-war atmosphere in which Nettl wrote, Theodor Adorno was articulating a strident critique of universalist assumptions in music writing. In his 1948 volume, *Philosophy of Modern Music,* Adorno historicises the development of Western music in a far less whimsical manner:

> The critics present their arguments as though the tonal idiom of the last 350 years had been derived from nature [...] whereas these ossified principles themselves are actually the very evidence of social pressure. The idea that the tonal system is exclusively of natural origin is an illusion rooted in history. This 'second nature' owes the dignity of its closed and exclusive system to mercantile society, whose own dynamics stress totality and demand that the elements of tonality correspond to these dynamics on the most basic functional level.
>
> (11)

Adorno's comments are in relation to the future of high-art music in the immediate post-war period. Certainly his contempt for manufactured popular culture was as great as his disdain for the ossified principles of late classical music. In anthems we find a meeting of the two – the state-orchestrated manufacture of populist music to serve the state's purposes. For Paul Nettl, hypostasising nation and 'national characteristics' as unanalysed abstractions in the eternal/universal category leaves us with a curious contradiction in the apparent similarity of so many 'national' tunes. Here is how Nettl approaches the problem:

> The fact that the national characteristics of a given melody do not restrict it to its country of origin would seem to be at odds with the idea of specifically national traits discernible in this or that country's national music. Surely, if it is correct that every nation is possessed of a specific and characteristic brand of music, it cannot but amaze us that precisely the national anthem – obviously destined to express a people's definitive characteristics – should have been borrowed so frequently from abroad [...]
>
> The very existence of an 'objective' anthem, that is, an anthem whose melody can be and has been taken over by other peoples, would seem to prove that the psychological impact of an anthem is not exclusively determined by the emotional appeal of its music.
>
> (29–30)

Then what determines the psychological impact of an anthem? 'The full patriotic appeal of an anthem is determined by both the tune and the lines – or if you will – the association and relationship between the two' (30). While this last truism is difficult to argue with, it does not quite follow – knowing what we know of nations and their investments in particular and in common – that 'every nation is possessed of a specific and characteristic brand of music'. Nettl's use of the word 'destined' is instructive. Our attention should be drawn here to all three of Benedict Anderson's key paradoxes of the national. Modernity and pragmatic response to a need ('we have to have an anthem to be a nation') are obscured by a pretended eternal right. The fact of nation as posited universal difference belies the 'identity of identities' to which Michael Billig draws our attention (92). Anthems demonstrate a strong expression of this principle. Lastly, the intellectual weakness of the abstraction is demonstrated in the weakness of Nettl's argument, his failure to resolve the contradiction to which he alerts us.

So we can see, in the reduction of the world's musical choices to a set of Eurocentric folk and pseudo-philosophic clichés, that the 'de-colonising phase' of the UN's existence entailed the dispensing of Europe's affective goods to the natives. That was the kind of medicine that went with the territory the natives were allegedly *re*-claiming. Getting to be a nation – in the sense of being de-colonised – entailed all manner of Westernisations, the most obvious of which were in the form of formal attributes able to be presented in series with those of other nations and especially the older members of the club. A nation needs in this sense the serious things that A.D. Smith has prescribed and many mundane items as well: a constitution, a coat of arms, an anthem, borders, citizens, passports, border guards, rule of law, citizens' rights, taxes, money, bureaucracy, souvenirs, postcards, postage stamps, teaspoons, snow cones, car stickers: whether a nation can objectively be claimed to have each of these attributes, it is clear today that 'peer group pressure' among nations is such that few states would claim to be getting by without these kinds of things. 'Rogue' states are conspicuous for making just such claims to legitimacy: there is a constitution, there were elections. There are stamps for the collectors but no one sends postcards and you won't find the teaspoons and this gives the game away.

There is a kind of world average in nation-ness – a uniformity – a country does well to aspire to, if wishing to avoid detection as a 'rogue' or 'pariah' state. It seems incredible that – with some notable exceptions – the music of anthems the world over is so uniform, until one recognises that much of the function of national symbols is in their *not* drawing attention to the particularity of a nationhood. Modernity has demanded the natives throw off their colourful garb. The costumes may be kept for ceremonial purposes or for spectacular appearances in the UN General Assembly (not that New York can be shocked), but modern warfare and the displays of preparedness on which it depends require pants and shirts and battle jackets, cut so that the armies in them are often difficult to tell apart. Consider a country like Burma, where the military have until recently been the only part of the population conspicuous for their Western style dress in the form of a military uniform. Third World populations have gone on being bullied by the same or very similar uniforms that bullied them in the colonial days. When the soldiers – and the schoolchildren – of the Third World line up and salute their symbols of nation, they are mainly saluting styles of icon that, in general, were brought to them by colonising powers. What we witness in the Third World's saluting of its own national symbols is mainly the worship of Western form, this in turn representing the abstractions borrowed for the world stage (as also for self-recognition) in order that the nation shows itself in a good light: with good governance, with freedom, with democratic rights.

The tragedy unacknowledged is the lack of an alternative. The colonised are never given back the country that was taken from them. They are given something better and worse, less distinctive, something permanently less their own. They are given the idea of nation and the fact of state power. They are given modernity, a commodity, that, while its nature entails mechanical reproduction, can only be sold to the extent that it reveals no place of origin.

In his essay, 'Postcoloniality and the Artifice of History', Dipesh Chakrabarty discusses the co-achievement of 'European imperialism and third-world nationalism': 'the universalisation of the nation state as the most desirable form of political community'. For Chakrabarty, 'the universalist propositions of "modern" (European) political philosophy' condemn the Third-World historian to knowing Europe as the home of the modern. From this follows 'the everyday subalternity of non-Western histories'. Traffic between the dominant and the subaltern narratives results in a collaborative project, that of 'provincialising "Europe", the "Europe" that modern imperialism and third-world nationalism have, by their collaborative venture and violence, made universal' (in Ashcroft et al., 385). Nation, in the modern sense, is a Western idea. Its acceptance as the basis of a world order of international relations has guaranteed the imitation of European models by other-than-European peoples. National symbols have naturally been a key mechanism for the competitive mimesis demanded of new polities wishing to enter the fold. Anthems, I would argue, have been the affective lubricant greasing the wheels to make functional the paradox of the uniformity of differences. As such we may see them as the principal site of betrayal of Third World peoples, a means of endlessly signing an inescapable subalternity. When you sing the anthem that is an imitation of a European anthem, which mimics the feeling such an anthem inspires, you invest your identity in the mimetic, rather than the unique. But the investment is not made merely for today; it is notionally for all time.

In her essay, 'Anthropological Perpsectives on Music and Emotion', Judith Becker writes, 'if we accept [...] the uniformity of passions, we condone the silences imposed upon subalterns of all times and places whose feelings were assumed to be isomorphic with those of the persons who controlled the writing of history, and we ignore the developing body of data supporting the cultural inflection of the emotions' (in Juslin and Sloboda, 139). This is precisely what the good unisonant of anthems does; s/he accepts the silences in favour of an anthem quality, something with universal appeal.

Is the universal appeal of anthem quality something to be scoffed at? Surely everyone deserves democracy, and surely human rights should be the universal inheritance of the Enlightenment, of the categorical imperative, of civilisation as lived thus far? It is a helpful truism that languages in their diversity are able to express what people who speak them need to say; or to put it negatively, if one language is expressively deficient then all are. The paradox of the uniformity of differences consists in the imposition of one set (a generally debased version of the Western classical set) of musical choices worldwide as if this were the only set of choices for the making of music through which a people's collective feeling could be produced.

To constitute oneself as a nation for international symbolic purposes is to accept modernity as evolved by (and as historically imposed by) the West. For the most part we can say that music and nation of the kind an anthem presents are pseudo-choices for other-than-Western populations. They are arbitrary impositions presented in the guise of motivated choices. Along the lines Adorno suggests, it makes sense to think of them as one-and-the-same pseudo-choice. If we believe that all of the world's populations have to be divided into bordered national entities and that these state entities must be represented through means of words and music obeying the one set of rules as handed down through Western tradition, then the spectre of cultural imperialism vanishes. One draws the line in ethics here between acknowledging and accepting a reality. There is a contradiction between the expression of a people's particular feeling and particular sense of identity-in-common (what makes us us) and the use of Western-only means of expressing such feeling. The contradiction is resolved by a simple rhetorical mechanism – that it is through means descended in Western thought and Western affective strategy that particular peoples of the world express the identity-in-common we know as national: national identity as we know it today is a Western construct expressed through Western means.

The rhetoric for the universality of rights suggests accepting the humanity of all members of our species; this suggests an equality-in-principle and in-prospect more fundamental than the economic conditions with which it is at odds. If we can make the playing field level to that extent then there is no need for empires in which the more powerful will rule the less. Does the current basis of international relations in general serve such a goal? Does the paradox of the uniformity of differences raise the weak and hungry to the level of those nations that have had a head start? Or does this paradox rather distract the wronged from their world-bettering mission by giving them the impression all are in the same boat? To put the question bluntly – is the singing of anthems part of the problem or part of the solution?

To recap on the paradox of the uniformity of purported differences: people are moved to express their purportedly unique national identity through a tune that, often as not, might easily be somebody else's. The issue of provenance here is occluded by the musical (and rhetorical) uniformity of anthems. Stories that tell of people and places who composed, who sang, who marched to the song – these particularities conceal a more general contradiction between nation and the forms in which devotion is sung to it.

In his 1963 collection *Quasi Una Fantasia – Essays on Modern Music*, Theodor Adorno writes:

> [T]he very music which aimed to preserve the distinguishing marks of its origins now falls under the same dominance of the universal which, as the music of the people, it revolves around, now that its substance has withered away. Nowadays the only music which can achieve concrete specificity is music which traverses the entire realm of reason right to its very end, preserving in it anything natural that has survived the experience.
>
> (19)

Adorno was not thinking of anthems particularly in this passage, which nevertheless helps to explain why anthems borrowing native folkloric elements may well still be arranged to sound the same as each other. He was though interested in the national aspect of music: of the formulation, 'such a nation especially can never perish', Adorno writes:

> a nation that allows itself to be addressed as 'special' is already doomed. The products of the American pop music industry shed some light on this abyss. The sheer idiocy of a mass product created especially for you assumes the character of a ghastly necessity. Individual needs have been so ruthlessly eliminated from the product that they have to be invoked like magic formulae to prevent the customer from becoming aware of the murderous ritual of which he is the victim.
>
> (44)

Adorno was scathing of the putative individual specialness of pop music. For him hit tunes were an aspect of barbarism (46). They 'allow modern barbarians to laugh at the past for which they yearn and to pride themselves on how far they have advanced' (47). Adorno was interested in quotational-sounding classics and in the nexus between banality and universalism, a nexus one may plausibly claim as characteristic of anthems. Writing of 'L'amour est enfant de Bohème' from Carmen's *Habanera*, Adorno observes 'a primeval quotation which sounded familiar to everyone hearing it for the first time'. He writes that 'only the profundity of such memories can justify such banalities' (25). And this is precisely what the classic national anthem offers – it presents the listener with the tune that is unique to the future of the nation in particular, but is loaded with evocative *déjà vu*, of the kind Plato elucidated in his theory of learning in the *Phaedo* (220-251). We can only learn great truths because they are already known to us. The eternity of the nation has just this quality of transcendent religious truth, something beyond expression in words. It is for the future – for the benefit of generations yet unborn – the living nation strives; it is for the future of those yet-to-understand and of the unborn that those for-the-nation-dead have sacrificed. In his essay on 'The Goodness of Nations', Benedict Anderson writes that though the unborn 'are not a collectivity with which the Great Religions were preoccupied, they figure 'significantly in the national imagining, because their existence is the only sure guarantee of the nation's quasi-eternality' (196). It is to the future we-the-living pass the baton of our unmistakable signs; we pass it from those who are lost to those yet to wake, in whom however we place our unconditional trust. We trust the unborn as we ourselves were once trusted. The sacredness of the procedure is not to be questioned, and so, should the emperor be standing naked during the proceedings, this is likely to go unremarked. We nod to the anticipated *déjà vu* of national signs, and these work their magic the way scientific jargon might on subjects long since wary of religion proper. Everything one needs to know in the way of national devotion has the feeling of being known from a former life; that former life is as much of the eternity of the nation as is its future. It is by such tunes and orchestration the dead and the unborn will know each other. They meet in the hearts, in the souls of those with the breath to sing.

As the tearful reunion of those who have never met, the nation requires some powerful affective medicine – a drug of the kind that leaves minimal traces and for which antidotes will not be easily found. Adorno writes of popular music more generally, 'the sentimentality that is common to all remains unaware of its universality' (41). This lack of awareness is essential to the magic of the national anthem; to be under the spell of the anthem is, to the extent of the subject's devotion, to live the unexamined life. Adorno goes on from his portrayal of an unconscious universal sentimentality to portray 'that knowing twitch at the corner of the mouth which denotes the willingness to show understanding for every form of hegemonic nastiness, so as to be the better able to forgive it' (41).

My nation is better, is greater, than others? This is the idea cruelly mocked in Borat's anthem for his parodic Kazakhstan[1]:

Kazakhstan greatest country in the world.
All other countries are run by little girls.

Kazakhstan number one exporter of potassium.
Other countries have inferior potassium.

(Borat, 2012)

The straw-dog claims of exotic others are easily mocked and the self-parodic hyperbole of so many anthems shows how the mocking is done. This is Adorno's hegemonic nastiness in action. But who gets to choose their nation? Not those – the world majority – who are born and die in the territory where their lives just happened to happen; the refugee, even the economic migrant, generally chooses her new nation from a very short list, or else has that choice made for her. Then why should anyone feel that theirs is greater than other nations? So much of the world's injustice today has borders. 'It wouldn't happen here', we say, meaning 'we are better than that'. I think we can say that the psychology of nationalism involves motivating ourselves as a collectivity with regard to arbitrary facts of who and where and how we are. To make arbitrary facts appear just or right or eternally apt involves some complicated not-giving-things-a-thought. The paradox of the uniformity of differences is a key means to this end.

The Automatisation of Powerful Affect

Motivating citizens to pride in the arbitrary (right or wrong) facts of their collective situation is a trick of the ideological kind; the illusions it requires will be better maintained through affective than through logical means. Citizens may spontaneously express devotion to their nation of birth or choice, but there is a need for states to maintain the loyalty of their subjects through feeling and through image association, and, because of the special powers of song, a special kind of song fits the bill: this is the national anthem.

In everyday speech, the repetition of a sentiment or a particular representation leads often to cliché or tautology resented as such. As we have noted in Chapter 3, an overplayed pop song torments the weary ear, but populations go on being moved, sometimes over long stretches of history and over vast territories, by the tunes of and words in their national songs. In surviving anthems we find instances of clichés and tautologies that are typically not resented. In choosing an anthem, a nation chooses to typify itself for purposes of domestic and international consumption. That choice amounts to finding or creating and then promoting what already is or will become a clichéd representation of the nation in question, of its people and customs and collective sense of self. My intention in noting this largely unnoticed fact is not to criticise nations in particular for the particular choices of cliché they make (though certainly much critique along those lines will be justified); rather it is to assert that there is something unavoidably kitsch about the making of, and adopting of, anthems. The process of cliché manufacture is often very deliberately undertaken and is most noticeable when government authorities decide, for whatever reason, that they need to switch from a set of clichés or value assertions that, for whatever reasons, have become unacceptable. A case in point is Switzerland, which, at the time of writing, has decided to swap its current anthem (dating to 1841) because this text is thought too old fashioned, with its references to mountains and sunshine and prayer and God. The Swiss are holding a competition in 2014 in which they wish entrants to express in a new anthem the values espoused by the constitution of Switzerland (Laurence).

It might seem *prima facie* unlikely that a strategy of cliché creation and management would effectively harness national sentiment for state-sanctioned purposes. But this is to underestimate the solidarity-building power of collocations readily recognised by a speech community. For Anton C. Zijderveld, in his 1979 study, *On Clichés: The Supersedure of Meaning by Function in Modernity*, 'clichés are magically convincing, i.e. produce a sort of enchantment which needs an emotional participation in the general cadence of the words and sounds' (66). Kurt Spellmeyer writes of cliché in terms of 'substratums' (sic.) in discourse that 'enable participants to recognise what they hold in common' (267).

For Ryan J. Sparks, in his essay, 'Clichés and Composition Theory', clichés are 'culturally convincing places in discourse'; they represent 'powerful connective pathos' (454). Sparks is interested in 'how discourse builds the sort of connective energy necessary for an ethical sensibility'. Cliché for Stark 'does not initiate paradigm shifts; rather the cliché verifies that one belongs to an existing paradigm, an operating discourse' (456).

What of other people's clichés? Just as children and non-native speakers of a language will by lack of habit not be apprised of the clichéd nature of many utterances they encounter, so they will tend to de-automatise those markers of paradigms in which they are not yet full participants; they will bring dead metaphors back to life. What will it mean for the non-native speaker then to embrace foreign cliché for his/her own purposes? In the case of the widespread nineteenth-century adoption of 'God Save the King' (or its tune), one might opine that the effort was to borrow British success – at national cohesion, at being taken seriously on the world stage. I think we can say that when Third World nations adopt this strategy they are making a claim to participate in the appropriated paradigm; they are claiming a stake in sameness, in the same cultural capital.

Anthem, as discussed in the last chapter, is phatic communion on the grand scale: a people greets itself by means of words it has remembered well enough to forget to understand: a kind of collective 'rote' memory. That memory is archetypically of some originary moment or primal scene. Words of the anthem are the words of nation, words to which the breath returns, gives life. Anthem is the breath and so the embodying – in unisonance – that gives a modern nation life. In anthems powerful affect is automatised because the unisonant know how the anthem makes them feel. Emotion remains and is even intensified after the meaning of the words has been forgotten.

We sing together, and as we sing the feelings engendered by the song strengthen. We forget what it is we are singing about; we forget the meaning of the words; perhaps we forget that words have meaning. Just as music transcends the representational drive of communication, of speech, so in singing the words together we pass beyond the need to communicate and into the music of the moment we make. In unison we are lost as individuals; we are merged in the moment. This being-one-voice-in-the-moment together is what matters when we sing the anthem. We identify with the form in which we participate when we sing because this is the way in which we are together. In the event of our singing, so many other like events are memorialised; and these were events in which we honoured, not merely the song or the nation of the song, but those who have fallen for the nation. At such empathic events we feel the power of pledges exchanged among ourselves and to the fallen and to the as-yet-unborn for whom they sacrificed, for whom we too should be prepared to sacrifice. In the event of unison we are *with* words to be beyond them, and yet – whatever is lost along the way – ultimately the procedure is replete with meaning. The powerful meaning that every working anthem carries is that we who sing are of and for the nation: the nation is what the anthem means.

The power of these symbolic arrangements is such that neither lyrics nor music need be of a quality that would account for the strength of feeling they appear to engender. The power of these arrangements accounts for the widespread emulation of national anthems in other-than-national spheres. The magic of anthem quality is so powerful that the makers of many kinds of song would like to cast such a spell.

In a national anthem strong feelings (of identification with symbols and with fellow citizens, of a strong sense of one's identity) are made automatic – are able to be taken for granted – because they participate in a tight symbolic circuit. As we saw in the flag/moment/nation/song loop in the case of 'The Star Spangled Banner', each article of faith – each link in the symbolic chain of nation – confirms all the others. And more than confirms; each makes the others sacred and so beyond question and so able to be taken for granted. If it is reasonable to describe such a procedure as magical, then how can we describe the mechanism by which the spell is cast?

Patriotism is the last refuge of the coward and sentimentalism is the affective trigger on which it regularly relies. The issue of sentimentalism goes to the ethical basis of anthem singing because it implies a question as to the sincerity of those who sing. Sentimentalising detected is thought cloying; revelation of sentimentalism is shown with a knowing look, a smile. But if the sentimentalist is smug so also is the knowing critic, who judges from a position above and who may well resort to sarcasm. What sentimentalising and its knowing opposite have in common is that each depends on an act of judgement at once equally excluding and including (which, as in the case of anthems, includes by excluding and vice versa): 'if you can't feel this then you're not a member of the club; if you can't see what soppy fools they're making of themselves then you're not a member of my club'. The one lot has no feeling; the other has no judgement. Each earns and returns the other's sneer, and so the last refuge of the coward and the lowest form of wit have, it turns out, more than a little in common.

What motivates the sentimentalist? Anthony Saville writes:

> What is the desire under whose guidance sentimental thought is conducted? Doubtless there are several answers to this question. The most straightforward seems to be that what the sentimentalist seeks is the occurrence of certain enjoyable emotions. And since no emotion can be felt except as supported by a certain thought about its object, an appropriate thought has to be entertained for the sake of the pleasure. Where the object

> itself does not properly support that thought I shall have to contrive it by projection. Thus for instance I may sentimentalise a duckling before eating it by falsely representing it to myself as eagerly waiting for the pot, and in so doing make possible a gratifying feeling of benevolence towards the bird and the natural order to which the bird belongs.
>
> (1995, 224)

For Saville, 'the sentimentalist achieves a certain kind of gratification by false-colouring an object in his thought', for instance by thinking of his nation as greater, or nobler, than others. Sentimentalising has the effect of offering 'a world in which he [the reader] is comfortably and protectively cocooned' (225). Saville quotes us Ruskin's example from his remarks in 1865 to the cadets of the Royal Military College at Woolwich:

> You don't understand perhaps why I call you 'sentimental schoolboys' when you go into the army? Because, on the whole, it is love of adventure, of excitement, of fine dress and of pride of fame, all of which are sentimental motives, which chiefly make a boy like going into the Guards better than into a counting-house [...] So far then, as for your own honour and the honour of your families, you choose brave death in a red coat before brave life in a black one, you are sentimental.
>
> (226)

Ruskin's point was in part that the cadets were in love, not with substance, but with a circle of qualities and attributes, with the feeling itself, rather than that which (queen and country?) might be supposed to inspire the feeling.

Sentimentality might be a key technique or a pervasive condition in both anthem lyrics and music; certainly it is a characteristic quality of anthems generally. Along with the awe-inspiring of the sublime it is part and parcel of the late-Romantic aesthetics that provide anthem quality to this day with its arsenal of techniques for wringing affect from the heart of the good national subject. In Oscar Wilde's definition sentimentality is affect unearned. Wilde's sentimentalist is 'one who desires to have the luxury of an emotion without paying for it'. Consider Wilde's infamous critique of the death of Little Nell in *The Old Curiosity Shop:* 'One must have a heart of stone to read the death of Little Nell without laughing' (in Fulweiler, 65). James Baldwin wrote of sentimentality as 'the ostentatious parading of excessive and spurious emotion', as 'the mark of dishonesty, the inability to feel [...] the mask of cruelty' (in Berlant, 58). For Saville the crucial belief commonly held with regard to sentimentalising is not so much about its being false or mistaken per se, but that it is 'arrived at as a result of active false-colouring' (224). The sentimentalist is, in other words, disingenuous. S/he knows the feeling is overblown, out of proportion – in Wilde's terms (in a long letter he wrote from prison to his former lover), it is emotion cheaply had (768). Anthems are full of this gratuitous affect and we may regard them, as such, in the light of state-sponsored sentimentalism. Where feelings are discounted there will be a risk that truths demanding attention will go unremarked. Sentimentalism in the context of national devotion may for instance be a convenient means to conceal a theft or other crime or the suffering or sacrifice of others (who are not on our team); sentimentalise our losses and suffering and we can forget about them and theirs. We feel nothing for them because our tears have already been shed. There are many instances of cosmopolitan feeling (Christmas across WWI trenches in France) where the rote observance of duty breaks down and affective assumptions are challenged or displaced, however briefly. Should we read such perhaps carnivalesque events as outbreaks of sincerity against the rule of form? What nauseates Oscar Wilde in the death of Little Nell is akin to what nauseates Nietzsche more generally about Christianity: the slave's morality is founded on the celebration of weakness we read in the lie to oneself as to how one is entitled to feel. Those for-the-nation-dead? To redeem ourselves, we have merely to worship their sacrifice for us and express our own willingness to ourselves be subsumed by such a sacrifice. The model for this mindset is of course Christ's sacrifice for all sins present and to come. If we can accept the idea that someone else can die for our yet-to-be-committed sins and, in so doing, atone for them then we can accept much of the 'logical basis' on which national affect is enacted. Sentimentalism amounts to a short in the affective circuitry of the citizen subject. This lapse in the usual sincerity protocols matters because nation is today the world's deadliest belief-inspiring abstraction.

The paradox of automatisation may present the unisonant with feeling that is overwhelming, deadening with affect that – shading into the sentimental parodic – cancels itself out. I believe though that, beyond the self-parodic danger zone, there is a depth of identification (of self-understanding) at which the feeling intended in the words returns. In that place too, there is anthem quality, and of a kind that appears to have survived some test of cynicism. At such a depth of feeling, one may listen again to the words and, if they have value, rediscover their meaning so that, in the right frame of heart and mind, nothing can undermine the sentiment through which one has come to understand oneself. In literature and in music, in art more generally, classics are texts that survive to be admired in such a manner: the parodist acknowledges the greatness of that which s/he was moved to imitate. Surely, the average anthem is bathos to this. And yet beyond scepticism and criticism, beyond disciplined analyses, there too is a point at which even the scholar-ironist of anthems will acknowledge, in the chosen song, the weight of meaning who I am, among those others who, in the national sense, are like me and among whom I belong. This is the magic of anthem quality that works with and survives the paradox of the automatisation of affect.

The Art and Accident of Parody – Humbug Exposed

To recap: key paradoxes of anthem quality are the uniformity of differences and the automatisation of strong affect. Perhaps it is easiest to account for the coordinated functioning of these paradoxes through an example of their parody. In the Marx Brothers'

1933 film *Duck Soup*, the pseudo-country of which Rufus Firefly (Groucho Marx) is Prime Minister comes equipped with the shortest 'anthem' of which I know. It consists of two lines of lyrics, as follows:

> Hail, hail Freedonia,
> Land of the brave and free.
>
> (Marx Bros, 2012)

Musically, the movement is from swelling refrain in the first line to grandiose closing cadence in the second. The memory-wearying stanzas, the epic story of heroic deeds done in the name of nation, the symbolic setting: these things simply are not there. In terms of generic classification, we good subjects, who would generously like to imagine ourselves unisonant, do not have enough time to work out whether to start marching or praying or appreciating the tableau. This is the anthem hollowed out for display, shown to be empty. Freedonia's anthem is not anyone else's but it could be. It has – in parodically abbreviated form – all that swells the prideful breast of nation. The overdetermined speech functions of the anthem are all there. Hailing Freedonia we assert its bravery and freedom, we commit to go on hailing it, we express the (mock-) national affect, we declare what Freedonia is and must be. The difference of 'Hail Freedonia' from other anthems is of the degree – is parodic of the degree – that allows this song to be a member of the series, anthems. In 'Hail Freedonia', automatisation of affect is parodied by being made too literal, too immediate. The band strikes up the anthem when and only when Rufus Firefly (Groucho Marx) comes on stage. Then everyone must stand to attention and join in the national devotions. Humour lies in Firefly's candid determination continually to make himself unworthy of those devotions, to thus make himself an unworthy symbol of the non-existent nation he is meant to represent.

The knee jerk here shows how the tune is stuck like a broken record; the tune that could be played for any country can be played for anyone who happens to be declared the leader. This Ruritanian nation-in-particular does not exist but the abstract reality of nation has powerful effects on those whose loyalty is demanded by the state: this is what 'Hail Freedonia' reveals. Moral of the story: the dignity for which the state calls distracts its citizenry from any business they might otherwise have had; rather they are consumed in the moment of avowing themselves. Not that we the audience know anything of them; we know them as we know ourselves because their difference from us is uniform with the affect we express when we represent – and when we welcome – ourselves to and as ourselves.

If *Duck Soup*'s 'Hail Freedonia' parodies the uniformity of differences that the cheerfully unisonant subject will fail to notice, then another much older American parody, Lydia Huntley Signourney's 'God Save the Plough', targets a particular form of oppression, an identification with which one might wish to part ways in order to become someone else, someone different. You know the tune.

See, – how the shining share
Maketh earth's bosom fair,
  Crowning her brow, –
Bread in its furrow springs,
Health and repose it brings,
Treasure unknown to kings,
  God save the plough!

The last stanza clarifies the political agenda:

Who are the truly great?
Minions of pomp and state,
  Where the crowd bow?
Give us hard hands and free,
Culturers of field and tree,
Best friends of liberty –
  God save the plough.

(in Gesner, 646–647)

Parody is by no means the only way of critiquing a text, and it will be an open question then as to whether we should regard 'America' ('My country, 'tis of thee') as in fact a parody of 'God Save the King/Queen'; presumably sincerity on its own terms is what saves it from parody status. Compare The Sexpistols' more recent – and somewhat less subtle – attack on the song.

God save the queen
The fascist regime
They made you a moron
Potential H-bomb

God save the queen
She ain't no human being
There is no future
In England's dreaming

The nihilist agenda is clear in the lyrics:

Don't be told what you want
Don't be told what you need
There's no future no future
No future for you

There is a reflexive turn too, and a bitter historicising gesture to justify conclusions already reached:

Oh god save history
God save your mad parade
Oh lord god have mercy
All crimes are paid

And there is identification: this time it is expressed in the unisonance of those who proclaim themselves as beyond the pale of the national unison:

When there's no future
How can there be sin
We're the flowers in the dustbin
We're the poison in your human machine
We're the future your future

Any lingering doubts as to sincerity are cleared up towards the end:

God save the queen
We mean it man
We love our queen
God saves

God save the queen
We mean it man
And there is no future
In England's dreaming

From the exclusion then a new unisonance is forged:

No future no future
No future for you
No future no future
No future for me

(Sexpistols, 1977)

In sum, I think we can say that the Sexpistols' 'God Save the Queen' is generically anti-anthem, rather than parody. In Chapter 6, I will explore some further examples of the anti-anthem.

***

Serge Gainsbourg's example demonstrates that the business of parodying national sentiment may be undertaken at personal hazard. Gainsbourg's controversial 1978 reggae version of 'The Marseillaise' resulted in death threats from right-wing veterans who were probably right to read this innovation as a de-sanctifying gesture.

One of the most interesting of anthem parodies is Jimi Hendrix's feedback-rich 1969 version of 'Star Spangled Banner' (Woodstock, 1970). A single lick really, one will be justified in asking how this can be a parody at all and what could be parodied by such means. Hendrix's rendition of the national anthem provided a critique of American national affect – his 'Star Spangled Banner' is parodic of the song's rootedness in a tradition that has certain unavowed parameters in terms of class and sense of musical propriety. Let us say that, in 1970, we imagine the unisonant of this song in a congregation, much like that of a church in terms of fellow feeling, and we imagine them as mainly white and we imagine the human voice – the evidence of unison – as the image of the sentiment expressed in the song. The ironising affect Hendrix's performances achieved can be explained by accounting for the context shift they involved. On stage was a black man making a solo psychedelic drug-hazed electric guitar version of something Americans associated with a conflation of items with race and class-based unspoken hegemonic qualities: white middle-class Protestant, civic-minded, mindful of the war-dead, appreciative of God's gifts, dutiful, filial. Sentimentalists had had all of this affect out of their national song without the least conscious effort. And now it had all been exposed as such and so negated, at great volume, by a single guitar riff, which was itself a kind of feedback.

In the context of Vietnam-protest-era music, this could not but be read as parody of the American national affect and its sentimental bases. By negating various unspoken terms of the average normal performance context, this particular performance draws attention to these and makes an audience realise that something has been concealed from them. Hendrix's was a revelation of false consciousness. His rendition gathers then a group, not of the unisonant, but of 'good listeners' who in the parlance of the day get to share 'right on' feelings about how things are in and with America. The power of this parody has to do with its tit-for-tat transcendence of the words. In terms of strategy, Hendrix, like those who object to him, does not bother to spell out assumptions or circumstances in which meaning are made. The power of Hendrix's 'Star Spangled Banner' is of evocation rather than representation.

***

By way of parody, we return to the idea of sincerity. When the veil of sentiment is cast aside, what is revealed as the real motivation behind anthem singing? Let us leave the last word on that question to Norman Lindsay whose Noble Society of Puddin' Owners sing the following anthem in his novel, *The Magic Pudding* (already noted in Chapter 3 for its treatment of 'God Save the King'):

The solemn word is plighted,
  The solemn tale is told,
We swear to stand united,
  Three puddin'-owners bold.

When we with rage assemble,
  Let puddin' snatchers groan;
Let puddin'-burglars tremble,
  They'll ne'er our puddin' own.

Hurrah for puddin'-owning,
  Hurrah for friendship's hand,
The puddin'-thieves are groaning
  To see our noble band.

Hurrah, we'll stick together,
  And always bear in mind
To eat our puddin' gallantly,
  Whenever we're inclined.

(44)

Note

1. The lyrics of Kazakhstan's real anthem are as follows:

    We are a valiant people, sons of honor.
    We've sacrificed everything to gain our freedom.
    Emerging from malicious grip of fate, from hell of fire,
    We scored a victory of glory and success.

    Soar high up in the sky, oh, the eagle of freedom.
    Call up to harmony, agreement and Accord!
    Since the hero's might and strength is in the nation.
    Just as the unity is nation's razing sword.

    (Xing Hang, 330)

   In March, 2012, Kuwaiti Olympic officials caused a scandal by playing the Borat parody in error (having found it online) for the gold medal performance of Maria Dmitrienko in the World Shooting Championships.

Chapter 5

Choosing and Chosen

the overt and covert us *and* them *of national devotions*

There are men whose words
Are as natural sounds
Of their places.

(Wallace Stevens, 51)

Imagine a city under siege. It is the capital of a nation just come into being. The city though is ancient, one that down through the ages has been a part of all sorts of kingdoms, empires, republics. Let's call it S. S is a city among ever shifting borders, a place where powers that be on all sides have recognised the line needing to be drawn because the others have gone too far. S is a city where local people have learned time and again to live peacefully with each other, despite the urgings of those faraway who, by asserted right of religion or race or empire, claimed them for their own. It is hard to live on the line between civilisations, but if you can learn how to do it then you will be culturally the richer for it; certainly you will have learned a tolerance – an openness – of which the metropolitan masters will never be capable.

But now the wars have come again and the city is under siege. During the siege, a song is popular. The song is about a girl from another town, in fact the capital of the invading country, the country laying siege to the town. Let's call the town B. The song is about the girl from that town, a fashion capital, one with a romantic history of songs like this, songs about tragic love. B is such a glamorous place the boys from S do not think twice about singing the song. Of course the song is popular with the boys from B; it is a popular song about their town and the 'girl from B' could be the girl next door. The boys on both sides hum it to themselves as they go about their arduous work of killing and of not being killed. In either case the song has no political meaning for the soldiers; but it is ironic they can kill each other and love the same sentiment about the same girl in the same song sung in the same language (which they each call something else now because national pride prevents them from admitting that they, and their adversaries, speak the same language).

There is another song popular in B at this time: a soldier's song, it is about being willing to die for your country. The refrain is along those lines: 'I will die for my country; I'm happy to die'. The boys from B, laying siege to S, sing this song and this song too becomes popular on the other side, in the city under siege, because the boys there, in the army of S are very happy to see the boys from B die for their country. 'Go on! Die for your country!' they echo back across the valley when they hear the song being sung. But taunts cannot touch the national pride of the B boys; they have been inoculated against irony. They will only sing louder because they express their patriotic commitment through this ultimate choice: a willingness to die in the cause of country, the cause that makes them who they are.

We sing the same words, but do they have the same meaning for us? The words of a song, like turns in a conversation, will never mean quite the same thing twice. The moment the song becomes part of – or subject to – a conversation, the risk of irony appears. Irony breaks the spell of eternity, the anthem-incantation that mesmerised the unisonant to think that what they sang was immutable. The spell is broken because dialogue is an unfolding in time, function of which is *inter alia* to undermine certainty of what was known. Otherwise, why speak? Singing together has a different function. If others sing with us, but sarcastically, then they have re-contextualised our devotion, by showing that it has an outside – a place beyond the belief we share. But, as noted in the last chapter, the spell can be mended, the song saved, depth of feeling deepened in the manner of a resolve redoubled against odds. Surviving a test of cynicism from the other side will be easier than facing off a fifth-column ironist's threat because the anthem and our unison already tell us the others are not entitled to sing. They can only sing sarcastically.

The context of the war gives the song a different, an opposite, meaning on either side of the lines. We sing from somewhere because we are who we are, but the singing itself is part of the living sense of self that makes us who we are. The magic of anthem quality is that singing the words (or humming the tune to connote the words) helps us to feel that we are the same people as those who sang the song before. The sentiment seems to be the same; we seem to be the same as the fallen of yesteryear. But can we be?

***

In his 1982 book, *Orality and Literacy: The Technologizing of the Word,* Walter Ong writes of the phenomenon of homeostasis in oral cultures. The term is adapted from biology and psychology, where it accounts for the means by which systems and organisms maintain continuity with an existing order and so resist dramatic change. Homeostasis, on Ong's reading (46–49) is the means by which a culture maintains a past appropriate to its present. We know about this phenomenon because of the understanding of oral poetry that has come from the early to mid-twentieth-century work of Albert Lord and Milman Parry and because of the investigations of literate anthropologists into the genealogies the (pre-literate) tribe has constructed in order to account for its present order. Ong writes of a process whereby 'oral societies live very much in a present that keeps itself in equilibrium [...] by sloughing off memories which no longer have present relevance' (46–49). The tribe claims to be preserving a knowledge of things as they always were, of the past as it actually was. But it turns out that they have changed the genealogies in order to justify the social and political order as it is today. The myths now explain that the people now running the show were the good guys before, that they always were. The literate anthropologist consults the records and discovers that this was not the story before. Fifty years ago the people now in power were not running the show and nor were they considered, by the powers-that-were-then, to be the good guys. The story has changed to accommodate the changed order. The anthropologist observes how the people studied have deluded themselves about the way things were, about how things came to be the way they are. You could say that these people are now deluding themselves about who they are because they are seriously mistaken about how they came to be *as* they are. There is no reason to see homeostasis as a consciously fomented plot; on the contrary, the remembering of a past that justifies the present is an unconscious mechanism with broad prevalence and one that perhaps has maximum efficacy in the absence of written records. In societies where national identity is invested in the idea of a generational continuity, the revision of anthems can serve the homeostatic function of allowing us to feel that we are the same people as those who, earlier on, were singing different words or words that, in their different context, had a different meaning. Anthem quality has a homeostatic effect on those who sing; it helps the unisonant to feel that they are participating in an eternal order; together they are singing the way things have to be. Where different traditions are available to a people, or those who order a people's devotions, changes in political climate may effect sudden changes in the self-perception implied by a particular anthem quality. Among the former Yugoslav republics a number of examples may be noted.

In the Balkans

Anthems are – *inter alia* – declarations of who we-who-sing are. The need to decide on a particular song among various possibilities will often bring into sharp relief different opinions as to identity-in-common. Serbia's case might, for present purposes, be described as 'a tale of two anthems', these being the royalist song 'Bože Pravde' ('God of Justice') and the pan-Slavic hymn, 'Hej, Sloveni' ('Hey, Slavs')[1]. Each has had anthem status and lost it at various stages in the history of Serbia, pre-, during and post-Yugloslavia. Neither song was originally intended to be a national song for Serbia; both have been in this sense 'accidental anthems'. 'God of Justice', originally a song in a patriotic stage play of the 1870s (commissioned to legitimise a young prince's accession to the Serbian throne), was the national song and later the official national anthem of Principality (later Kingdom of) Serbia from 1872 to 1919 and then, in a changed form, part of the national anthem of Kingdom of Yugoslavia from 1919 till 1941. It was resurrected in 2006, in again a changed – republican – form to become the national anthem of the Republic of Serbia. The pan-Slavic 'Hey, Slavs', written in 1842, emerged, a century later, as a national song of the Communist-led resistance movement in Yugoslavia in 1942, and it later became an unofficial national anthem of the Communist-ruled Yugoslav federation; only becoming the official anthem of the Socialist Federal Republic by virtue of a constitutional amendment in 1988. The song survived the violent disintegration of that federation in 1991 to serve (once again unofficially) as an anthem of the rump Yugoslavia from 1992 to 2006.

'Hey, Slavs' was written in 1834 by Samuel (Samo) Tomašik, a Lutheran minister of Slovak origin, a writer and an ardent promoter of Slav culture and unity. Originally written in Czech or Slovak (at the time the boundaries between the two languages were not yet firmly established), it was addressed to the Slovaks and it celebrates the Slovak language and spirit. The song was written initially as an act of defiance against the dominance of the German language in the Czech capital, Prague. Shocked by the refusal or reluctance of fellow Slavs to speak their Slavic language, Tomašik wrote the song in one night as a celebration of the native tongue and as an assertion of its glorious future, this in spite of the menacing threat of another unmentioned language – one may assume to be German. The music for these lyrics was in part borrowed from the already famous Polish marching and fighting song – 'the March of Dabrowski'. For the purposes of Tomašik's song, the march, based on a lively folk melody or mazurka, was slowed to a paean, dedicated to a language allegiance. The Polish song was written in July 1797 by Josef Wybicki, a friend of General Jan Dabrowski, and entitled 'The Song of the Polish Legions in Italy'; later it became known by its first verse 'Poland has not yet perished'. General Dabrowski at the time commanded Polish volunteers fighting under General Napoleon Bonaparte in Italy against Austria-Hungary, one of the three states that partitioned Poland in 1795. 'Poland has not yet perished' attained the status of a national anthem in the newly independent Poland in 1926, much earlier than 'Hey, Slavs' did in Communist Yugoslavia (1945).

In sum, the story of 'Hey, Slavs' is that a Slovak in Prague, annoyed to hear German, gets a Polish marching tune stuck in his head, and this becomes a vehicle for lyrics that have proved very portable for the purpose of expressing pan-Slavic spirit. Perhaps it was the very disunity of the Slav peoples of Yugoslavia – which was already in the process of disintegration – that made this a desirable official anthem in 1988. By 2006 each of the formerly constituent peoples of socialist Yugoslavia had its own state and anthem (or at least a state-like entity with an official anthem); there was, by that time, for those former-citizens of the former Yugoslavia no possible use for a song of Slav unity. 'God of Justice' – a number from a pro-monarchist musical – now serves a democratic republic – the Republic of Serbia – as its first official anthem. Why should such a notionally superior political entity (genuinely democratic as opposed to monarchic or authoritarian) identify itself and its citizenry through a miasma of confused imagery and the defensive investments of a past that bears little resemblance to the present? The easiest answer to this question will be that, however vacuous a solution this may seem, the only imaginable alternative was simply no longer viable. Serbs could no longer maintain an identity-in-common expressed through the vehicle of Slav unity; events leading to Serbia's isolation had made the idea ridiculous. And so, along the lines of Anderson's first paradox, their only alternative was to identify with each other on the basis of a spurious tradition requiring renovation for the purpose.

The choice between 'God of Justice' and 'Hey, Slavs' was effectively between a monarchist prayer and a populist liberatory march, between a king's song and a fellow-feeling foreigner's song. At any point in the story of Serbia, we can say the choice between these songs was made on the basis of political expediency. 'Hey, Slavs' was an idea appropriate to maintaining the existence of the Yugoslav federation; once that hope was lost the song seemed silly. Still, from the point of view of Serbian democracy today, there is something equally ridiculous in the origin of each of these songs. It is for the sake of appearance of tradition and continuity that such nonsensical choices are made.

***

As with Serbia (and as with many states), in the case of Slovenia two songs contended for the position of national anthem. In this instance an apparent ideological gulf masks perhaps a more essential temperamental divide: the bellicose army song versus the happy drinking 'all together …' number. Vacillation between 'Zdravljica' ('A Toast') and 'Naprej zastava slave' ('Forward, Flag of Glory': its refrain, 'let the rifle speak') might be taken as reflecting the ambivalence with regard to potentially hostile others one reads attributed to Jesus Christ in the gospels of Matthew, Mark and Luke: *who's not with me is against me/who's not against me is with me*. The difference in orientation of these two songs also reflects an ongoing left/right animosity in contemporary Slovenian politics. It is interesting that the militarist song was able to enjoy anthem status in Slovenia under both Yugoslavias (i.e. the kingdom and the federal republic), when many and various separatist songs were proscribed. The 1989 adoption of 'A Toast' (lyrics courtesy of Slovenia's national poet France Prešeren) is strongly suggestive of an outward looking state, one hoping for a place in a cosmopolitan Europe. 'Forward, Flag of Glory' has remained the anthem of the Slovenian army and so is far from being discarded for the purpose of asserting Slovenian national spirit. Perhaps retaining it in this minor role has been necessary because 'A Toast' is a song that – at least as it is presently sung – de-emphasises national aspiration to a degree unusual for the anthem genre. In a crossroads of Europe dominated historically by the national (or imperial) aspirations of larger and more powerful political entities, 'A Toast' is a song that tests the limits of what an anthem can be by holding out a hope of rising above the national.

In 1989, the fledgling sovereign state of Slovenia needed briefly to assert to itself and its neighbours a preparedness to fight for its independence; that struggle over, the identity-in-common of Slovenians was pragmatically re-invested in cosmopolitan spirit, because Slovenia saw that its future interests would best be served by joining Europe as quickly as possible. Prešeren's Toast provided the new nation with lyrics perfect for the purpose. The original (1844) poem begins:

Friends, again the vines bore well!
Let sweet wine liven our veins,
And clear our hearts and eyes,
Drown cares.[2]

Set to music,[3] we have here a drinking song, written by a drinker and for the benefit of others who will imbibe. It is a poem primarily for heterosexual males who are drinking together (the 'brothers' of the third and of the final stanzas, those who collectively admire the comely maidens of the fifth stanza). The poem's sentiments are mixed, mercurial, as those of drinkers and drunks often are. Or, one might say that there is a rambling distractedness, true to genre in these lyrics. To gloss them in their spirit, so to sum up, the idea of the poem is more or less this: *Let's drink up, forget your cares/don't be sad. Drink to whom? To us, of course! We're Slovenes. Let lightning strike anyone who gives us trouble. Let's be free, as our ancestors were. Let's all love each other and live in peace; that way there'll be honour. And our girls our matchless! And their sons will be brave! Young men – you'll defend the land! We're all brothers. Let's have a drink!*

Considering the poem all in all, compared with canonic anthems of the Western world, one is impressed with the range of tone and mood in 'A Toast'. There are lyrical and bellicose passages; there is admiration of beauty, both of the season in the vines and of Slovenian womanhood. There are sad thoughts to put aside; there is the image of enemies vanquished. There is the promise of neighbourly fellowship (as modelled by the circumstances in which the song is ideally sung). No matter your mood or politics on the day, there is something for every Slovene in here, but especially for the male of drinking age. At every turn and for every purpose, there is an inducement to drink. Indeed, one is tempted to draw an analogy between the stages of drunkenness and the moods of the nation as portrayed in the song. It should be noted that this observation would be true of these lyrics' reference to any nation in the modern European sense, because with very little substitution of phrases this is a song that could be sung by drinking age males of just about any European country with a few grapes to harvest. The final stanzas essentially contain no national sentiment at all; rather they are transcendent of the national world view. It is of further interest that the most cosmopolitan stanza in the song, the seventh, is the one the Slovenian government, in 1989, chose alone to be the lyrics of the national anthem. One may be tempted along these lines to see the singing of 'A Toast' as something in the light of a parody of national sentiment. And yet one may be sure both that Prešeren's intention was sincere (sincerely patriotic in its way) and that those who sing the song today do so to sincerely express their devotion to Slovenia as the sovereign state in Europe that it has become. The seventh stanza – that is to say, the present Slovenian anthem – is, in the official government translation, as follows:

> God's blessing on all nations,
> Who long and work for that bright day,
> When o'er earth's habitations
> No war, no strife shall hold its sway;
> Who long to see
> That all men free,
> No more shall foes, but neighbours be.

(Government of the Republic of Slovenia, 2010)

Every anthem is at once self-addressed as an expression of solidarity as well as an address to (or display for) others. As we have seen in the case of 'Hey, Slavs', solidarity can leak across borders to be at least notionally shared with neighbours. In Slovenia's case the chosen lyrics appear unusually outwardly oriented. For reasons I will now explain, I think though that this appearance is something of an illusion.

One is tempted to regard Prešeren's toast as an unambiguously cosmopolitan text, thus contrasting with the relatively unselfconscious patriotism of the anthems of neighbouring states. If we consider which of Prešeren's words are in and which words are out of the anthem as officially sung, one will see that it is the more bellicose parts that have been omitted. For instance in the third stanza, where the protection of the deity is invoked: 'Let lightning out of clouds strike down/All our people's foes', and in the fifth stanza where young Slovene men should strike terror in the hearts of enemies.

The fighting words and the words suggesting the exclusive qualities of those singing are not in the official song; they will nevertheless be in the minds of those singing. That is because this poem – at the core of the Prešeren canon – is one that all Slovenian schoolchildren would have had to commit to memory, during their schooling, at any time since the creation of the Kingdom of Yugoslavia in 1918. If an anthem simultaneously represents a people-as-nation to itself and to the world at large, then (as we have for instance seen in Holland's case) sentiment thus expressed and understood within the family of nation is likely to differ in some degree from that which the outsider will perceive. In this instance we can see that there is a subtext to that manner of representation, one that will operate largely at an unconscious level for the subject-in-unison. In 'A Toast' the call for sacrifice precedes what is sung and all those singing would have this in mind. So one may argue that there is a covert militarism in this anthem. To most non-Slovenes (though perhaps not to all citizens of former Yugoslav states), the words not sung are unknown and so irrelevant; they are though at the back of the minds of those singing. So, to sing the Slovenian National Anthem is, in some degree, to concur with the ideas expressed in the parts of the poem omitted from the official text. One might also contend that it is to participate in a covert rite of exclusion (*those only listening cannot know the whole of the story of what we are singing*).

The uniqueness of Prešeren's poem-cum-song lyric is in encapsulating a Slovenian spirit of pragmatism in the geopolitical sphere. Pragmatically putting behind them the question of identity, Slovenians in singing a snippet of Prešeren's toast ironically position their national identity as other-than-national. In what might be thought a quest not to offend, they perhaps give the European Union its least problematic (one might say most politically correct) of anthems, one to which no other nation could possibly object. When one considers how problematic the idea of unisonance has been for Europe or at least the European Union, one sees Prešeren's toast in the light of a helpful gesture to the EU from the enthusiastic newcomer. Allowing our view to take in the other 'end' of the former Yugoslavia, considering the self-symbolisation difficulties Macedonia has had with neighbouring Greece, Slovenia's anthem choice is a Balkan success story.

Slovenia's current anthem represents perhaps a unique example of a universal mechanism, expressing Anderson's second paradox: the anthem appeals to the universality of sentiments implying the participation of national entities in a cheerful *cosmopolis* – a *glocality* of neighbours and friends. One might well speculate that Slovenia's anthem thus transforms the anthem's usual object of national devotion – the clearly bounded nation state – into a diffuse feeling of universal solidarity with national subjects in general. The synecdoche implied suggests drinkers gathered convivially under vines are the model of good international relations. In this manner, Slovenian nationhood (brotherhood among nations) is implied by a particular proven facility for brotherhood – the capacity to imbibe. Through these rhetorical means one might claim that, in the Slovenian anthem, the object of Slovenian national devotion is nationhood in general. The objective of the song is acceptance of Slovenia as brother-nation among neighbours. As the least war-disrupted and most economically advanced and Europe-integrated of the former Yugoslav states, the success of Slovenia's self-symbolising strategies is clearly demonstrated. It has been a reflexive and postmodern strategy. Slovenia was able to cite its own Romantic text from the golden age of nation and anthem, and from this text produce a new artefact that would provide both an effective storefront for Europe-integration purposes and a subliminal nationalist message for Slovenians.

Who is Addressed in an Anthem?

A comparison between Slovenia's anthem and that of its immediate former-Yugoslav neighbour, Croatia, reveals an impressive contrast in the sense of an addressee, as presented to and by the unisonant. If Slovenia's chosen (and edited) anthem speaks overtly of friendship, as one included voice to a world of (apparently included) others, Croatia's 'Ljiepa Nasa' ('The Croatian Homeland') is avowedly self-addressed and lacks the covert (insiders' as opposed to outsiders') reading we observed in the case of 'A Toast'[4]. Three of the four stanzas speak of the Croats' unquenchable love for their homeland; the remaining stanza extolls the beauty of the place. By addressing the homeland's rivers and the sea directly, its singers appropriate this geography and so demarcate the borders of the much-loved country. The anthem thus asserts Croatia's unity (against potential pretenders) and its unbreakable ties with its people. In contrast, the original fourteen-stanza poem 'The Croatian Homeland', written by Antun Mihanovic in 1835, is a song of praise for the Croats' relationship with nature, their simple life and bravery – the romantic virtues of pure national souls. On their path to anthemhood, the four stanzas drawn from this poem have undergone significant modifications and additions, the result being a song that is doubly reassuring: it reassures the singers first of the people's love for themselves as a people, and second that this love is the means by which the 'natural' territory of the homeland is maintained. In contrast with Slovenia's 'A Toast', 'The Croatian Homeland' is a song unconcerned with the opinions of non-Croats. If anthems reflect, they also produce the temperament expressed in them.

Slovenians swapped 'let the rifle speak' for 'friends, let's have a drink'; Croatians have gone on loving their country and speaking to its parts – metonymic anthropomorphisms of the Croat collectivity (the peopled place that is the Croat homeland). How conscious a decision has this been? In Croatia's case there have not been other songs seriously contending for anthemhood; but the revision of 'The Croatian Homeland' has been a deliberate and politically motivated process. Perhaps, as we have seen with a number of well-travelled anthems (for instance 'God Save the King/Queen' and 'Hey, Slavs'), it will be fair to say that a song chooses its singers and for reasons they might not have anticipated. This, I will argue below, seems certainly to be the case with Australia's unofficial national song, 'Waltzing Matilda'.

To whom are anthems addressed? In the case of 'God Save the King/Queen' it may be better to ask, who is intended to hear them (or overhear them)? This complication points to the dual conscious/unconscious, overt/covert aspect of anthems and their lyrics. The fact that a tune carries the meaning of words even in the absence of those words already suggests that there may generally be something subliminal taking place when anthems are sung. In the national tableau, as in Croatia's anthem, the imagery of the beautiful country shines through the tune; in a march (like 'The Marseillaise') we hear the passage of feet and we know the cause that binds us in our progress towards a common future; a prayer song such as 'God Save the King/Queen' focusses the mind on the throne, the crown and the symbolic nation-centring person of the sovereign. We do not need to hear or to sing words to have these images in the mind's eye or to recognise the tone of feeling intended. The suggestion is already planted; and as we have seen in the case of the Marx Brothers' 'Hail Freedonia', the tune can set off a series of devotional activities that are automatic and unconscious.

There are exceptions to the pattern of tune-connoted lyrics (for instance, in the case of Spain, where there are no well-established lyrics to connote by way of what would otherwise be accompanying music). Before we leave the Balkans we should briefly consider the case of Bosnia, a country that has been seriously challenged by the problem of how to address itself and that has, thus far, not been able to officially sanction lyrics for its new national anthem. Lyrics have been written for the official anthem, 'Intermezzo', by one of its composers, Benjamin Isovic. Till date however, the Bosnian legislature has not made these official, and, in terms of popular recognition, parodies of the song (composed prior to the writing of the 'serious' lyrics) are probably better known than the 'real' words. Zoran (Zoka) Ćatić's, the best known of the parodies, concludes with the stanza:

> Bosnia dear mother, Herzegovina –
> Please forgive us our existence.
> You will always be the land and we the manure.[5]

In *Musicophilia,* Oliver Sacks writes of aphasic patients who have in many normal circumstances lost the ability to know themselves and to represent themselves in language.

Following on from discussion of the case of an elderly patient who had for a long time remained speechless following a major stroke, Sacks writes that though 'singing is not propositional communication, it is a very basic existential communication. It not only says "I am alive, I am here," but may express thoughts and feelings that cannot be expressed, at this point, by speech' (233–234). Sacks goes on to observe that 'being able to sing words can be a great reassurance to such patients, showing them that their language capacities are not irretrievably lost, that words are still "in" them, somewhere, even though it may take music to bring them out' (234). Perhaps connotation-free words will provide a people with a way of finding a voice? In the case of Bosnia today, we may well witness the circumstances of an 'aphasic nation' that will, as in Sacks' observations, find itself through singing. Sing and the words will come. In the case of Spain, perhaps humming along will in time bring forth the needful words; and if these cannot be agreed then might not the condition of postmodernity be well expressed by the principle – each to his/her own anthem? Or might we simply let the humming mean what it means for each?

As we have seen with 'God Save the King/Queen', because of the questionable nature of the speech act involved, the prayer-type of anthem brings to the fore the question of covert messages and addresses to unnamed parties. Argentina's anthem presents us with the overt opposite of a prayer: the (1814) song originally titled 'Marcha de la Patria' is addressed to mortals in general; it tells the world about the peoples of South America and, we may infer, about a South American people in particular. The lyrics today, as standardised in 1924, are as follows:

> Mortals! Hear the sacred cry;
> Freedom! Freedom! Freedom!
> Hear the noise of broken chains
> See noble equality enthroned.
> The United Provinces of the South
> Have now displayed their worthy throne.
> And the free peoples of the world reply;
> We salute the great people of Argentina!
> And the free peoples of the world reply;
> We salute the great people of Argentina!
>
> May the laurels be eternal
> That we knew how to win.
> Let us live crowned with glory,
> Or swear to die gloriously.
>
> (Bristow, 35)

The original version of the song could be read as entirely reactive; it said nothing about Argentina as a nation, it was all about independence from Spain. As one might expect, this original version was popular throughout Spanish-speaking South America. In terms of address however these lyrics offer an extreme example of a people identified with the outside world watching. In 'Advance Australia Fair', discussed below, there is a spectacularism to the tableau presented ('in history's page, let every stage Advance Australia Fair'), but the people addressed in that song are the people who are becoming Australians. In Argentina's national hymn those singing objectify themselves through third-person-pronominal reference; they sing in the voice of the world recognising the birth of Argentina: 'We salute the great people of Argentina!' Only after this world-identification do we come to the now validated avowal, 'Let us live crowned with glory, / Or swear to die gloriously'. Should these arrangements be read as the expression of cosmopolitan humanism ('To address ourselves we must first address the world') or parochial cringe ('We're not worth talking to until the world's been told')?

In Austria's anthem we find a progression, through the stanzas, from objectification from the outside ('Land of mountains, Land on the River'), through the land addressed as from the outside ('You are a home of great sons'), through value judgement (again as if made from the outside), until in the last stanza we move to the first-person plural:

> Watch us striding free and believing,
> With courage, into new eras,
> Working cheerfully and full of hope,
> In fraternal chorus let us take in unity
> The oath of allegiance to you, our country,
> Our much beloved Austria, our much beloved Austria.
>
> (Bristow, 41)

It is as if those singing have, by this time (and presumably through the process of singing), convinced themselves that they are Austrians, that though they have been distracted by other credible points of view, their collective discovery is that this is in fact the thing that they have in common; and it was necessary to do some thinking out loud in order to reach this conclusion. The emphasis however remains on a spectacle presented to the world: 'Watch us'.

Argentina's and Austria's anthems draw attention to the question of authority as it relates to the form of address taken in an anthem. Where so many prayer-anthems in monarchic states simply rely on the assertion of an arbitrary link between God and king, republics have often had to work harder in their lyrics to justify themselves to themselves. As we saw in Chapter 2, anthems worldwide are preoccupied with such abstractions as heart or soul or blood or death; these stand for the nation and are putative sources of authority for action and sentiment. But of course many republics rely on the authority of a deity to justify the identification called for in the anthem. Consider Tagore's lyrics for the anthem of India[6]:

> Glory to thee, ruler of our hearts and of India's destiny!
> Punjab, Sind, Gujarat, Maharashra,

The land of the Dravids, Orissa, Bengal,
The Vindyas and the Himalayas, the Jamuna
And the Ganges and the ceaseless waves of the Ocean
All arise at thy fair name and seek thy blessings,
Singing their hymn of praise to thee.
Glory to thee, oh Goddess of India's fortune!
Hail, hail, to thee forever!

(Bristow, 271)

Sri Lanka's anthem avows the worship of 'Mother Lanka', a figure of harvest plenty (Bristow, 520), but in India's anthem, the nation is apotheosised in the form of a goddess (along the lines of Athena for Athens, Britannia for Great Britain, Liberty for France and the United States). In the second stanza, the statue-like figure of the first comes to life: 'Day and night thy call spreads over the land/ And we hear thy voice of salvation'. The mystery of the opening lines (Who could be the ruler described? The British Empire? The UN?) is resolved in a complex circular manner: apotheosis meets avatar in the process of symbolising the nation as entity worthy of worship. In the land of innumerable deities, the nation is represented (as it might be elsewhere) by a statue-evoking figure of a goddess. This goddess has a voice (the unisonant are urged to imagine) and she uses it to call the faithful to the salvation that will be achieved through the process of hailing the goddess. Perhaps the function of this roundabout is to avoid any impression that the people are, as per Durkheim's claim with regard to nations in general, merely worshipping themselves?

Covert Argument

There are among the anthems of the world numerous examples of surreptitious or circumlocuted thinking or argument in the framing of the national devotions. We have already seen this with the example of The Dutch anthem, 'The Wilhelmus' (dating to the sixteenth century and so arguably the world's oldest). One trawls through the fifteen stanzas of the song to get a sense of the story, which is basically a first-person account of William of Nassau's thinking in deciding to fight for what would eventually be Dutch nationhood. The point William of Nassau insists on is that it was not his idea. In the first stanza he tells us that he pledged lifelong loyalty to the Spanish king, in the last stanza he tells us that he never despised the Spanish king. The lyrics are all about loyalty and god fearing and doing the right thing, and from all this we need to garner that things were desperately not alright with the Spanish king's minions in the low countries. And so an independence struggle was necessary. Although there was, for factional reasons, a long period during which 'The Wilhemus' was not the national anthem (from the foundation of the Kingdom of the Netherlands in 1813 until 1932), for today's Dutch citizen that historical/political business is ancient history and so nothing much is contested here. During the song's almost five hundred year history there have been many folkloric moments, we might say, in which the Dutch have been inspired by 'The Wilhelmus'. And so it appears as a strange but acceptable tradition that the Dutch sing of their long-established independent identity by giving voice to a particular nobleman's 500-year-old ambivalence about a kingdom to the south of France.

The case of Japan's 'Kimi Gayo' ('The Emperor's Reign') is equally interesting, and one notes that this song has likewise a claim to being the world's oldest anthem. That claim is on the basis of the antiquity of the lyrics, which are from a Heian era (794–1185 CE) *waka*, sung to a Meiji era melody, chosen in 1880. There is no official translation of the words, but their meaning is something like this:

> May you reign
> For a thousand and for eight thousand generations,
> Until pebbles
> Become moss covered boulders.

Though it cannot compete with 'Hail Freedonia', 'Kimi Gayo' is clearly one of the world's shortest anthems in use. Unlike the case of Holland, the choice of retaining 'Kimi Gayo' as Japan's national anthem has been extremely controversial. Japan is an ancient country/kingdom/empire, the words of 'Kimi Gayo' are genuinely ancient. Their use in the anthem is coextensive with the various phases of Japan's modernity and nationhood (in the modern sense). What can the fuss be about? Surely, however, implausible it may seem, no one can object to pebbles growing into boulders, or the idea that a thousand years ago the Yamato clan were quite taken by such a metaphor? If the Dutch can get over the old religious conflict implied in their anthem, then 'Kimi Gayo' would appear, on face value, to present its unisonant with a genuine and harmless continuity in tradition. The problem for the song is association. This was the anthem during the decades of Japan's imperial aggression in the last century; it supports the cult of the emperor, which was what allowed or encouraged fanaticism, war crimes, crimes against humanity. It is this kind of continuity with which many Japanese people would rather not be associated[7]. The emperor has remained but with a vastly altered role; the emperor seems much more mortal to most Japanese than he did prior to the bombing of Hiroshima and Nagasaki in 1945. So why then continue to sing a song that hypostasises the making eternal of a temporal power? Why sing an anthem that, a little reflection shows, revives the imperial cult, suggests that it is alright to think of the emperor as a god? The comparison with 'God Save the King', with its contractual caveats ('and ever give us cause to sing …'), is instructive. Today, very few even extreme right-wing Japanese nationalists could think of the emperor as a god; the Japanese people nevertheless are torn between those who see 'Kimi Gayo' as a tradition and continuity worth maintaining, and those for whom its associations are so distasteful and so anti-democratic that, even to hear the tune, will fill them with loathing. Some others in East Asia will have similar feelings if their memories are long enough or are able to be stirred in this cause.

In Germany's case, the anthem has been just as contentious. 'Deutschlandlied' ('The Song of Germany'), has remained in service since 1922 (in other words, through the Weimar, Nazi, post-Nazi Cold War [for West Germany] and post-reunification periods). The solution to the controversy associated with lyrics many would rather not have to sing has been (as with Slovenia) to cut the song down to a single stanza (the third stanza of the original text) to which no one could possibly object. That stanza is translated as follows:

> Unity and right and freedom
> For the German fatherland;
> Let us all pursue this purpose
> Brotherly with heart and hand.
> Unity and right and freedom
> Are the pledge of happiness
> Flourish in this blessing's glory,
> Flourish, German fatherland.
>
> (Xing Hang, 253)

The problem for the song had been its opening lines, in German: 'Deutschland, Deutschland über alles, / Über alles in der Welt' ('Germany, Germany above everything, / Above everything in the world'). When those lines were in official use (until 1945), many non-Germans had taken 'Deutschland über alles' to be the title of the song. The words 'über alles' (which Nietzsche criticised as the stupidest in the world) have been widely misunderstood as implying that Germany should rule over all other nations in the world, whereas in fact they were intended to mean that Germans should recognise their collective identity and put Germany before other interests of their own in order to unite as a nation. The misunderstanding is aggravated by another problem with the first stanza, the fact that the lyrics suggest somewhat grandiose borders for the devoutly-to-be-wished nation of German speakers: 'From the Meuse to the Memel, / From the Adige to the Belt' – a space that would take in quite a bit of neighbouring territory, including large parts of Denmark, Holland and of course, German-speaking Austria.

The music dates to the eighteenth century, having been written by Haydn for the birthday of Austrian emperor, Francis II. The lyrics, by German poet August Heinrich Hoffmann von Fallersleben, date to 1841. A symbol of the March 1848 revolution and so of the cause of German unification, it was chosen as anthem by the Weimar Republic for its radical liberal and republican sentiments. (In fact, Germany could not have made use of the song as a national anthem prior to the dissolution of the Austro-Hungarian Empire in 1918 because, thanks to its original purpose, it was still in use in Vienna, until that time, as a royal anthem.) The Nazis kept the song but only the offending first stanza, following it up with the Nazi Party anthem, 'The Horst Wessel Song', also known as 'The Flag On High' – a lyric lauding storm troopers and expressing the hope of millions in the swastika. After the war, for some years neither Germany had constitution or state symbols or an anthem. When West Germany began using 'Deutschlandlied' again officially in 1952, it was agreed that only the third stanza would be used. To this day, all stanzas may be used for unofficial purposes. Due to two world wars and a devastating association with fascism, the radical liberal-republican aspect of 'Deutschlandlied' has been mostly lost for non-Germans. Certainly, this is a song that, in the twentieth century, has had little of the cosmopolitan appeal of France's 'The Marseillaise'. The ease with which the lines 'Deutschland, Deutschland über alles, / Über alles in der Welt' have been misinterpreted in the light of German aggression must certainly have played a role in confining sentimental attachment to this song within German borders.

During the pre-unification Cold War period (from 1949), East Germany's anthem had been 'Auferstanden aus Ruinen' ('Risen from Ruins'), and it is interesting that some consideration was given, at the time of reunification, to the idea of combining lyrics from both songs. Though the idea was ultimately rejected, along the way it became widely recognised that there would have been no serious metrical problem in combining these lyrics. There never had been any problem in fitting the lyrics of 'Auferstanden aus Ruinen' to Haydn's tune.

Things were easier anthems-wise after World War II for the third Axis power, Italy. Italy's present anthem 'Il Canto degli Italiani' ('The Song of the Italians'), composed in 1847, was a song of the unification struggle; it is also variously known as 'Inno di Mameli' ('Mameli's Hymn'), after the author of the lyrics, or 'Fratelli d'Italia' ('Brothers of Italy'). The song never enjoyed any official status prior to Italy's becoming a republic, almost a century after its composition, because post-unification (1861), it was the 'Marcia Reale' ('Royal March') that, as the official song of House of Savoy, remained in service through the Mussolini years. In 1946, Italy no longer being officially a kingdom, it had no further need of a royal song. In 'Il Canto degli Italiani' there was an untainted song of national unity available for service to the new republic.

In Italy's case, we see that the problem of how to address oneself as a citizenry was simply resolved in terms of an understanding of the form of the state and the nature of the citizen's relation to state authority. In the case of both Germany and Japan, demands of tradition and a legacy of wartime aggression have left a bad taste in the mouths of some of those singing and of some of those listening. In the case of Holland, we see that where there is no bad taste in the mouth and no self-image issue to resolve in terms of recent-past aggression; it will not matter if a tradition is maintained, even to the point of retaining little meaning of present relevance for those singing. In such a case, the symbol in question serves an arbitrary function distant social-historic connotations need not distress.

The Ethics of the Invisible Man

The second half of the nineteenth century was the golden age of European nationalism (and imperialism), and anthems worldwide today are for the most part either surviving nineteenth-century nation-making artefacts or imitations of that kind of text. Ancient authority may generally be sought by modern states in their quest for self-symbolisation (the naming of Australia being an unnoticed example of such a process), but it is typically late-Romantic music and diction that is indicated for anthemic purposes today wherever the high-tide mark of Western influence remains. In the history of anthems there are many cases of politically motivated alteration and omission as lyrics have passed down through generations. A classic early case of conscious omission is the leaving out of the anti-Spanish verses of the Argentine national anthem. Slovenia and Croatia each also furnish examples of a carefully calculated revision of national sentiment as expressed in the official words of the anthem; there are many more.

Australia's official national anthem, 'Advance Australia Fair', dating to 1878, is a prime example of the anthem as late Romantic artefact and another re-written song. As a putative work of art, its failings are exemplary. In the rest of this chapter I will draw some contrasts between this song and 'Waltzing Matilda', a song that, though having no official status, is much better loved by the Australian people.[8] Various continuities and discontinuities are implied in the century-long journey of 'Advance Australia Fair' from popular to official status. It should be recognised that, however British Australians now regard this song to be, its acceptance (in the 1970s/1980s) over 'God Save the Queen' marks a break from Australian self-recognition as British. The 1984 revision of the song removed its overt British content. Celebrating – in the song's sense of advancing – Australia now entails promoting a new becoming-national entity – a white, English-speaking, self-governing democracy – an entity that gradually supersedes the colonial entities that had in turn superseded the uncivilised state the white colonists believed they had found when they first came to the 'fair' shores of the Great South Land or New Holland: the territory that would not be popularly known as Australia until well into the nineteenth century.[9]

Let us briefly consider the revision of 'Advance Australia Fair' prior to its taking on unambiguous and permanent anthem status under the Hawke Labor government in 1984. Comparing the original with the now-official version of the lyrics canvasses a question as to whether there is an implied racist investment in Australian nationhood and self-symbolisation. 'Advance Australia Fair' was politically corrected (not a phrase in use at the time) when re-instated as Australia's national anthem in 1984. It had had national anthem status in the previous decade during the latter part of the Whitlam Labor government (1972–1975). The 1984 re-write was largely with a view to giving the fairer sex a fairer go. The revision of the lyrics was done by the National Australia Day Committee in consultation with two of the Boards (Music and Literature) of the Australia Council for the Arts. The original opening line of Peter Dodds McCormick's nineteenth-century song was: 'Australian sons let us rejoice / for we are young and free'. The complete 'official' anthem is now officially as follows:

Australians all let us rejoice
For we are young and free.
We've golden soil and wealth for toil
Our home is girt by sea.

Our land abounds in nature's gifts
Of beauty rich and rare.
In history's page, let every stage
Advance Australia Fair.

In joyful strains then let us sing
Advance Australia Fair.

Beneath our radiant Southern Cross
We'll toil with hearts and hands
To make this Commonwealth of ours
Renowned of all the lands

For those who've come across the seas
We've boundless plains to share.
With courage let us all combine
To Advance Australia Fair.

In joyful strains then let us sing
Advance Australia Fair.

(Australian Government)

What of the original is missing from the revised version? The second stanza of the original song is as follows:

When gallant Cook from Albion sail'd,
To trace wide oceans o'er,
True British courage bore him on
Till he landed on our shore.
Then here he raised old England's flag,
The standard of the brave;
With all her faults we love her still,
'Britannia rules the wave'.

(McCormick, 1–4)

Contradicting the idea of 'boundless plains to share' with new arrivals, the fifth and last stanza of the original 'Advance Australia Fair' was concerned with preventing others from coming to the country. It describes what Australia would be defending itself from in the case of war:

Should foreign foe e'er sight our coast,
Or dare a foot to land,

We'll rise to arms like sires of yore
To guard our native strand;
Britannia then shall surely know,
Beyond wide ocean's roll,
Her sons in fair Australia's land
Still keep a British soul,
In joyful strains and etc.

(McCormick, 1–4)

The 'correction' of 'Advance Australia Fair' is noteworthy given the emphasis the song places on a self-conscious effort at nationhood. McCormick's text had a British nationhood in mind. The old and new lyrics situate a collective effort at being a nation in the 'act' of being seen to be one, being worthy of the name. The claim is justified on two grounds: possession and intention. Australians have golden soil, wealth, youth, the ability to toil, freedom, a beautiful country possessed of nature's gifts, boundless plains and so on. They make no particular claim to have done anything as yet but have good intentions, specifically to toil with hearts and hands to make their nation (now Australia) famous as such. The setting of the song then is temporally ambiguous, one might say vaguely forward looking: we have *x* and we're about to *y*. The big questions one might ask this far into the song are naturally: 'Who are *we*?' and 'How did *we* get to be in a place that needs to be sung about by us in this way?' 'What effect does it have on us or on others, that we sing this particular song about ourselves?'

The 'we' is, I think, the (mainly) white nation, under construction in Australia at the time of writing (1878), under construction at the time of the song's official revision (1984) and still under construction today. The ongoing framing of an identity, as revealed in the revision of this song, demonstrates instructive continuities and discontinuities in the evolution of Australia's self-image. A paradoxical investment is entailed in the symbolic means of the nation's construction. The white man is a spectacle embodying human progress. To be white is to aspire, to be beheld aspiring. Whiteness, on the other hand, is invisible. It functions as norm only to the extent that it is overlooked as a quality of those who possess it. It is able to be overlooked by and large because it is white people who do the looking. Or at least an unmarked point of view and narrative style in Australia has systematically presupposed and privileged a white man's view of the world. The unmarked category (white) goes without saying as normative because (apparently) lacking ethnicity. Who lacks ethnicity becomes autochthonous, by virtue of a rhetoric that only works as long as it is not spelled out (as it might be, for instance, by the equally covert gesture we find in Jimi Hendrix's 'Star Spangled Banner').

The re-writing of 'Advance Australia Fair' foregrounds the paradox of the spectacular and the invisible in the investments of whiteness and of nation. The emptying of the country of its former cultural content has been accomplished by those who have progressively spread out to occupy the land and at once made themselves rhetorically less visible in the process. In the terms Robert Frost set out in 'The Gift Outright' the newcomers have become possessed by the land over which they have claimed possession.

A postmodern global human-rights rhetoric allows us to speak of individuals as racially unmarked in a way that would have been implausible in the nineteenth century, or even before the Second World War, in mainstream Western societies. Thanks to the value of whiteness as unmarked category, this rhetorical shift may, far from opening the range of humanity to all races and ethnicities, rather have the effect of rendering white subjectivity both invisible and universal (i.e. normative) in one stroke. In the musicology of anthems more generally we see an analogy for this effect. Whiteness confers unearned privileges on those who happen to be white. This systematic privileging does not apply only to individuals, but as well to nations. There was no 'Australia' in the continent prior to the coming of white people. Nevertheless the continent was invaded, and is still occupied, by forces that absolve themselves for responsibility in the process; their main means of absolving themselves is that of absenting themselves from the action.

The depth of contradiction in the present and official version of 'Advance Australia Fair' (its 'look at me, I'm not here' quality) leaves some of those who sing it a little uneasy as to the question of what they have meant by singing it. Still, one need not dig deep to unearth the contradictions. In terms of form, the song begins as if it were a hymn or a prayer, with the formula: 'Let us (pray/sing?)', but the formula is given without the locutionary force of an appeal to God (cf. 'God Save the King/Queen'). It is a pseudo-hymn. Who is addressed? *We* are. The temporal setting of the hymn is substituted with the imminence of an imperative: 'Let us rejoice'. Rejoicing is something we should all do for a long list of reasons; that being the case, 'let us sing'. In 'Advance Australia Fair' it is the imminent future to which voices attend in their act of unison.

Who is this 'we' the unisonant cannot see because they are so busy singing when they are not toiling, when they are not rejoicing? These gestures become empty as they become normative. The invisibility of those singing is assured by their identity with themselves. Who in Australia in 1878 can sing a song in English praising Captain Cook for his nation-making role? Who can sing the song with Cook absented today? In the re-writing of 'Advance Australia Fair' we attend to a vanishing spectacle, a spectacle into which Australians vanish in becoming themselves. It is through that act of vanishing that authority comes to be unassailable.

The emptiness posited by 'Advance Australia Fair' is deeply ironic. It represents a refusal of the ethical question that must lie under European presence in Australia. Australians have land to share because they took land. They sing from an emptiness wrought on themselves in the act of emptying, the emptying of the land and at once the popular consciousness: emptying it of the fact of the emptying. So emptying themselves of truth becomes the basis of the collectivity on which a polity is asserted.

Learning the song that makes you Australian means learning not to ask certain awkward questions. It is an induction into an ambivalence. Australians are embarrassed by the unresolved ethics of their presence. And so they sing this embarrassing song. It is not merely a matter of substituting tradition for intention. Tradition is, in this tune, emptied of intending. 'Look at me, now! How good of me just to happen to be here'. One gets through the embarrassment and the contradiction by refusing a reflexive engagement with the terms of questions begged but that go unasked.

The central ambiguity in the title and refrain of 'Advance Australia Fair' is such that when Australians sing the song they do not know whether they are describing how things are or how they should be. Are they singing to keep things the way they are or to make things the way they ought to be? Advance Australia because it is fair or so that it will be fair or for both reasons: to keep the fair, fair? This speculation begs the question about the meaning of the word 'fair'. Of all the various dictionary entries for the word *fair*, the three that seem to coalesce in this usage are: fair as in beautiful, fair as in just and fair as in white.

In the third critique, Kant writes 'the beautiful is the symbol of the morally good' (547). Kant's views on race (as for instance expressed in his 1775 essay 'On the Different Races of Man') – though perhaps atypical of the anthropology of his time – demonstrate a powerful conviction that the white race was superior to the other three races Kant imagined as encompassing the human types. Kant particularly viewed black people as inferior, unintelligent (in Eze, 38–48). There is no doubt that for Kant the beauty and goodness he conceived coalesced best under a white skin (and no doubt, the appropriate civilised garment). Today's human rights and rule-of-law rhetorics are fuelled by a universalising spirit (spirit of the categorical imperative) that no longer wishes itself to be seen as imperial or chauvinistic. The provenance of such rhetorics is hidden not merely in the manner of blank whiteness, it is hidden behind blank whiteness of the kind that the re-writing of 'Advance Australia Fair' exemplifies.

Today we take racial prejudice as presenting a problem for the categorical imperative. How can one act only on a maxim one can will to become universal law while dealing unfairly – unequally – with other humans (i.e. the rest of the human universe)? Kant's universal rule seems to be contradicted by his own prejudices. But there was no contradiction along these lines for Kant. Acknowledging the ongoing validity of Kant's ethics means recognising the continuity between an imperial (and racist) mindset and today's individual-universal-rights rhetoric.

The beautiful inhabit a just polity. A just polity is a white polity. This is the advance, in the song, that is happening, or has happened, in Australia. In fact this is the advance that the European word (Latin made English down here) constitutes for the continent formerly known to Europe as New Holland: *Australia* is becoming a white man's country. In terms of Kant's categorical imperative, this particular people have become universal and normative (have transcended their particularity) just to the extent that they are invisible. Mediating between imperial mindset and today's individual universal rights/rule-of-law rhetoric is the modernity of nation: the mainly banal and unanalysed great good that powers anthems.

The original version of 'Advance Australia Fair' is about historical consciousness. It may not be a contemporary Australian consciousness of history, but it tells a story about how it is Australians are where they are. Rhetorically, the key is in the synecdoche expressed in the line 'In history's page, let every stage …'. Unpacking the synecdoche reveals nation and national aspirations as textually framed textual artefact. Nation is word or image – word as image – to be read. History is a book consisting of pages. One of these pages stands for the book. On each page a scene is presented, in which stage, in the spectacular sense, coincides with the notion of a phase or of epoch. Word and image, action and depiction, are parts of the ongoing cycle invoked by the turning of the pages of a book, the reading of which conjures images, the writing of which is nation-making.

As to the event of Australians singing themselves into the 'fair' future: three connotations – just, beautiful, white – conflate in an ambiguity where through repetition, through emphasis and through the dignifying effect of an anthem setting, they come to imply each other. The unspoken terms of the song suffice to imply the conflation: the white person (now standing for *all* the people) toils to make the land beautiful and just. Whether this is an accomplished fact or an uphill battle, regardless of who is now included in this mission, there is no doubt that this notion of progress as 'Australia-making' is owing to the coming of the white man. Importantly, this 'man' – the hero of the story – is able to go unmentioned and unexamined because he is invisibly (and indivisibly) white.

Song of a Story of a Haunting

Nation survives with us from a time when the racial kind of superiority carried with it deep convictions of moral superiority. It is because of that 'natural' connection – one not needing to be argued – that there was nothing hypocritical for the eighteenth- and nineteenth-century British mind in those possessing acts we now think of as dispossessing. The British in Australia were establishing law, order, land tenure, the cultivation of crops, writing, progress (and so with hindsight, history) where none of these good things had been before. For the benefit of English colonists in Carolina, John Locke had developed, in these terms, the self-justifying ethical basis of the *terra nullius* doctrine, the idea that Europeans had a right to occupy land that they could not see as having heretofore been cultivated.[10] Although press and politicians toil hard to have us see things otherwise, an overview of world events suggests that the 'might is right' assumptions of earlier world empires persist strongly in the West's *weltanschauung* today. Are we disingenuous to imagine ourselves as having morally surpassed the old imperial stage of human development?

An irony of 'Advance Australia Fair' is that despite the effort at historical consciousness (in the original version) and its failure to focus on a present situation as having arisen from historical circumstances (in both versions), the homeostatic effect of the song is to keep the present stuck; the means to that end is to distract us from paying attention to the present. 'We have this and that: let's party now, toil later'. The past enabling is missing from the picture for the simple reason that in order to feel proud of where and what they are, Australians (like the postcolonial whites of new Europes everywhere) find it more comfortable and convenient to gloss over what makes them and their present position possible.

'Waltzing Matilda' is a song, by contrast, set in the epic past – not in one of Bakhtin's peak times, when all was golden – but in a fragment of memory, apocryphal perhaps and yet authentic. The story of the song is set in a forensic landscape of possession and dispossession; there is in it the acceptance of doubtful assertion, there are voices spoken for and over. In each of these cases the unisonant is provided with a primal scene that is hauntingly Australian. 'Waltzing Matilda' is a ghost story – the story of a ghost's becoming – set in the nowhere of bad times that corresponds with the depression and the shearers' strike of 1890s outback Queensland. How much of that provenance remains in any rendition of the song today? The laconic landscape of sparse events remains. Its secrets may be few but neither are they easily rendered up. Here is the text of the A.B. Paterson version (arguably the original) of the song[11]:

Waltzing Matilda
(Carrying a Swag)

Oh! there once was a swagman camped in a Billabong
Under the shade of a coolibah tree;
And he sang as he looked at his old billy boiling,
'Who'll come a-waltzing Matilda with me?'

Who'll come a-waltzing Matilda, my darling,
Who'll come a waltzing Matilda with me?
Waltzing Matilda and leading a water-bag–
Who'll come a waltzing Matilda with me?

Down came a jumbuck to drink at the water-hole
Up jumped the swagman and grabbed him in glee;
And he sang as he stowed him away in his tucker-bag,
'You'll come a-waltzing Matilda with me.'

Down came the squatter a-riding his thoroughbred;
Down came the policemen–one, two and three.
'Whose is the jumbuck you've got in your tucker-bag?
You'll come a-waltzing Matilda with me.'

But the swagman, he up and he jumped in the waterhole,
Drowning himself by the coolibah tree;
And his ghost may be heard as it sings in the Billabong
'Who'll come a-waltzing Matilda with me?'

(1921, 213)

Here is a quick gloss of the story to remind us of events on and suggested by the record:

> An old swagman, carrying all his few belongings on his back (the swag, which he calls 'Matilda'), decides to camp in a dry creek bed. He makes a fire, brews some tea and dances with his blankets, his various few implements, imagining music, imagining his bedroll is a female companion. Of course he's got an appetite and about then a sheep happens by, and naturally the hungry swagman grabs it without thinking too hard on the *whose sheep*(?) issue. Unluckily for him, in all this vast wilderness to wander in, the sheep-owning farmer and some police at his beck and call just happen by, when there are still some pieces of undevoured sheep in the swagman's possession. There is a waft of singed wool in the air. The authorities challenge the swagman, and rather than face them, he searches out a puddle in the creek bed and drowns, perhaps drowns himself. If you go past this place today you can hear his ghost. You can hear his ghost singing as he dances with the bedroll. The ghost is singing the whole story over and over, like a stuck record.

There is something hypnotic in this text, in the manner of the missing horse-shoe nail of the nursery rhyme. One thing leads to another, but as with every good story, in a way you could not have predicted. Swagman does away with himself rather than face justice at the hands of the police at the behest of the owner of the sheep the swagman stole to feed himself. Everything fits, falls into a circle. But is the fit convincing? Does the circle make sense?

The characters of 'Waltzing Matilda' are unnamed types; the place is merely the site of the action: a mysterious theft, a strange death. This lyric has the oneiric logic of the Old Testament. That is how the ever-thus of an unarguable past is established as in the logic of a patriarch's prophetic dream. This is the white man's dream of the vast obscure of the anonymous moment, the blank slate of beginning: the dream of *terra nullius*. When sung it is the primal scene of the Australian nation and even of any nation circumstantially like Australia. Details, even main events, must be missing. But this much is got right: the story of the nation's beginnings is about a confusion of crimes for which restitution has not been made.

Whether the 'story' is persuasive or not, the text convincingly evokes the haunting of a place. This is appropriate as the story in the song is one eternally retold by the ghost it frames as telling the tale. This ghost inside and outside of the story is thus a kind of *genius loci* for the unknown place of the tale's provenance, the place that would be recognised by one passing, were one to hear the song or at least the refrain. Everything fits in a manner predetermined, circular, in epic manner. The story is always already known. Would that not be the case with every much-sung story? Must it not be the case with any anthem, with any expression of patriotic sentiment?

Two things radically distinguish this context from that sung in the two other (radically different) songs charged historically with the responsibility of representing Australia: 'God Save the King/Queen' and 'Advance Australia Fair'. What is different here firstly is that there is a credibility gap between the events offered a reader, as if fact and the form of address (even self-address) of the refrain that implies a dialogic or more physical proximity, as in a waltz. How does this set-up fit the more generally applicable intersubjective tactics of the patriotic song? The typical 'reader' is in the case of an anthem implicated in the sense that s/he asserts whatever is asserted in the act of unisonance that paradoxically brings the words to attention and at once wears them away. The wearing away is relevant to the banality of the song as institution cum icon. There is something to care about here only if you think about the story. And it is easy not to. What is offered as fact in 'Waltzing Matilda' appears to be from the point of view of someone ambiguously on one side or the other, inside or outside of the dance. It is not quite clear which or whose point of view applies at any point. To that extent a confused, or at least, unstable unison is indicated. And yet point of view in the story/song is singular, it appears to be interested. Interest is indicated through the asking of questions: 'Whose is the jumbuck you've got in your tucker-bag?'; 'Who'll come a-waltzing Matilda with me?' The point of view remains singular, but it shifts. In any one utterance, a particular character inside or outside the story must be speaking. The question is, which (?).

Note the generic difference between this song and the present and past Australian anthems: this is narrative plus question, in the Paterson version, or instruction, in the Cowan. Either way, 'Who'll come / You'll come a-waltzing Matilda with me' is not the kind of exhortation the prayerful make of their God or the citizenry make of themselves apotheosed as nation. For the phrase 'waltzing Matilda' to have national significance, it must be read metaphorically. (This is a fact of the text's present framing against which anything known in the way of authorial intention will be irrelevant.) Depending on which version we read/sing, the song then exhorts us or at least asks us to do something of an undisclosed symbolic/metaphoric nature in order to recognise ourselves. When we observe how the meaning of the metaphor shifts through the song, with the various situations it has us envisage, we see that there is a peculiar kind of self-identification demanded of those who sing this song. 'Waltzing Matilda' is something you could do by yourself, with a sheep if you were a swagman, with a swagman if you were a squatter or a policeman, by yourself again if you were a ghost. In every case you would be demanding or asking of someone – someone anonymous – that they join you. In no case would you be envisaging a dance floor with a female partner.

This song's complexity is tied up in the framing of the narrative and the shifting of the persona. The story is self-addressed by those who sing it. In the more popular version (the Cowan) they address themselves in the second person: 'as you pass by that billabong'. In that case there is an intersubjective bridge between the inside and outside of the story. Inside the story the *you* addressed is in turn the sheep and then the swagman, outside it is the *you* who is the listener to the story/song, who also happens to be the singer, the anonymous unisonant subject of the song. One might read the line in Banjo Paterson's published version, 'And his ghost may be heard as it sings in the Billabong' as an awkward attempt to avoid the building of the interpersonal bridge that links the inside and the outside of the song. Without such a bridge it is easier to regard what the song delivers as 'just a story', nothing to do with the reality of lives as lived.

To recap: in 'Waltzing Matilda' there is a credibility gap between the narrative content and the manner of its delivery. The contradiction between the two serves to generate doubt. 'God Save the King/Queen' and 'Advance Australia Fair' do not have enough story to have that kind of credibility problem. Neither would 'The Marseillaise' or 'The Internationale'; anthems do not conventionally impart a story in the sense that 'Waltzing Matilda' does. We have seen shifting point of view in, for instance, the anthems of Argentina and Austria, but this is unusual. Nor is manner of address typically as unstable as in the case of 'Waltzing Matilda'. In 'Waltzing Matilda' there is an uncomfortable conflation of narrative certainty and doubt of a personal nature. The re-iteration of the text, through verse and refrain, expresses an ambivalence between a past fixed forever as originary, as explaining us, and a future act foreshadowed ('Who'll ...? / You'll come a-waltzing') in which the metaphor accounting for us will be enacted.

That enactment could have an interpretive consequence. Consider the metaphoric/euphemistic 'waltz' series proposed in the song. This genteel act, ideally of men and women, is envisaged in a place where all it requires is lacking. There is no woman, no dance floor, no music. So, if you were a swagman you could – or rather you would have to – do it with yourself, if you were a sheep it could be done to you. If you were a swagman (going on foot) with a sheep in your tucker bag it could be done to you by a coalition of squatter and policeman and thoroughbred (by the folk on horseback, one could say). If you were a ghost, again, you could do it with yourself, but you might be looking for company. That is where the listener/singer of the song comes in. The ghost is who does it to the unisonant of the song. As long as Australians remain *in* the song, addressing themselves, through the shifting personae of the series and ultimately as a (collective) ghost, the possibility of an interpretive consequence is forestalled. Here I think is a key ambivalence that applies to the self-addressing singer of this song. Singing, we address ourselves and each other, both as ghosts and as persons to be 'waltzed' with.

The euphemism implies oppressive power relations of some to-be-guessed form. At least it implies this in the two clearest cases, that of what is intended for the sheep and what is intended, by the powers that be, for the swagman. As long as we keep singing, we forestall the danger that we might ourselves be threatened (as we would as parties addressed); we forestall that danger by threatening others – in the final instance, we threaten them with haunting. Thus you might say that 'Waltzing Matilda' is a song that keeps its subjects singing for fear that if they stop or step outside of the lyrics they sing (for instance to reflect), they will run the risk of being recipients of their own curse. We can read the song as a case of 'keep cursing or be cursed'.

***

The contrast, along these lines, between 'Waltzing Matilda' and 'Advance Australia Fair' could not be greater. 'Advance Australia Fair' had the intention of spectacularising the Australian story and Australia's presence on the world stage. Something *more* sinister seems to be at stake in 'Waltzing Matilda'. If the song/story is allegorical, then what does the dance represent? Who are its partners, how do they change? What social or sexual implications may be read into the events one might imagine from the allegory? Is the obscurity of the setting a case of hoping to persuade people that Australians are not worth paying attention to and so hoping that no one will notice what they are or have been up to? Again, that reading would make the story and song, by intention, the anathema of 'Advance Australia Fair', that song being centrally obsessed with justice and with self-justification, with the rendering of the moral right of nation as spectacle.

In 'Waltzing Matilda' the story played out by the invocation of the ghost, from now to eternity, is an account of the last moments of someone's life. The ghost may be heard. Perhaps the ghost of the swagman tells his story. But is it the story we have already heard, or is there another gospel we are never privileged to hear? As one might say in a thieves' argot of latter day Australia, it is as if this ghost has been 'verballed'[12]: he can sing till eternity, there is very little he can say.

The question of the official versus the unofficial[13] is brought to the fore in 'Waltzing Matilda' because whoever understands the story is likely to entertain doubts as to who in it should be believed. Doubts the song delivers in the story are mirrored by doubts among singers and listeners, as to whether this song can, officially or otherwise, represent Australians. 'Waltzing Matilda' is certainly no less important to Australian sense of self than is an official anthem. The difference between the intention expressed by each song might be articulated in the following terms: 'Advance Australia Fair' expresses an overt Australian nationalism, 'Waltzing Matilda' expresses Australians' covert ideas as to who they might be. 'Advance Australia Fair' is what Australians sing officially because this is who they think they are supposed to be: the kind of people well-enough endowed with nationhood to possess a classic national anthem from the golden age of nationalism. For all that, 'Advance Australia Fair' has the whiff of a self-conscious effort to assert an identity that seems to have been pre-chosen for Australians, as one in the series available to British-made nations. 'Waltzing Matilda', by contrast, expresses fears and doubts as to the true identity of Australians, but it rings true in its uniqueness. No other anthem is a ghost story. 'Waltzing Matilda' is a song about not knowing what happened. Australians sing this song with greater gusto because it much more accurately accounts for the mystery of who they are.

We saw in the case of *Casablanca* that the connotative range of a song can become permanently disconnected from its history, from authorial intention, from the apparent denotation of the lyrics as sung. It is interesting that, in the case of 'Waltzing Matilda', the voluminous scholarship (and pseudo-scholarship) devoted to the text through the twentieth century and beyond has been obsessed with questions of provenance (both of music and lyrics), to the virtual exclusion of any seriously posed question as to what Australians mean when they sing the song (Wood, 1943; May, 1944; Mendelsohn, [1996, first published 1964]; Semmler, 1988; Magoffin, 1995, 1998a, 1998b, 2001; Radic, 1996). The obsession has been with authorising a text as authentic. In diverting those interested from the substantive question of meaning, it will be fair to say then that this copious meta-narrative is as authentic as the song itself. Yet, much in the manner of Hendrix's 'Star Spangled Banner', Australians who sing this song refuse the offered absolution of a ready-made text, 'Advance Australia Fair'. Offered a song in the anthem series, Australians would rather be moved by the authentic mystery of who they are and for all the ethical perils that emotional investment entails.

But perhaps each of these texts is, in its way, overblown, a little too serious for the people singing it. In that case perhaps the truth in the averaging between them might be in those lyrics of Norman Lindsay's we met in the last chapter, in the anthem he penned for his Noble Society of Puddin' Owners:

> Hurrah, we'll stick together,
> And always bear in mind
> To eat our puddin' gallantly,
> Whenever we're inclined.

(44)

Notes

1. For a more detailed account of these songs and their historical role in national devotions in Serbia and Yugoslavia, see Kelen and Pavkovik (2010).
2. Hidetoshi's (1988) article, 'Flag and Anthem, Symbols of Distress' gives an account of attitudes to 'Kimigayo' and the 'Hinomaru' flag, at a time of heightened controversy over these symbols due to the conflict between a resurgence in nationalism and the nation's 'peace constitution' (152–156).
3. Translated by the author, with Aleksandr Pavkovic.
4. For a detailed account of this song and its historical role in national devotions in Croatia, see Kelen and Pavkovik (2012).
5. Composed in 1905 by Slovenian composer, Stanko Premrl, adopted by the Slovenian Assembly as the official anthem on 27th September, 1989.
6. Translated by the author, with Merima Didjarevic.
7. Tagore also authored the lyrics for Bangladesh's national anthem.
8. The observation is made notwithstanding Australians having clearly voted for this as anthem of choice over 'Waltzing Matilda' and several other contenders, in a 1977 plebiscite to choose a national song. 'Advance Australia Fair' polled 43% to 'Waltzing Matilda's' 28% in that vote.
9. Though the coining of the word (or at least the donation of the name) 'Australia' is traditionally credited to Matthew Flinders and dated to 1804 (Manning Clark, 1992, 182), the term is in fact much older. A 1794 work, *The Zoology of New Holland,* by English naturalist, George Shaw, refers to the whole of the continent as Australia. The adjective Australian is somewhat older, having been applied to the fictitious (aboriginal) inhabitants of Australia in a 1676 novel by a Frenchman, Gabriel de Foigny: *La Terre Australe Connue* (translated

into in 1693 as *A New Discovery of Terra Incognita Australis, of the Southern World*). The 'Advance Australia' motto (found, for instance, on pre-decimal coinage up till 1966) dates to the 1820s and was the banner on the front page of the *Sydney Gazette* from 1824. The idea of 'Advancing Australia' is roughly contemporary with Matthew Flinders' popularising of the idea of Australia itself.

10. In the (1690) *Second Treatise on Government,* Locke wrote 'As much land as a man tills, plants, improves, cultivates, and can use the product of, so much is his property. He by his labour does, as it were, inclose it from the common' (v, 32).
11. For the purposes of reference and comparison I include here the lyrics of the 'other' or 'Marie Cowan' version of the song, thought by some (e.g. Russell Ward) to be the traditional version of which the Paterson is a variant.

    Once a jolly swagman camp'd by a billabong,
    Under the shade of a coolibah tree,
    And he sang as he watch'd and waited till his billy boiled,
    You'll come a waltzing Matilda with me

    Waltzing Matilda, Waltzing Matilda,
    You'll come a waltzing Matilda with me,
    And he sang as watched and waited till his billy boiled,
    You'll come a waltzing Matilda with me.

    Down came a jumbuck to drink at that billabong,
    Up jumped the swagman and grabbed him with glee,
    And he sang as he shoved that jumbuck in his tucker bag,
    You'll come a waltzing Matilda with me.

    Up rode the squatter mounted on his thoroughbred,
    Down came the troopers, one, two, three.
    Whose that jolly jumbuck you've got in your tucker bag?
    You'll come a waltzing matilda with me.

    Up jumped the swagman, sprang into the billabong,
    You'll never catch me alive said he,
    And his ghost may be heard as you pass by that billabong.
    You'll come a waltzing matilda with me.

    (Radic, 20–21)

12. In Australian vernacular, verballing is the extraction of a confession by authorities through threat of, or resort to, violence.
13. On one occasion, Prime Minister Robert Menzies was welcomed in France by band of the Republican Guard playing 'Waltzing Matilda'. The band leader was apparently staggered when told that 'Waltzing Matilda' was not the Australian national anthem.

Chapter 6

Anthems for a Better World

cosmopolitan and postcolonial hymns

There is a word
Which bears a sword
Can pierce an armed man.
It hurls its barbed syllables, –
At once is mute again.
But where it fell
The saved will tell
On patriotic day,
Some epauletted brother
Gave his breath away.

(Emily Dickinson, 88)

Words of the anthem are words to which the breath of the citizen-patriot returns, and so gives life. Anthem is the life-breath of the nation. In anthems powerful affect is automatised because, despite some deep mysteries and doubts, the unisonant know how the anthem makes them feel. The portability of songs like 'God Save the King/Queen' provides a convenient illustration of the paradox of *uniformity of differences*. Conversely, songs like 'The Marseillaise' and 'The Star Spangled Banner' show that an apparently particular national sentiment can have a powerful affective/ideological impact away from home. The Slovenian anthem, 'A Toast', discussed in the previous chapter, is a rare anthemic instance of libidinous pragmatism, and demonstrates the potential utility of a cosmopolitan hymn to a nation-in-particular. This paradox is more pointedly observed in the case of 'The Internationale', a song that (as well as serving the international communist movement) provided Russia and the Soviet Union with an anthem for many years.

Anthems inspire parody because their self-seriousness seems (at least to the cynic) to be begging to have the piss taken. This no doubt has more than a little to do with perceptions of, and attitudes to, sentimentalism, as discussed in Chapter 4. The more serious the anthem, the greater the parodist's temptation to revise it. Motive and opportunity are frequently strong for the citizen who entertains doubts as to the unisonance expected of him or her, and whether these doubts relate to the idea of nationalism, the policy of a particular government or the quality of a particular song. Being made to stand and sing words dinned into one's head is too powerful an enticement for many free-thinking spirits to resist. The flag-centred playgrounds of the world must be the principal site for the fashioning of anthem parodies, and it would certainly be an interesting comparative study, to collect the spontaneous anthem parody efforts of school children from various countries.

Poems, in general, are words to which their makers hope the breath will return. Thinking of the schoolyard rhyme, we remind ourselves that anthems are poems and that, even in the case of those made by government-appointed committees, a creative process has gone into their making. The relation of poetic texts to their predecessors has been famously theorised by Harold Bloom, in *The Anxiety of Influence*. For Bloom, 'to imagine is to misinterpret' and so mistakenness is definitive: 'Poetry [...] is misprision, is a disciplined perverseness. Poetry is misunderstanding, misinterpretation, misalliance' (93–95). From one context to another, poetic meanings are re-read, revised; poetic truths may thus be of the homeostatic kind, adjusting tradition to present circumstances and beliefs. It is not only the survival of anthems-in-particular we may read in this light; the persistence of the anthem idea is itself a tenacious truth of the poetic kind.

Romanticism and the Anthem Idea

From where does the self-seriousness of nations come? The authority and authoritarianism states invest in demanding sentimentality, in insisting on rote devotions, of their citizen subjects, has a basis in authoritarian governance and religion of ages past – 'this is the song you sing here, this is how it is sung'. How did the religious feelings of ages past become invested in the quasi-religiosity of national spirit? I think anthems had much to do with this, as did the self-seriousness of poets and poetry. And it was the ideology of Romanticism that facilitated the neat transfer of affect from the song sung in unison devoted to God to the song sung in unison devoted to the nation.

Coleridge's 1795 'The Aeolian Harp' is a poem one might see as setting the tone for a Romantic interest in the connection between music and things of the soul. In lines 26–33:

> O the one Life within us and abroad,
> Which meets all motion and becomes its soul,
> A light in sound, a sound-like power in light,
> Rhythm in all thought, and joyance every where –
> Methinks, it should have been impossible
> Not to love all things in a world so filled;
> Where the breeze warbles, and the mute still air
> Is Music slumbering on her instrument.

Pantheism encourages synaesthesia, and Coleridge's esemplastic spirit shows us light in sound, rhythm in thought, imagination in all things created. The senses are promiscuous where they seek universal love and joy and central to this soul-work is the naturalness of music, its expression of the divine. Music in these circumstances becomes the perfect metaphor for and the perfect expression of the sacred. In lines 44–48:

And what if all of animated nature
Be but organic Harps diversely framed,
That tremble into thought, as o'er them sweeps
Plastic and vast, one intellectual breeze,
At once the Soul of each, and God of all?

(103–104)

It is in the poetry of Coleridge's friend, William Wordsworth, we begin to get a sense of how nation fits into the Romantic picture of a relationship with the divine. In Wordsworth's 1802 sonnet, 'Great men have been among us', thinking of England's literary past the reader is told that these men (Sidney, Marvell, Milton and others) 'taught us how rightfully a nation shone/ in splendor' (in Auden and Pearson, 191). The sonnet goes on to bemoan France's lack of any such 'master spirit'. In 'London 1802', we see that the nation is, for Wordsworth, something fallen into ruin and needing revival:

MILTON! thou shouldst be living at this hour:
England hath need of thee: she is a fen
Of stagnant waters: altar, sword, and pen,
Fireside, the heroic wealth of hall and bower,
Have forfeited their ancient English dower
Of inward happiness. We are selfish men;
O raise us up, return to us again,
And give us manners, virtue, freedom, power!

(182)

'Altar, sword and pen': religion, power and imagination may have, in the poet's present, been forfeited; we see in their conflation the means of state authority on which the nation depends, without which the nation languishes. Though he wrote nothing official in that capacity, Wordsworth did spend the last years of his life with a national role, as poet laureate. Like Blake, Wordsworth contributed to the material record of the English ethnoscape, and one reads, particularly in *The Prelude*, the connection made, as per the etymology of 'nation' (the Latin *natio* – that which has been born) between childhood as state to which the poet yearns to return, and the love of country, as that which the poet's pen might revive.

The days gone by
Return upon me almost from the dawn
Of life: the hiding places of man's power
Open; I would approach them but they close.
I see by glimpses now; when age comes on,
May scarcely see at all; and I would give,
While yet we may, as far as words can give,

Substance and life to what I feel, enshrining,
Such is my hope, the spirit of the Past
For future restoration.

(in Auden and Pearson, 223)

The Prelude expresses Wordsworth's sense of affective synergy in the line, 'So feeling comes in aid of feeling'. For Wordsworth, as for Coleridge, music – and its evanescence – is central to this heart/soul work, as is of course, memory. In the closing couplet of 'The Solitary Reaper':

The music in my heart I bore,
Long after it was heard no more.

(168)

We find a similar idea in an 1824 poem of Shelley's: 'Music, when soft voices die,/Vibrates in the memory' (in Auden and Pearson, 336). And in Keats' 1819 'Ode to a Nightingale', a contrast is spelled out between the immortality of song (the soul poured forth in ecstasy) and the transience of its reception: 'Still wouldst thou sing, and I have ears in vain –/ To thy high requiem become a sod'. The bird was not born for death, its voice was heard 'in ancient days by emperor and clown'. The poem concludes:

Forlorn! the very word is like a bell
To toll me back from thee to my sole self!
Adieu! the fancy cannot cheat so well
As she is fam'd to do, deceiving elf.
Adieu! adieu! thy plaintive anthem fades
Past the near meadows, over the still stream,
Up the hillside; and now 'tis buried deep
In the next valley-glades:
Was it a vision, or a waking dream?
Fled is that music: – do I wake or sleep?

(in Auden and Pearson, 385)

If culture is a kind of dreaming together then in Keats' poem we see that, under the spell of so natural a thing as song, the listener cannot tell whether s/he wakes or sleeps; nor can the place of the 'anthem' be precisely discerned, rather it is 'past' and 'over' places and 'buried deep'. Keats, I think it will be safe to say, did not have a national anthem in mind when he wrote the 'Ode to a Nightingale', but in transferring the idea of the anthem from its liturgical context to the broader church of nature he helped to make it available for the love of landscape and so ethnoscape. Across Europe, Romanticism went on to privilege the sublimity of landscapes, which would increasingly, through the nineteenth century, be seen to be national; it privileged folkloric traditions (easily assimilated to nationalist agendas, and now able to be standardised and disseminated through print); and it invented the 'national epic' – the 'ancient' poem, which country by country would justify Wordsworth's hope in *The Prelude*, of 'the spirit of the Past/For future restoration'. Of course Rome had had *The Aeneid* and Portugal had had *The Lusiads* available for such a purpose since Camoens had, centuries earlier, made the effort, for national purposes, to hark back to Virgil. But now the Anglo-Saxons had *Beowulf* complete, the Russians had *Igor's Campaign*, the Finns the *Kalevala*, the Armenians *Sasuntzi*, the Poles *Pan Tadeusz*. And the Homeric epics had a new national significance for the Greeks. These and the national folkloric texts now avidly collected across Europe, together with the cult of the sublime helped to sacralise the homeland and its myths and legends, as worthy of quasi-religious observance.

A nation is a people and a people casting off the shackle of thinking that kings had a divine right ran the risk of being left without a sense of connection to the divine. As Durkheim and Gellner and Smith have all observed, the advent of nationalism was of the people's self-worship. However, it is difficult to imagine many nineteenth-century Romantics or Nationalists countenancing that idea.

Beyond an apparent squaring of the circle, enlightenment thinking had given way to a new state-directed religiosity – the worship, in lieu of nature, of the putative place *in* nature a people occupied with its distinctive language and customs and culture – the national God-given space of a particular people. New forms of art were needed for the new observances, and the more respectable their traditional credentials the more persuasive they would be. Where word and sound meet in art, God seems already a presence. With hindsight, it seems the idea of evanescence Coleridge gives us by way of his Aeolian Harp presages the age of mechanical reproduction that will, by the end of the nineteenth century, make all song potentially rote, able to be reproduced at will by a machine devised for the purpose.

I think we can say, from this brief excursion, that the passage of authority and identity-making from religion to nation state, was greatly facilitated in Europe, through the nineteenth century, by the Romantic ideas that made a certain kind of song available for the purpose. If Romanticism may be blamed for laying the ideological foundation for state worship, then it will only be fair to note that we do also find a critique of the nation–state nexus at its source. Writing halfway through the Industrial Revolution, Blake certainly warned his readers of the dangers of state power and of the coming mechanical age. Blake may have written 'A War Song to Englishmen' (44) but in what would become an alternative anthem for England, the 1804 preface for *Milton*, 'And did those feet in ancient time', some bold subversive questions are asked:

And did the Countenance Divine
Shine forth upon our clouded hills?
And was Jerusalem builded here
Among these dark satanic mills?

(in Auden and Pearson, 24)

The question form for the suspicion asserted here is instructive. Was God here? Was this place part of a divine plan? It is implied that something went wrong. And in the last stanza we learn, through the model of the poem's persona, that we (later the unisonant) can play a role in setting things to rights. As with Wordsworth's idea of 'future restoration' in *The Prelude*, there is salvation in a sentiment, there is hope in reviving an imagined spirit of the past. For Blake the battle, with the 'bow of burning gold' and 'the arrows of desire', was explicitly an ideological one, a kind of English *jihad*: 'I will not cease from mental fight'. But if, for Blake, it is national sentiment that will save us, then it is the state from which nation and citizen need protection. In 'Auguries of Innocence':

> The Whore & Gambler, by the State
> Licenc'd, build that Nation's Fate.
> The Harlot's cry from Street to Street
> Shall weave Old England's winding Sheet.

(171)

Corruption is associated with the state; the nation (which for Blake has a biblical/contemporary resonance) is what needs to be saved from corruption. It is the people – the *I* singing – who need to do the saving. The anthem quality of Blake's anti-industrial rant seems curiously at odds with the progress-oriented empire-rhetoric that would make the UK the world's most powerful state by the end of the century and into the twentieth. Still, had England become a republic at any time in the century since Hubert Parry set Blake's words to music, it is difficult to imagine that this song would not have become the national anthem. The self-seriousness of English national sentiment had much to do with the Romantic idea of an uncorrupted Edenic condition (a place-based God-given Christ-redeemed right) to which the citizenry en-masse might return.

Whitman's and Ginsberg's Americas

For a New World perspective on the idea of a citizenry *en masse* we may turn, a half-century later, to Whitman's 1855 'Song of Myself':

> One's-Self I sing, a simple separate person,
> Yet utter the word Democratic, the word En-Masse.
>
> Of physiology from top to toe I sing,
> Not physiognomy alone nor brain alone is worthy for the Muse, I say the Form complete
>   is worthier far,
> The Female equally with the Male I sing.

Of Life immense in passion, pulse, and power,
Cheerful, for freest action form'd under the laws divine,
The Modern Man I sing.

(22)

Whitman's embodied self, not facelessly of the crowd, is the modern voting difference-making man. In his own way as oracular as Blake, in *Leaves of Grass* Whitman revises for his readers anthem after anthem for the democratic spirit, for the one deciding with equal others, how variously to be. In his 'Prayer of Columbus', Whitman closes, in the voice of the explorer, by beginning with a question many readers will equally have asked of his work and of Blake's:

Is it the prophet's thought I speak, or am I raving?
What do I know of life? what of myself?
I know not even my own work past or present,
Dim ever-shifting guesses of it spread before me,
Of newer better worlds, their mighty parturition,
Mocking, perplexing me.

And these things I see suddenly, what mean they?
As if some miracle, some hand divine unseal'd my eyes,
Shadowy vast shapes smile through the air and sky,
And on the distant waves sail countless ships,
And anthems in new tongues I hear saluting me.

(338)

Whitman's orientation to the nation-devotional role of the poet has as much religious spirit as Blake's. His Columbus is a battered, wrecked, ancient mariner crazed with his devotional duties to God, the insistent 'thee' of the poem. But the anthems Whitman's Columbus hears through the shadowy vast are a salute and so a vindication of the difference-making individual – the poem's persona and equally avatar of the New World nation. Whitman's anthem quality is not about reviving or yearning to return to Eden, it is looking forward from an imagined past to an enlightened future, to a better and self-bettering world. As with Blake there are many moods but no lack of self-seriousness in Whitman. Still, his poetics will lay the foundation for a devastating critique of national sentiment and its dangers.

The parodies we have considered in Chapter 3 (especially 'Hail Freedonia' and 'The Puddin Owners' Anthem') mock either the rote pretensions of nation or of anthem singing or of both. Parodies need not propose serious alternatives, nor need their purveyors entertain more than the necessary moment's doubt in order to imagine a world other than that which is assumed in the official text and through the affect it generates.

An anti-anthem is, I think, by contrast the kind of text we find in Allen Ginsberg's 1956 poem 'America'.[1] This text does not parody an existing anthem; rather it plays with, in order to expose, the kinds of assumptions that imbue the cosy WASP singalong of American national culture, which Hendrix would attack a decade later.

America I've given you all and now I'm nothing.
America two dollars and twenty-seven cents January 17, 1956.
I can't stand my own mind.
America when will we end the human war?
Go fuck yourself with your atom bomb.
I don't feel good don't bother me.
I won't write my poem till I'm in my right mind.

(146–148)

Ginsberg's 'America' starts off sounding like a state of the nation address. But it turns out to be a description of the state of mind of one citizen – one simple separate person – addressed to the nation he acknowledges. The poem is part confession, part accusation, argument, monologue (mock-mad talking to oneself); it is a plea, a prayer, a defiant stance, a pledge, a question, a kind of heckling, a long quibble that breaks into invective. First and foremost though, this is the voice of one whom nation has infantilised, and it is a voice asking why. Not 'my country, tis of thee I sing', but 'I have questions to ask of my country'. Where speech had become wooden and rote, now the voice of the worldly wise and well read – the voice of the self-historicising subject – takes the nation to task. Putting a certain anthemic logic to the test, the poem is addressed as if the nation were a sentience in its own right. The ironic effect of that false impression is that, once recognised as such, attention is drawn to the impossibility of the speech act posited. America cannot answer or even witness in the univocal manner of an interlocutor. And yet we feel from the onset of the poem that America is a collection of weighty and singular opinions bearing down on the persona. Irony engages the poem's reader in a critical disclosure of all of the metonymic paraphernalia of nation. You could say that the (mock) patriotic title belies the subversion of patriotism in the poem. But at a deeper level Ginsberg's poem *is* a truly patriotic gesture. It asks Americans of the Cold War not to look for 'reds under beds' but to look into their own souls to see who they are, to look at the bizarre contradictions and the mad-seeming mood swings that are expected of the loyal citizen. The poem is asking America to make sense of itself, of what and how it includes and excludes. That is subversion and it is also love: desperate love of the type Auden promoted, the 'love one another or die' kind. It is work, which though of a different rhetorical order, has a number of affinities with Whitman's project in *Leaves of Grass*.

Subversion is an act of rhetorical refusal. It succeeds – where it succeeds – as a refusal to be constrained to the position that appears to have been prepared for the subject now speaking. This poem changes the world that made it possible because it takes apart the patterns of words it is given and it fits that world's means of meaning back together to suit itself, rather than the categories it began with. It is in this way Ginsberg's 'America' expresses the ambivalence of Whitman's words: 'myself disintegrated, every/one disintegrated yet part of the scheme' (144). Scouting out the anathema of American anthem qualities, Ginsberg presents a genre-opposite: the idiosyncratic personal in lieu of the apparently objective collective of the unisonant. Yet Ginsberg's 'America' ends with a curious expression of commitment to nation:

> I'd better get right down to the job.
> It's true I don't want to join the Army or turn lathes in
> precision parts factories, I'm nearsighted and psycho-
> pathic anyway.
> America I'm putting my queer shoulder to the wheel.
>
> (84–87)

In the poem's context, this is as if to say 'you, my nation, may not acknowledge gay Jewish left-leaning poets with drug-taking proclivities; I may be your anathema, and yet I am not only part of the nation, but my work is nation-making, as well'. The reversal nicely foreshadows the more pedestrian one John F. Kennedy will make at his inauguration in 1961, when he urged Americans to ask not what the nation could do for them but what they could do for the nation.

There are many parodic elements in Ginsberg's poem, but can the poem *in toto* be classified as parody? Is it anti-anthem, anthem-anathema? Ultimately there will be little point in quibbling over labels: Jimi Hendrix's parodic rendition of 'Star Spangled Banner', though wordless, had a similar eloquence. Ginsberg's is one of many texts by famous poets from the Romantics on, which have been explicitly interested in the idea of anthem and anthem quality. Most have recognised in anthems something of the Barthesian mythology[2] and so, we may say, an anathema of what poetry, since Modernism, has become.

If however there is a need to define by example what an anti-anthem might be, then I think we can find no better instance than in 'Lithuania, Bloody Land' – a song sung in the Kovno Ghetto during the Nazi Occupation in World War II. Jews had made up one-third of the population of what had been the between-the-wars capital of Lithuania. Few of them survived the pogroms, massacres and deportations that followed the German invasion of 1941. But while they were fighting, they managed to create this curse in the form of a song, authorship of which remains anonymous.

> Lithuania, bloody land,
> May you be cursed through the centuries,
> Let your blood flow
> Like the blood of Jewish children.
>
> Let your sons suffer
> As you made Jewish sons suffer;

When your dark days end
May no one find your grave.

You hope the Germans will grant you favours,
But you will end up in the Ninth Fort.
What you wish for us should happen to you:

Let your cities burn,
And your villages and farms;
You should die as you made us die,
Through all eternity!

(Werb, 25)

And End the Vanity of Nations

It is important to distinguish parodies and anti-anthems from cosmopolitan and anti-national anthems. The most celebrated of cosmopolitan anthems is in the music Beethoven set to Schiller's 'Ode to Joy' for the last movement of the Ninth Symphony. For Theodor Adorno, it is in this work of Schiller's that Kant and Beethoven meet. In *Quasi una Fantasia* Adorno writes, 'In "Ode to Joy" Beethoven composed, programmatically, the Kantian postulate of the Categorical Imperative' (22).

The song has had a long, complex and often contradictory career (as spelled out in Esteban Buch's 2004 book, *Beethoven's Ninth – A Political History*). It has been used in all sorts of contexts, was the anthem for the United German Olympic Teams in the fifties and sixties, was at one stage the anthem of Rhodesia and – without lyrics – has served Europe as an anthem since 1971. In a 2007 *New York Times* article, following the Treaty of Lisbon, Slavoj Zizek writes of it as an 'empty signifier':

> The 'Ode to Joy' is more than just a universally popular piece of classical music that has become something of a cliché during the holiday season (especially, oddly, in Japan, where it has achieved cult status). It has also been, for more than a century, what literary theorists call an 'empty signifier' – a symbol that can stand for anything.
>
> (www.nytimes.com/2007/12/24/opinion/24zizek.html)

Zizek points out that song has served such diverse functions as celebrating Hitler's birthday and representing proletarian solidarity during the Cultural Revolution in China. Bucher, in his book-length study, is impressed with Beethoven's symbolic survival of Nazism, in contrast with Wagner's fate. Zizek reminds us of the exclusive aspect of the original lyrics: in Schiller's last couplet, 'Und wer's nie gekonnt, der stehle/Weinend sich aus diesem Bund!' –

'Those who cannot join in the joy, should creep away into the shadows'. Just as Kant's categorical imperative cannot have been intended for other-than-white races, so Schiller's cosmopolitan God was never really world embracing. Nevertheless, the lyrics and the music that now suggest their spirit are in praise of a brotherhood of men, from which none are, by virtue of identity, excluded.

Freude, schöner Götterfunken
Tochter aus Elysium,
Wir betreten feuertrunken,
Himmlische, dein Heiligtum!
Deine Zauber binden wieder
Was die Mode streng geteilt;
Alle Menschen werden Brüder,
Wo dein sanfter Flügel weilt.

Joy, beautiful spark of the gods
Daughter of Elysium,
We enter, drunk with fire,
Heavenly one, your sanctuary!
Your magic reunites
What custom strictly divided.
All men become brothers,
Where your gentle wing rests.

('Symphony Number 9', 2012)

As Zizek reminds us: 'In early twentieth-century France, the Nobel laureate Romain Rolland declared it to be the great humanist ode to the brotherhood of all people, and it came to be called "The Marseillaise of humanity"'.

The Esperantists' hymn, 'La Espero',[3] is another, though little-known song, with this pretension. The words, by L.L. Zamenhof himself, were set to music by Félicien Menu de Ménil in 1909. In English, these are rendered as follows:

Into the world came a new feeling,
through the world goes a powerful call;
by means of wings of a gentle wind
now let it fly from place to place.

Not to the sword thirsting for blood
does it draw the human family:
to the world eternally fighting
it promises sacred harmony.

Under the sacred sign of the hope
the peaceful fighters gather,
and this affair quickly grows
by the labours of those who hope.

The walls of millennia stand firm
between the divided peoples;
but the stubborn barriers will jump apart,
knocked apart by the sacred love.

On a neutral language basis,
understanding one another,
the peoples will make in agreement
one great family circle.

Our diligent set of colleagues
in peaceful labor will never tire,
until the beautiful dream of humanity
for eternal blessing is realized.

('La Espero')

Though perhaps less inspiring, Zamenhof's lyric shares with Schiller's the hope that it might not be to the sword thirsting for blood the human family will be drawn.

The other song with serious (if less peaceful) pretensions to be 'The Marseillaise' of humanity is the 'The Internationale', a song adopted by the Second International and which subsequently had numerous uses in cosmopolitan, socialist and anarchist causes. Originally written in French by Eugène Pottier, the words were first intended to be sung to the tune of 'The Marseillaise'. A score specifically for the song was composed by Pierre de Geyter in 1888,[4] and this has been the basis for the music by which the song has generally thereafter been known. The first stanza of the original lyrics is as follows:

Debout, les damnés de la terre
Debout, les forçats de la faim
La raison tonne en son cratère
C'est l'éruption de la fin
Du passé faisons table rase
Foule esclave, debout, debout
Le monde va changer de base
Nous ne sommes rien, soyons tout
C'est la lutte finale

Groupons-nous, et demain
L'Internationale
Sera le genre humain.

('The Internationale', 2012)

The song has often been loosely translated, for instance indulging idiomatic differences, and there are many versions allowing different political emphases. For example, in English, the first line has been rendered: 'Arise ye prisoners of starvation'; alternatively, 'Arise, ye workers from your slumber'; alternatively, 'Stand up, all victims of oppression' ('The Internationale', 2012). 'The Marseillaise' is the original of the grievance-focussed late Enlightenment anthem; it is ideological precisely where 'The Star Spangled Banner' is not. The (bourgeois) class loyalties 'The Marseillaise' proposed offered a clear parallel with the international selling power of 'God Save the King/Queen'; in either case were (opposed) sentiments that would travel well regardless of national origin. No doubt the revolutionary fervour of 'The Marseillaise' appealed to Eugène Pottier when he set his lyrics to it, but it was because of its bourgeois associations the tune of 'The Marseillaise' would quickly prove unsuitable for 'The Internationale'. 'The Internationale' is a lyric that seeks to employ the power of the anthem for the purposes of not only a critique of nation but in order to propose a practical and urgent alternative to nations. As with 'Ode to Joy', we can say that the putatively post-national anthem recaptures the pre-national spirit of the old English anthem: this is a song for co-religionists, rather than patriots.

If 'Lithuania, Bloody Land' presents us with the anti-anthem of the excluded and persecuted minority, 'The Internationale' is the archetypal anti-national anthem; its function, we may say, is to turn anthem quality on its head, to use proletarian fellow feeling and cosmopolitan spirit against nations in particular and in general: 'The Internationale unites the human race'. The controversial suggestion is that the people in general (the masses) are the persecuted excluded of the nation and that nations, as such, exist for the benefit of their ruling classes. And yet the title itself shows the intellectual failing of the idea; 'The *Inter*-nationale' implies that nations will continue. Are not nations the problem? Then how can the solution be *inter*national? Should the song not have been called 'The Cosmopolitain'? In Billy Bragg's version:

Let no one build walls to divide us
Walls of hatred nor walls of stone
Come greet the dawn and stand beside us
We'll live together or we'll die alone
In our world poisoned by exploitation
Those who have taken, now they must give
And end the vanity of nations
We've but one Earth on which to live

('The Internationale', 2012)

In the original lyrics for the fifth stanza, the anti-national sentiment had been expressed: 'Ils sauront bientôt que nos balles/Sont pour nos propres généraux' – 'They soon shall hear the bullets flying,/We'll shoot the generals on our own side' ('The Internationale', 2012). It is not difficult to imagine how that kind of lyric might not survive a transition from insurgent to official status. In fact, after the Bolshevik Revolution, the 1902 Russian translation of Aron Kots was revised to remove the now redundant future tenses; after all, the rule of the tyrants had officially ended. As for turning the guns 'on our own generals', the fifth stanza then became:

> Enough of the will of kings
> Stupefying us into the haze of war!
> War to the tyrants! Peace to the people!
> Go on strike, sons of the army!
> And if the tyrants tell us
> To fall heroically in battle for them –
> Then, murderers, we will point
> The muzzles of our cannons at you!
>
> ('The Internationale', 2012)

If we seek to evaluate the utility of 'The Internationale' for stirring cosmopolitan socialist sentiment on the world-scale, then it faces a contradiction analogous to that observed in Stalin's claimed paradox of 'socialism in one country'. The anthem that would be anti-national in nature becomes the anthem of one nation, a power post-1945 as imperial as Czarist Russia ever was, a nation that – as the world's longest running totalitarian state – internally and externally exercised some of the worst excesses of the national kind of the twentieth century. One should note that the 'The Internationale' was the anthem of the Soviet Union only from 1918 to 1944, when it was replaced by 'The Hymn of the Soviet Union' or 'The State Anthem of the USSR' (now known as 'The National Anthem of the Russian Federation'), the (non-Stalinist) lyrics of which (dating from 2000) now commence:

> Russia, our holy country!
> Russia, our beloved country!
> A mighty will, a great glory,
> Are your inheritance for all time!

These words followed by the refrain:

> Be glorious, our free fatherland!
> Eternal union of fraternal peoples,

Common wisdom given by our forebears,
Be glorious, our country! We are proud of you!

(Xing Hang, 530)

In fact the progression, away from internationalism and towards Russian nationalism was well under way during the Soviet era, particular from the sixties, when the whole of the Eastern Bloc was becoming more overtly nationalist. Allowing nationalism elsewhere would eventually promote Russian nationalism at home, much in the manner that devolution in Britain has allowed the re-emergence of a distinctly English nationalism (witness the prevalence of the Flag of St George today, a generation ago long since vanished). Sergei Mikhailov's 1944 version of the state hymn had praised Stalin as Lenin's successor, and began as follows:

United forever in friendship and labour,
Our mighty republics will ever endure.
The Great Soviet Union will live through the ages.
The dream of a people their fortress secure.

Due to de-Stalinisation, there had been a long period during which the anthem was played without lyrics at all. At last the author was called upon to update his lyrics. Mikhailov's 1977 revision of the song begins:

Unbreakable Union of freeborn Republics,
Great Russia has welded forever to stand.
Created in struggle by will of the people,
United and mighty, our Soviet land!

(*Sounds of the Soviet Union*)

The vanity of nations seems to be firmly ensconced in these words. With Stalin, critical consciousness had left the stage, the dream of a better world free of strife between nations had gone up in smoke, as ideals so often do. Perhaps, along these lines, it will be appropriate to end this discussion of anthem anathemae with a song which is unquestionably an anti-anthem, The Who's 1971 'Won't Get Fooled Again':

We'll be fighting in the streets
With our children at our feet
And the morals that they worship will be gone,
And the men who spurred us on
Sit in judgment of all wrong
They decide and the shotgun sings the song.

I'll tip my hat to the new constitution,
Take a bow for the new revolution,
Smile and grin at the change all around me.
Pick up my guitar and play,
Just like yesterday
And I'll get on my knees and pray
We don't get fooled again!
Don't get fooled again!

Change it had to come,
We knew it all along.
We were liberated from the fall that's all.
But the world looks just the same,
And history ain't changed,
'Cause the banners, they all flown in the last war.

Refrain

I'll move myself and my family aside
If we happen to be left half alive,
I'll get all my papers and smile at the sky
For I know that the hypnotized never lie.
Do ya?

There's nothing in the street
Looks any different to me
And the slogans are replaced, by-the-bye.
And the parting on the left
Is now the parting on the right
And the beards have all grown longer overnight.

Refrain

YAAAAAAAAH!

Meet the new boss
Same as the old boss

(*Who's Next*)

Pete Townshend's devoutly cynical lyrics render in these last lines the familiar Orwellian *Animal Farm* trope: the new boss is the same as the old. Throughout the song though, we read a reflexive and thoroughgoing critique of anthem quality, of religion and equally of the promises of revolutions (of their pseudo-religious quality).

> I'll get all my papers and smile at the sky
> For I know that the hypnotized never lie.

The persona of this song is owning up: the finger is pointed, certainly, but it is pointed at the crowd of the unisonant that includes the self-singing. One might say that this is only disingenuously so, that this is a voice which leads by pretending not to. But this voice is (perhaps ironically, for rock stars) a voice *of* the people; this persona understands the need, for the purposes of survival, to maintain an impression of solidarity with the state that demands unison of its citizens.[5] Roger Daltrey's legendary scream before the closing couplet leads the otherwise unisonant past the fatalistic promises of revolution to the song's truth, which is not of any ideal, but rather of simple observation – a Brechtian plea for self-respect. All things considered, this postmodern text is truly an anti-anthem. For contrast, John Lennon's 'Imagine' might be read as antithesis to the older religious conception of anthem; like 'Ode to Joy', it is a cosmopolitan hymn.

The Postcolonial Problem of Choosing a Nationhood

In the previous chapter, I dealt at some length with the postcolonial anthem choices of one new Europe or settler-society, Australia. In the rest of this chapter, I will look at the anthem choices of several other-than-white countries de-colonised in the post-war years (and so under the UN's de-colonisation regime). It is interesting to look at the lyrics of these songs in the light of the sentiment expressed in 'Won't Get Fooled Again', because so many of the facets of a postcolonial anthem are critiqued in that song. Despite notable and interesting exceptions (India, Bangladesh, Japan, Tibet), as I have argued in Chapter 4, through the reduction of the world's musical choices to a set of Euro-centric and pseudo-philosophic clichés, de-colonising entailed offering Europe's cut-price affective goods to the natives. The irony is that this was the kind of medicine that went with the territory the decolonised were allegedly *re*-claiming. The revival delusion (the idea that a precolonial polity is available to return to) has widespread currency as a postcolonial rubric of Anderson's first paradox. The choice of an anthem among contenders (as discussed in the previous chapter) may be seen as explaining the nature of national investments, but in postcolonial circumstances there may be more fundamental issues at stake. And so in some postcolonial anthems, ambivalences are revealed, which go to the question of a nation's viability, and likewise the viability of the abstract relations on which national entities depend, including rule of law, inviolability of borders, human rights.

The strident tone of 'The Marseillaise' and 'The Internationale' is prevalent among postcolonial anthems. Consider the 'Arise ye prisoners of starvation' opening of 'The

Internationale': something close to that idea is to the fore in the anthems of Belize, Benin, Chad, Congo, Djibouti, Kiribati, Kyrgyzstan, Mali, Vietnam, Niger, Nigeria, Papua New Guinea, Tonga, Senegal, Togo. Consider Algeria's anthem, originally the song of the 1950s liberation front; it tells the story of why liberation was necessary – so that the nation might live:

We swear by the lightning that destroys.
By the streams of generous blood being shed.
By the bright flags that wave.
Flying proudly on the high djebels.
That we are in revolt, whether to live or to die.
We are determined that Algeria should live.
So be our witness – be our witness – be our witness!

We are soldiers in revolt for truth
And we have fought for our independence.
When we spoke, nobody listened to us.
So we have taken the noise of gunpowder as our rhythm
And the sound of machine guns as our melody.
We are determined that Algeria should live.
So be our witness – be our witness – be our witness!

From our heroes we shall make an army come to being.
From our dead we shall build up a glory,
Our spirits shall ascend to immortality
And on our shoulders we shall raise the standard.
To the nation's Liberation Front we have sworn an oath,
We are determined that Algeria should live.
So be our witness – be our witness – be our witness!

The cry of the Fatherland sounds from the battlefields.
Listen to it and answer the call!
Let it be written with the blood of martyrs
And be read to future generations
Oh, Glory, we have held out our hand to you.
We are determined that Algeria should live.
So be our witness – be our witness – be our witness!

(Bristow, 17)

The call to witness is the call to arms. The state is founded on apparently oppositional terms. The anthem recalls the originary moment of nation. This might as easily be said of China's

'March of the Volunteers' (one of the world's shorter anthems), China being a nation which though perhaps not strictly speaking, postcolonial, has (and for sound historical reasons) one of the most strident of anti-imperialist lyrics:

> Arise, ye who refuse to be slaves;
> With our very flesh and blood
> Let us build our new Great Wall!
> The peoples of China are in the most critical time.
> Everybody must roar their defiance.
> Arise! Arise! Arise!
> Millions of hearts with one mind,
> Brave the enemy's gunfire,
> March on!
> Brave the enemy's gunfire.
> March on! March on!
> March on!
> On!
>
> (Bristow, 137)

The Great Wall is perhaps an ironic image to choose to inspire national sacrifice and perhaps a classic example of a Hobsbawmian 'invented' tradition. Although barbarian-deflecting walls in the north of China date back to antiquity, the 'Great Wall' is essentially a Ming Dynasty construction designed to deter the Mongols (who had ruled China for the duration of their own dynasty, the Yuan). It was the Manchus who marched over the wall to rule China in 1644, and whose dynasty, the Ching, continued until the Chinese Republic was established in 1911. In the Ching, the Manchu rulers of an empire that now extended far beyond the Great Wall did use parts of the structure to control migration movements of the Han Chinese, who from that point of view can be seen as having spent the previous dynasty building themselves a prison. Certainly the Great Wall would provide an apt symbol for the feudal exploitation of the peasant class. Whichever way one considers it, and without reference to Franz Kafka's hyperbolic treatment in his story of that name, The Great Wall of China is a spectacular long-term failure of foreign policy (Waldron, passim). But heroic failure has a special role in the evocation of national sentiment, such as we see in the growing veneration of the First World War Gallipoli catastrophe, among Australian patriots. And so perhaps this is an excellent lyric for suggesting the unconditional nature of the patriot's love of country. Macao poet, Yao Feng, asks in his volume, *In Brief*:

> every time I hear the national anthem
> my blood runs hot
> before my eyes
> the martyrs moving on

through the enemies' cannon fire
'get through the enemy's fire, move forward!'
why is it always on our land?
why do we always have so many enemies?

(20)

One reads in the lyrics of 'The March of the Volunteers' the fact that Algeria's and China's experiences of foreign domination have a deal in common. Continuities between the pre- and post-'colonial' state of China become more apparent with time, and with the return of Confucian thinking to the avowed state-sponsored ideology. Algeria's need is to assert the fact of its birth as a nation, and the memory of the sacrifice enabling that birth. The difference in these songs is that China's anthem recalls a permanently dire state of affairs, delivering a 'price of liberty is eternal vigilance' message. Despite (or because of) this, China's permanence as a political entity can be taken for granted. Algeria's anthem, by contrast, is evoking the originary moment of the nation – the conditions and the mindset from which the nation would arise. In Angola's anthem, the moment of the nation's baptismal fire is lauded very specifically:

O fatherland, we shall never forget
The heroes of the Fourth of February.
O fatherland, we salute your sons
Who died for our independence.
We honor the past and our history
As by our work we build the New Man.

(in Bristow, 25)

This anthem offers the unisonant the narrative that explains the holiday that remembers the sacrifice that enables the nation. It helps the citizen to understand the meanings and expectations that are a part of the national habitus for Angolans. Some of the postcolonial anthems are very direct in their ideological appeal. Consider the lyrics of the first chorus of 'Total Independence', the national anthem of Sao Tome and Principe:

Total independence,
Glorious song of the people.
Total independence,
Sacred hymn of combat.
Dynamism
In the national struggle,
Eternal oath
To the sovereign country
Of Sao Tome and Principe.

In the last stanza of the song:

> Working, struggling, struggling and conquering,
> We go ahead with giant steps
> In the crusade of the African peoples,
> Raising the national flag.
> Voice of the people, present and united,
> Strong beat in the heart of hope
> To be a hero in the hour of peril,
> A hero of the Nation's resurgence.

(in Bristow, 480)

Portugal being the former coloniser of Angola and Sao Tome and Principe, for the purposes of comparison, consider the tone of Portugal's anthem, 'A Portuguesa' ('The Portuguese'):

> Heroes of the sea, noble race.
> Valiant and immortal nation,
> Now is the hour to raise up on high once more
> Portugal's splendor.
> From out of the mists of memory,
> Oh Homeland, we hear the voices
> Of your great forefathers
> That shall lead you on to victory!
>
> To arms, to arms
> On land and sea!
> To arms, to arms
> To fight for our homeland!
> To march against the enemy guns!

(Bristow, 450)

Another lyric of revival harking back to past glory, another song lauding the moral value of walking into gunfire, these words were written by Henrique Lopes de Mendonça in 1890. The song was essentially a patriotic march inspired by British bullying of Portugal over the extent of Portugal's African colonies. It became an important symbol of the republican cause and replaced the monarchist 'Charter Anthem' as Portugal's national anthem when the monarchy was deposed in 1911.

Portugal's and Sao Tome and Principe's anthems are both themed around the idea of a national revival. What is it that Portugal would be reviving? Presumably, the revival would be of the imperial moment celebrated by the national poet in the national poem, the sixteenth-century *Lusiads* of Camoens. Here the world conquering exploits of Vasco da Gama are fantasised in epic form, and celebrated as establishing Portuguese greatness on the world stage. This was a glory much lauded in the resistance to de-colonisation, which, under the aegis of Luso-tropicalism,[6] we witness in the latter stages of the Salazar dictatorship. What Luso-tropicalism suggested was that the Portuguese were nicer imperialists and therefore deserved to retain their empire while the rest of Europe was de-colonising. The Carnation Revolution of 1974 ended the fantasy-in-practice, but as we see in the Portuguese anthem, nostalgia for the idea remains, though in a form vague enough to not cause much offence.

Then what is it Sao Tome and Principe would be reviving? No doubt, in 1974, this poor Lusophone cocoa-dependent, ethnically African country was overdue for liberation from its colonial master. That liberation – the 'total independence' – of the new nation was achieved because the new democratic government in Lisbon decided to decolonise and immediately began treaty negotiations with parties that would form new governments in various possessions to be shed, all around the globe. And what of Sao Tome and Principe prior to the reign of the colonial oppressor? Both islands were uninhabited when the Portuguese first arrived in the fifteenth century and began building a slave plantation society there. It is participation in the pan-African struggle for independence from Europe that makes credible the idea, in Sao Tome and Principe's context, of being a hero of the national 'resurgence'.

So we see both coloniser and colonised, in defining the national unison, as possessed of unanalysed and unconvincing delusions of grandeur. Amicable and uneventful post-'liberation' political and economic relations between Portugal and Sao Tome and Principe show how unimportant such delusions may be in practical terms.

Hyperbolic claims are par for the course among postcolonial anthem lyrics. Consider the emphatic imagery of what was, until 2009, the first stanza of Peru's national anthem[7]:

For a long time the Peruvian, oppressed.
Dragged the ominous chain;
Condemned to cruel serfdom.
For a long time, for a long time.
For a long time he moaned in silence.
But as soon as the sacred cry of
Freedom! was heard on his coasts.
He shook off the indolence of the slave.
He raised his humiliated,
his humiliated, his humiliated head,
He raised, he raised his humiliated head

(Bristow, 439)

In the second stanza we hear the roar of rough chains of three centuries of horror. Perhaps the most strident of anti-aggressor/oppressor lyrics are in Libya's Gaddafi-era anthem:

God is greatest!
God is greatest!
He is above the plots of the aggressors,
He is the best helper of the oppressed.
With faith and weapons I shall defend my country,
And the light of truth will shine in mind.

In the last stanza are lyrics that arguably make this a suicide bomber's song:

And should I be killed,
I would kill him with me.
Sing with me –
Woe to the imperialists!
And God is above the treacherous tyrant.
God is greatest!
Therefore glorify Him, O my country!
And seize the forehead of the tyrant
And destroy him!

(Bristow, 332)

As we have seen, plenty of anthems extol the virtues of being *pro patria mori*; Lybia's was the only one that appeared to be fomenting a plan along these lines. Fatalism and the sense of history to be written are common features of the postcolonial anthem. Take the second stanza of Honduras' anthem, for instance:

To guard this sacred emblem
We shall march, oh fatherland, to our death;
Our death will be honored
If we die thinking of your love.
Having defended your holy flag,
And shrouded in its glorious folds,
Many, Honduras, shall die for you,
But all shall fall in honor.

(Bristow, 260)

Willingness to sacrifice one's life in the patriotic cause need not suggest any overpowering animosity for an oppressor. The first stanza of Honduras' anthem tells the story of national beginnings by painting a very forgiving picture of the coloniser, and indulging his (sic) point of view:

> Like an Indian maiden you were sleeping,
> Lulled by the resonant song of your seas,
> When, set in your golden valleys,
> The bold navigator found you;
> And on seeing, enraptured, your beauty,
> And feeling your enchantment,
> He dedicated a kiss of love to the blue hen
> Of your splendid mantle.
>
> (Bristow, 260)

Many postcolonial anthems are reconciliatory. In the second stanza of Guyana's for example:

> Green land of Guyana, our heroes of yore,
> Both bondsman and free, laid their bones on your shore.
> This soil so they hallowed, and from them are we,
> All sons of one mother, Guyana the free.
>
> (Bristow, 251)

One strives not to see a self-parodic comic book quality in the image of the 'heroes of yore' laying 'their bones on your shore'.

We have already noted the reconciliatory feat of the South African anthem, in combining the Apartheid era and ANC songs into the one text. The theme of bad old days being behind us is a common one. As we saw in the case of Peru, the memory of slavery is frequently evoked (in the anthems, for instance, of Guatemala, Guyana, Haiti). Many anthems express self-doubt as part of the national unison (for example, those of Burundi, Central Africa, Costa Rica, the Dominican Republic, Ethiopia.) The sense of protesting too much is palpable in the Ethiopian anthem:

> Respect for citizenship is strong in our Ethiopia;
> National pride is seen, shining from one side to another.
> For peace, for justice, for the freedom of peoples,
> In equality and in love we stand united.
> Firm of foundation, we do not dismiss humanness;
> We are peoples who live through work.
> Wonderful is the stage of tradition, mistress of proud heritage.
> Mother of natural virtue, mother of a valorous people.
> We shall protect you – we have a duty;
> Our Ethiopia, live! And let us be proud of you!
>
> (Bristow, 210)

This is a text of a people engaged in persuading itself that the national business is all happening. There are a number of other nations (for instance, Vanuatu and Uzbekistan) that place emphasis on the need to get on with the job as a way of telling the populace who to be. Panama seems to address itself, more or less in the boss's voice, with a 'get back to work (!)' imperative.

> Ahead, with spade and stone-mason's hammer!
> To work, without more delay!
> In this way we shall be the honour and the glory
> Of this fertile land of Columbus.
>
> (Bristow, 425)

Anthem is as we have noted a *sine qua non* of nationhood. Its aversion to music, and so the idea of an anthem, was one of the set of aberrances that made Afghanistan's Taliban regime stand out on the international stage. One of the embarrassments of new nationhood would be being discovered to lack an anthem. This might indeed indicate that the natives were not living up to their newly won *inter*national task, to present the world with the symbols suggesting worthiness of membership of the club of nations. Paul Nettl tells the story of how, in 1853, Costa Rica, embarrassed to learn that dignitaries visiting from Great Britain and the United States were expecting to be welcomed to the country with the Costa Rican national anthem, set about to get one. The strategy was simple. The country's foremost practising musician, Manuel María Gutiérrez, was detained by the authorities until he produced an anthem; which he duly did, and which remains to this day the national anthem of Costa Rica. According to Nettl, 'The poor devil insisted that he knew nothing about the art of musical composition. But that did him no good. He was thrown into prison and promised that he would not be released until he produced a usable piece of music' (185). Nettl admits the tale he tells may well be apocryphal; still one cannot help thinking it may have been in the back of the mind of the lyricist, Jose Maria Zeledon Brenes, when in 1903 he penned these, perhaps ironic, lyrics for the song's last stanza:

> Oh, sweet country, our refuge and shelter;
> How fertile your life giving soil!
> May your people contented and peaceful
> Unmolested continue their hard work.
>
> (Xing Hang, 158)

Japan's 'Kimi Gayo' was another anthem hastily put together because of the perception of a symbolic lack. In this case the observation that Japan needed an anthem was on the part of a visiting Irish band leader, John William Fenton, who may have influenced his acquaintances in the Satsuma clan to choose lyrics vaguely similar to those of 'God Save the Queen'. Fenton's original melody was discarded because it lacked solemnity, but the lyrics of the Heian *waka* chosen were, as we have seen, retained for what remains Japan's anthem.

Yet another anthem born of similar necessity was that of Malaysia. At independence, in 1957, each of the Malay States had its own anthem, and an international competition was held to choose a national anthem for the Federation. All entries were found wanting. So an all-star cast of composers was called in (including Benjamin Britten and William Walton) and their efforts were also rejected. What was chosen for the national devotions was the State Anthem of Perak. The story behind this song is that:

> The song had been very popular on the island of Mahé in the Seychelles, where the Sultan of Perak had formerly been living in exile. He heard it at a public band concert on the island, a song to a popular French melody, originally composed by the lyricist Pierre-Jean de Béranger (1780–1857), who was born and died in Paris. When Sultan Idris Murshidul'adzam Shah, who was the Ruler of the State of Perak from 1887 to 1916, represented the Malay Rulers of the Federated Malay States at the installation ceremony of King Edward VII in 1901, his protocol officer was asked what his state anthem was. Realizing that his state did not in fact possess an anthem, he, in order not to appear backward in front of his hosts, proceeded to hum the aforementioned tune. Thus was an anthem born.
>
> ('Negaraku')

By contrast, Indonesia's 'Indonesia Raya' ('Great Indonesia'), dating to 1928, has a history co-extensive with the independence struggle and is thus unequivocally the song that expresses the soul of the becoming nation. That goal is reflexively present from the first stanza of the song, with the words 'bangunlah jiwanya' – the aim of those singing is to 'create the soul' / 'raise the soul' of the Indonesian nation, to create the nationality for the people by uniting the people (Bristow, 275).

The earliest of the postcolonial East Asian anthems is that of the Philippines, thanks to that country's abortive late nineteenth-century attempts at independent nationhood. The title of the Philippine national anthem, 'Lupang Hinirang', has been rendered in English as 'The Chosen Land'. The (1899) words of the song present a tableau praising the nation; these were penned to accompany an (1898) score for a march. The anthem *in toto* we may describe as a late Romantic artefact. Its original function was to honour a nascent postcolonial nationhood, that of the first Republic of the Philippines, an entity that came to grief with the American occupation of the country (1898–1946), following the Spanish-American and Philippine-American wars. There are several ways in which 'Lupang Hinirang'/'The Chosen Land' is a curious title for the song. It is neither the popular name of the song, nor a translation of the original title. The song's popular name, in Tagalog, derives from its first line, 'Bayang magiliw', which may be translated as 'Beloved land'; this would appear to be a faithful translation of 'tierra adorada', with which the first line of the lyrics in Spanish commences, the song having originally been titled 'Filipinas'.[8]

The rest of the lyrics I have translated with my research collaborator, Ruth Jordana Pison, as follows:

Beloved Land,
Pearl of the East,
My heart's fervour
Lives in your breast.

Chosen land,
Cradle of heroes,
You will never submit
To invaders.

In seas and on mountains,
In the very air, in blue of sky,
Splendour in the poem
And the song of our loved freedom.

It is victory
That shines in your flag,
Stars and sun
That never dim.

Land of the sun, of joyous love,
Life is heaven with you.
Our greatest joy, be there oppressors
Would be to die for you.

There are certain questions begged by the title of the song; in particular – in what sense can the Philippines be thought a 'chosen land'? Might the choice of this title for the song be read as a case of over-identification with the coloniser (the Philippines considered 'a chosen land' in the sense that both Spain and the United States chose to occupy them)?

The song emerges from the originary moment of the Philippine national mythology. The lyrics therefore need to be read in the light of key events and icons of that period, in particular the 1896 martyrdom of the national hero, Jose Rizal. The language history of the song is of particular interest, and especially the apparent irony of Filipinos vowing in Spanish (just as the Spaniards are leaving and the Americans arriving) that their land will never be invaded. Although Filipino law now demands that the song only ever be sung in Filipino, the original Spanish lyrics were translated into English before they were translated into Tagalog. The song was banned by the American authorities until 1919.

Considering questions of self-efficacy as reflected in the anthem and its title, one might speculate as to whether the Filipino national consciousness might be founded on a fear of not being chosen; whether 'A Chosen Land' might thus be considered an attempt at the creation, for purposes of national identification, of a self-fulfilling (and pseudo-biblical) prophecy – that this far-flung place would be a promised land, its people a chosen race. Again, such a reading pre-supposes the song's identification with the coloniser's point of view, as perhaps implied by the original Spanish version of the lyrics.

***

A key paradox of subalternity for the subject throwing off the colonial yoke is the degree to which the collective emergence from this state is to be in the image of the coloniser; that is, as a modern state, notionally on a par with the mother/father country. That state on a notional par may – in terms of symbolism – be something more in the manner of an imitation. The paleness of the imitation is reflected in many of the bland or hyperbolic lyrics we have surveyed through this chapter. Blandest of all must be the lyrics of 'May Singapore Progress'[9]:

> Come, fellow Singaporeans,
> Let us progress towards happiness together.
> May our noble aspiration bring
> Singapore success.
> Come, let us unite
> In a new spirit.
> Let our voices soar as one.
> Onward Singapore!

(Bristow, 502)

Can anyone doubt that Singapore has marched on? By almost any socio-economic measure, Singapore has, from its inception as a nation, set standards for its near neighbours and for the Chinese and wider worlds. Progress, happiness, success, unity: the state enlists its citizens in the worship of the usual nation-making abstractions. But what can these rote lyrics that could be anyone's have to do with the soul of that city or with the real aspirations of its people? The success of Singapore is corporate, state facilitated; it is the competitive ethos and opportunism of the state that has made Singapore one of the world's most successful cities. And Singaporean nationhood is in this mold. The anthem provides us with the streamlined model of national affect. Look, no imagery! None is required. On we march, we for whom the appropriate vision will be provided at the hour the state appoints, or perhaps not at all.

Does the singing of anthems make for better worlds? Taken at face value, anthem lyrics would lead us to that conclusion. In so many cases though, the new boss has been as bad as (or worse than) the old. And so one is tempted towards the conclusion that the anaesthetic muzak of the anthem is among those factors making it possible for peoples to be taken for granted by the states that regulate them. This is not to say that anthems, in varied circumstances, might not provide the unisonant with opportunities for resistance, for alternative readings of reality and for critical challenges to authority. Anthem parodies and anti-anthems (as discussed in Chapter 4) provide cogent examples of performative instances that run against the grain of anthem quality, but these need to be understood as essentially oppositional phenomena.

By means of state power (the sanction of official symbols as such), the nation worships itself. Who and what and why do they worship? The nation *is* the citizenry and, in singing the anthem, it is the individual citizen who must join with others in reverenced anonymity to worship the state so worthily represented by the individual who stands on the dais to wear a medal at the Olympics, or who rests anonymously in the tomb of the unknown soldier. Anthem singing makes it possible for people not to bother exercising democratic thinking in working out who they are. That is because in reverencing their own self-symbolisation they agree it is decided who they already are. The anonymous figures whom the citizens worship have their corollary and origin in ancestor cults and, as well, in the divinity of Christ. The ancestors and the saviours of the nation are those, it is the task of the citizenry to emulate, however arduous that task might be. They are the apotheosis of the state and they are its avatars; as is, in substance, each who sings. Everyone who sings borrows the mystery of the deified nation to be the living substance – and anthropomorphic representation – of that abstraction that takes in both those for-the-nation-dead and those unborn for whom the deeds of nation are done. Singapore's anthem, with its spectacular refusal of mythology, hollows out the whole procedure. Does it then present a critique of national sentiment of the kind one might read in Slovenia's 'A Toast'? I think, in Singapore's case, this is pragmatism, pure and simple: the nation is an abstract idea for which a duty statement, some further abstractions and a little logic are mandatory; imagery would be surplus to requirement. And so we can say that Singapore's anthem is maximally sincere. The idea of voices soaring is of course a flight of fancy, but a concession to the fact that singing is necessary in the case of an anthem.

If the world's citizen subjects are to be protected from excesses of national sentiment and equally from bland erosion of a sense of self, then it will be the critical work of devout ironists, case by case, to fashion antidotes.

Notes

1. Cf. As discussed in Chapter 2, The 'America' of *West Side Story*, a New York Jewish-written mock argument among Puerto Ricans as to the relative virtues of the mainland United States and Puerto Rico. In this text, unison is displaced by direct contention, revealing dialogue as a species of anthem anathema.
2. In *Mythologies,* Barthes explored an opposition between the function of poetry in the classical and in the modern senses, such that while we might think of poetry today as myth's

anathema, this could not be said of classical poetry. In Barthes' words: 'Poetry occupies a position which is the reverse of that of myth: myth is a semiological system which has the pretension of transcending itself into a factual system; poetry is a semiological system which has the pretension of contracting into an essential system'. For Barthes, poetry 'attempts to regain an infra-signification, a pre-semiological state of language' (133).

3. In the Esperanto original the lyrics are as follows:

En la mondon venis nova sento,
tra la mondo iras forta voko;
per flugiloj de facila vento
nun de loko flugu ĝi al loko.

Ne al glavo sangon soifanta
ĝi la homan tiras familion:
al la mond' eterne militanta
ĝi promesas sanktan harmonion.

Sub la sankta signo de l' espero
kolektiĝas pacaj batalantoj,
kaj rapide kreskas la afero
per laboro de la esperantoj.

Forte staras muroj de miljaroj
inter la popoloj dividitaj;
sed dissaltos la obstinaj baroj,
per la sankta amo disbatitaj.

Sur neŭtrala lingva fundamento,
komprenante unu la alian,
la popoloj faros en konsento
unu grandan rondon familian.

Nia diligenta kolegaro
en laboro paca ne laciĝos,
ĝis la bela sonĝo de l' homaro
por eterna ben' efektiviĝos.

4. Echoes of this composition can be heard in de Ménil in his 1909 music for the Esperantists' anthem.
5. Townshend found it odd that his 'cautionary piece' should be taken up in an 'anthemic sense' and in a 2006 interview stated that: 'It is not precisely a song that decries revolution – it suggests that we will indeed fight in the streets – but that revolution, like

all action, can have results we cannot predict. Don't expect to see what you expect to see. Expect nothing and you might gain everything. The song was meant to let politicians and revolutionaries alike know that what lay in the centre of my life was not for sale, and could not be co-opted into any obvious cause. [...] From 1971 – when I wrote "Won't Get Fooled Again" – to 1985, there was a transition in me from refusal to be co-opted by activists, to a refusal to be judged by people I found jaded and compliant in Britain' ('Pete's Diaries').

6. According to the theory's key proponent, Gilberto Freyre, Lusotropicalism can be explained as follows:

> The Portuguese colonizer, basically poor and humble, did not have the exploitive motivations of his counterpart from the more industrialized countries in Europe. Consequently, he immediately entered into cordial relations with non-European populations he met in the tropics. This is clearly demonstrated through Portugal's initial contacts with the Bakongo Kingdom in the latter part of the fifteenth century. The ultimate proof of the absence of racism among the Portuguese, however, is found in Brazil, whose large and socially prominent mestiço population is living testimony to the freedom of social and sexual intercourse between Portuguese and non-Europeans. Portuguese non-racism is also evidenced by the absence in Portuguese law of the racist legislation in South Africa and until recently in the United States barring non-whites from specific occupations, facilities, etc. Finally, any prejudice or discrimination in territories formerly or presently governed by Portugal can be traced to class, but never colour, prejudice.
>
> (in Bender, 3–4)

7. Provenance of this stanza had been in doubt at various points in the past and there had been previous attempts to remove it because of its aggressively anti-Spanish attitude; however, it was not officially replaced until 2009 by the relatively inoffensive lyrics of the new first stanza (formerly the seventh):

> On its summits may the Andes sustain
> the two-color flag or standard,
> may it announce to the centuries the effort
> that being free, that being free
> that being free gave us forever.
> Under its shadow may we live calmly
> and, at birth of the sun in its summits,
> may we all renew the great oath
> that we rendered, that we rendered
> that we rendered to the God of Jacob,
> that we rendered to the God of Jacob, the God of Jacob...
>
> ('National Anthem of Peru', 2012)

8. The official Filipino version of the anthem is as follows:

Bayang magiliw
Perlas ng silanganan
Alab ng puso
Sa dibdib mo'y buhay.

Lupang Hinirang
Duyan ka ng magiting
Sa manlulupig
Di ka pasisiil.

Sa dagat at bundok
Sa simoy at sa langit mong bughaw
May dilag ang tula
At awit sa paglayang minamahal.

Ang kislap ng watawat
Mo'y tagumapay na nagniningning
Ang bituin at araw niya kailan pa ma'y
Di magdidilim.

Lupa ng araw
Ng luwalhati't pagsinta
Buhay ay langit sa piling mo.
Aming ligaya na pag may mang-aapi
Ang mamatay ng dahil sa iyo.

(Serbisyo Philippine Government e-services Portal, 2008)

9. Interestingly these pedestrian lyrics were inspired, according to their maker, Zubir Said, by a beautiful Malay proverb: '*Di mana bumi dipijak, di situ langit dijunjung*' ('You should hold up the sky of the land where you live') (2007).

Conclusion: The Soul and Its Un/Official Stirrings

A little string speaks for a crowd of voices.

To sing jubilas at exact, accustomed times,
To be crested and wear the mane of a multitude
And so, as part, to exult with its great throat,

To speak of joy and to sing of it, borne on
The shoulders of joyous men, to feel the heart
That is the common, the bravest fundament,

This is a facile exercise.

(Wallace Stevens, 398)

Anthems express emotions and they elicit emotions. They do both at the same time. In singing the anthem, persons who might otherwise be in conversation, or dissension, or nervous worry or silent contemplation, abandon other modes of being and being together. They abandon other habitual ways of being for a moment of self-recognition, of mutual agreement and of self-congratulation. They express these for each other and they elicit these from each other. However rote the circumstances in which this expressing and eliciting takes place, compared with the usual 'good morning/how are you/fine/fine' forms of phatic communion, anthem singing would appear to be profoundly meaningful and even deeply moving, on occasions, for those who catch themselves in the act. Are the emotions expressed and elicited in every case the same? It is difficult to countenance that kind of uniformity of feeling, but such a question is foregone in the act of unison. Fellow feeling is what acts of unison assume. Is it a good thing? Fellow feeling in general would, tautologically at least, appear to be a powerful force for amity and goodwill, for harmony among humans. But is the assumption of fellow feeling (and of implied inclusions and exclusions, motives and caveats for it) a healthy idea?

Though it was never my intention to begin with, I believe I have, through the pages of this book, diagnosed a number of closely related (and largely unnoticed) world-chronic malaises. The singing of anthems involves large populations in collective amnesia, mass hallucinations, and particularly in dangerous delusions of grandeur, all of which might lead, in the wrong circumstances, to unwarranted aggressive behaviour. It needs also to be seriously asked whether children are being emotionally abused when their thinking and feeling is taken for granted through the expectation that they should participate in anthem performances. Following Oliver Sacks' observations of patients, we have seen in the case of Bosnia (and perhaps Spain) that lacking able-to-be-agreed lyrics might indicate that a nation is suffering from a form of collective aphasia. These observations by way of analogy may lack rigour but they are helpfully suggestive of a question worth asking, namely – how seriously should we take the pathological character and effects of anthems and anthem singing? A number of interesting recent phenomena around the world draw attention to the question of a nexus between nation and unison and pathology, and likewise draw attention to its humorous potential. The Finnish Shouting Men (Mieskuoro Huutajat, established 1987), themselves anthem parodists, and the Birmingham Complaints Choir (established 2005), and a range of other derivative Complaints Choirs around the world, would certainly be worthy of scrutiny as such. At the time of writing, perhaps the most notable of the world's anthem parodists are the gaoled Russian girl group, Pussy Riot, with their incendiary anti-anthem, 'Mother of God, Cast Putin Out', as performed by them in February 2012, in Moscow's Cathedral of Christ the Saviour. This is Carol Rumens' translation:

Virgin Mary, Mother of God, banish Putin, banish Putin,
Virgin Mary, Mother of God, banish him, we pray thee!

Congregations genuflect,
Black robes brag gilt epaulettes,
Freedom's phantom's gone to heaven,
Gay Pride's chained and in detention.
KGB's chief saint descends
To guide the punks to prison vans.
Don't upset His Saintship, ladies,
Stick to making love and babies.
Crap, crap, this godliness crap!
Crap, crap, this holiness crap!
(Chorus)

Virgin Mary, Mother of God.
Be a feminist, we pray thee,
Be a feminist, we pray thee.
Bless our festering bastard-boss.
Let black cars parade the Cross.
The Missionary's in class for cash.
Meet him there, and pay his stash.
Patriarch Gundy believes in Putin.

Better believe in God, you vermin!
Fight for rights, forget the rite –
Join our protest, Holy Virgin.
(Chorus)

Virgin Mary, Mother of God, banish Putin, banish Putin,
Virgin Mary, Mother of God, we pray thee, banish him!

(*The Guardian*, 20th August, 2012)

Pussy Riot certainly took the religious origins and anchoring of anthemic sentiment seriously, and they accordingly took their performance to the source – arguably one of the holiest places in Russia, certainly a church with a history embodying the struggle between religious doctrine and its anathemae. This performance was so annoying to those who did not wish to be disturbed in the continuity of their state-religious devotions that the parodists had themselves to be cast out of society, for a time at least.

The Slovenian rock-band Laibach are similarly of interest for their overt and covert critiques of anthem quality, especially through quirky re-situated performances of anthems, as in their 2004 album of that title. The Shouting Men and the Complaints Choirs are performance-oriented place-based institutions for highly voluntary unison. Whether we should regard them as anti-anthemic or anthem-parodic, performances of these choirs de-automatise the unspoken assumptions, which worldwide, make anthem singers compliant and complicit in rote performances of national devotion. These critical performances make productive a tension between the energy of collective assertion and a desire not to be spoken for or taken for granted.

In her conversation with Gayatri Chakravorti Spivak, *Who Sings the Nation State (?)*, Judith Butler speaks of singing as the assertion of a right to rights. This is specifically in the context of debates over the singing of 'The Star Spangled Banner', in Spanish, in the United States. Butler entertains the hypothesis that 'there can be no radical politics of change without performative contradiction' (66). The contradiction in this case would be that which is revealed through the reversal of the covert exclusion implied by the taken-for-granted language-exclusiveness of the US anthem. Through the simple rhetorical strategy of translation, a hegemonic routine is overturned. The state excludes by means of its citizens' collective avowal of inclusion; here the excluded use their language to avow that they are here, and perhaps only because they are here. Lo and behold: *e pluribus unum*, the tired, poor huddled masses and so forth: the hypocrite state hoist on its own petard. In Butler's terms then we should acknowledge that Hendrix also translated 'The Star Spangled Banner', and into a language he was at the time creating for the purpose: the uniqueness of his enterprise makes the achievement all the greater.

Butler tells us that, 'To exercise a freedom and to assert an equality precisely in relation to an authority that would preclude both is to show how freedom and equality can and must move beyond their positive articulations' (66–67). As in the case of the Hendrix version of

'The Star Spangled Banner', 'the contradiction must be relied upon, exposed and worked on to move towards something new [...] This involved a deformation of dominant language, and reworking of power, since those who sing are without entitlement' (67). What Jimi Hendrix, the Complaints Choirs, Laibach, Pussy Riot have in common is that they rely upon the exposure of the contradiction inherent in the eternity of nations: the truth that is meant to go without saying turns out to be something needing to be said, needing to be performed. Perform the truth (or even parts of it) a little differently (in a different context or a different language) and those who watch may begin to see the mobile army of metaphors, metonymies, anthropomorphisms; they may begin to see, that is, those illusions of which, as Nietzsche tells us, one has forgotten that they are illusions.

The confusion of patriotism and its intellectual weakness is the assumption that a community is the result of a meaning it exists to generate. We did not, by and large, decide how to be a people. Rather we find ourselves in a certain place, at a particular time, with a range of meanings and actions constitutive of and available to us. Anthems are a kind of text that systematically distracts populations from both the objective conditions in which they function (or live dysfunctionally), and from the mutability of those objective conditions. For better and worse, it was power politics – on the local and on the global scale – that created the circumstances in which we find ourselves. Those antics, conventions and the like, by which we play at constituting ourselves as such, mainly function to conform to the observation that *we're here because we're here*. A poet's duty is to rub noses in those contradictions (noticed or not) by which we breathe. The conclusions for the state might be gloomy as in the case of Auden's disowned poem 'Spain':

> The stars are dead. The animals will not look.
> We are left alone with our day, and the time is short, and
>   History to the defeated
> May say Alas but cannot help nor pardon.
>
> (in Cunningham, 97–100)

These are lines not to rally the national spirit. Anthem lyrics are the opposite and the anathema of this; they are mythologies in the Barthesian sense.

Now it is time for the poet who wrote this book to step out of the *trompe l'oeil*. How and why do I feel when I sing those songs with which I identify on the basis of their anthem quality? I wrote this book, not because I am a cynic but because I am a sucker. Many times I have been moved to tears in the course of my research, and often that has been through the process of dealing closely with materials about which I may have otherwise had some cynical thoughts. Certainly, I have felt my spirit stirred by anthems with which I have no personal connection. It is true that the paradox of automatisation presents us with feeling overwhelming, deadening, with affect that – shading into the parodic or self-parodic – cancels itself out. But as suggested in Chapter 4, there is a depth of enquiry at which the feeling in the words returns. The reason for this, I believe, is that these words and the accompanying music are so heartfelt. Beyond cynicism, beyond disciplined analyses, the return of the feeling too is a function and result of the de-automatising move one might make shuffling between the shoes of poetry and theory.

Speaking in the first person of anthems is entirely appropriate. The response anthems require of us is, like prayer, in the category of the individual anonymous. We have seen how anthems provide the unisonant with a wall of *the sound of us*, a wall with the unobserved function of shutting out the other. Anthems are something of the past – a spell cast collectively in order to effect a kind of collective possession: anthems are our means of declaring ourselves in charge of what is ours. They are a naturally tautological expression of the soul. They are the kind of expression that makes viable the kind of abstraction we meet in a term like 'soul'.

Nations are hypostasised entities, which is to say that if everyone were to concertedly cease imagining them, then they would be no more. There is little risk of this happening in any global way in an immediately foreseeable future. Nations may be reifications – imaginings made solid – but they are reifications with a life of their own, and which live in the flesh and the blood and (most importantly for present purposes) the breath of their citizens. Their defining moments – of self-recognition or realisation, of amnesia, of guilt or of absolution – are ongoing, and symbolically self-sustaining. Nation is what A. Dirk Moses calls a collective ego ideal (in Manne, 338).

The proud swelling of the breast, which an anthem effects, unites people the world over in the manner of very old kinds of imagined community. To hear of the courageous deeds that made our world possible is to understand who and how we are. To ritually sing of these with unknown others – having together memorised their form in words – is to sanctify oneself as the bearer of a particular identity-in-common. Anthem in general is in this sense the answer to the questions, Who am I (?), How is my 'soul' stirred (?). Anthems are world framing identifications: they make common a certain kind of voice, as mine.

Music is the abstract form which carries that kind of emotional investment. And 'anthem quality' in music is today far more widespread than could be implied by particular investments in identity as national. 'Anthem quality' is attained wherever moral certitude and the symbolisation of events are made to coalesce – conveyed in abstract musical form – with quasi- or pseudo-religious authority, of which the tune 'The Star Spangled Banner' is exemplary, as has been much of Hollywood's product up to the present day. Through means of musical interludes in film, as in the participatory rituals of national life, the noble – like the patriotic – spirit takes part in a collective self-hailing, a welcoming home of the self.

The emotions are dangerous but, as Plato noted in the *Republic*, harnessed strategically for official purposes, can serve long-term and stabilising interests. The unisonance of an anthem sung represents a moment of affirmation and re-affirmation, like a perpetual wedding of the citizenry to itself. The public and collective expression of emotion in an anthem thus contrasts with the mainly banal and inert everyday flaggings of nation, expressed by the passage of coins, (and once upon a time) the wearing away of the face on them.

Plato dispensed with the dangerous makers of tall tales in the original imagined state. And yet the Platonic republic could not do away with music and poetry altogether, for the simple reason that the state itself requires praise. Hence, the two musical forms Plato's Socrates wishes to retain: the Doric and the Phrygian, the warlike and the peaceful; these corresponding to the alternative conditions of the state[1] (331). Plato did not want troublesome poets in his fictional country; he rather acknowledged a need for a kind of classical *muzak*: an inoffensive background strumming that would keep the guardians and the rest at their posts. And today, this is what anthems mainly are. Plato's interest in inclusion and exclusion is apposite in thinking of anthems because their *modus operandi* are often along the lines of feigning inclusion to hold off the world beyond borders, and whether those borders are real or imagined. Since the Romantics, poets of the kind who have been taken and who take themselves seriously, have, for their part, frequently been interested in anthem quality, and in the ideas of identification-in-common that anthems carry. What poets of the last two centuries (Shelley's 'unacknowledged legislators') write of anthems should be the subject of a future study. One can say of anthem lyrics, in general, that they conform in the broadest terms with Oscar Wilde's famous dictum that all bad poetry is sincere (889); the apt rejoinder for this perhaps being that good poetry is also sincere. Cutting through the productive cynicism one applies in the study of genre such as the anthem, one concedes that sincerity must be a key to its affective success. Heartfelt words may well be memorable. When others believe those words to be the right words and feel what those words convey they may wish to adopt them as their own, and even perhaps independent of any state-sponsored urging. The common assurance of bad poetry is though that it works from unanalysed (and usually unschooled) assumptions as to what a poem should be, what it has to do. To return to my earlier mock-forensic investigation, the psychoanalysis of anthems would I think reveal a phylogeny of self-esteem challenges: the nation-by-nation divulging of chips on the shoulders, the doubts and misgivings each designated people has with regard to being itself. For all of the rote similarity we have seen in the anthems surveyed in this book, some remarkably different attitudes and interpersonal conceptions of imagined community have also been revealed.

The various examples of anthems dealt with through this study have shown a wide range of affective investments and rhetorical strategies produced and reproduced for and by acts of national unison – the singing of the nation together. Which tunes and which words (which stories) stick in one's head and why? How can these satisfy for the subject-in-unison the paradoxical demand of expressing both national feeling and its particularity (the feeling of belonging to a particular nation)? However obvious or obscure, opaque or transparent the meaning of these devotions to those inside and those outside of the singing polity, one nevertheless discerns in them the clearest and most dominant signs there are today of place-based poetic identifications – the self-expressed identifications of subject-citizens who sing to tell us and to tell themselves who they are and where they should be. Everyone's nation and anthem and football team are best, and it is interesting to compare the manner in which such claims in particular may be supported. Temperament and self-image are revealed when unison stirs the singer's soul, and one may well ask in which cause/s these are employed, and what prospects they afford the big ticket items of *cosmo-polity*: liberty, dignity and self-determination.

We live in an information age and yet two great powers in the world today are national force and multinational capital. Cosmopolitan convention and cooperation – the obvious paths to a fairer world – come a poor third. It is easy to see how this works: international cooperation is 'naturally' regimented along national lines; the UN consists of nation state members for most practical purposes. The complicity we note here is such as to, despite the flowery rhetoric, always ensure that there will be more rich people and also more poor people in the world. Importantly for our purposes the complicity is symbolic and ritual. A song like 'We are the World', by USA for Africa, helps to keep those concerned with poverty from identifying with the UN or with NGOs as the answer. How could a distraction like the UN be necessary when *we* are already the world? It is a curious fact of the globe's present operating system that a cosmopolitan ethos has – as under other empires before – been stymied by a universalising spirit. Such complicities and machinations and their diabolical effects suggest the urgency of efforts to inspect the mechanism of sentiment that keeps nationalism alive as a way of working the world in the interests of its great dominating powers.

A concluding note on the nation–state relationship as reflected in, and as facilitated by, the anthem phenomenon. I have earlier noted the effective synonymy of these terms for many purposes, and their connotative difference. There may be exceptions to prove the rule, but on the world scale the nation is what makes the state palatable. What sins of the state can national pride not, for a need, forgive? *We don't agree with the war but we all join in praise for our brave boys at the front who are doing no less than their duty.* Nation and state are two sides of the one coin. Or, to offer another Janus-face metaphor – they perform a kind of soft cop–tough cop routine, of the kind Blake bemoaned, with his lines 'The Whore & Gambler, by the State/Licenc'd, build that Nation's Fate'. Whatever you do not like about the way the country is going, blame it on the State; but the lovely fellow feeling you get from national anthems is just human sentiment of the universal (and universally diverse) kind. The nation is us. It is – we, the people. The state imposes on us, on we, the people. This arrangement would not work if people did not want to believe in it. People want to believe in nations because – as was the case with the world embracing religious communities of the former age – they do not wish to be left out in the cold.

Symbolic machinery is the affective glue that keeps the two sides of the nation–state coin circulating in one piece. Among all the semantic-affective means available to the nation state the anthem is the most embodied – it is the voices of everyone concerted together. The anthem is the voice of the people. What the people express at the ballot box (if they are so fortunate) is, by contrast, the extent of their dissension. To follow an apt religious metaphor and continuity, national feeling is absolution for perceived excesses of state power. The Soviet Union tried internationalism in that place, but the switch was unsuccessful and so there was a return to national feeling: socialist, Stalinist, post-Stalinist and now otherwise.

If national feeling absolves the citizen for participation in the sins of the state then anthems are the sacrament through which the absolution is administered.

If patriotism is the last refuge of the scoundrel then the national anthem must be the music of that scoundrel's soul. The tear on the cheek, the chill down the spine, the genuine willingness to sacrifice, genuine animosity for perceived threats: however manipulable national feeling may be, there is no doubting the reality of the affect nations can inspire. An organ grinder makes the monkey dance, just with a twist of the wrist. The West's world dominance today is more banal even than that of any nation; at its simplest reflex it is able to be wound up at will by a few bars of music.

Anthems today are largely ignored, because they are taken-for-granted, phenomena. Taken for granted because of their banality, they are central to systems of faith and ideas of identity that are world-grounding and that those singing are therefore loathe to challenge or even acknowledge. It is because of this and because of the deadliness of nations that anthems require urgent and thorough investigation. And a note of warning here, for those who would take on this pastime: if there is one thing more dangerous than investigating a holy icon, it is the investigation of an icon the devout refuse to admit that they are worshipping. My hope is that this book will offer some impetus for the more serious study of what it is people mean when they sing together of themselves and so present a collective image to the world.

Note

1. Aristotle in his *Treatise on Government* writes, 'The Socrates of the *Republic* is wrong in retaining only the Phrygian mode along with the Dorian, and the more so because he rejects the flute; for the Phrygian is to the modes what the Dorian is to the musical instruments – both of them are exciting and emotional. Poetry proves this, for Bacchic frenzy and all similar emotions are most suitably expressed by the flute, and are better set to the Phrygian than to any other mode' (548).

Bibliography

Adorno, T.W. (1973), *Philosophy of Modern Music* (trans. Anne G. Mitchell and Wesley V. Blomster), London: Sheed and Ward.

——— (1994), *Quasi una Fantasia - Essays on Modern Music* (trans. Rodney Livingstone), London: Verso.

Althusser, L. (1972), 'Ideology and Ideological State Apparatuses', *Lenin and Philosophy and Other Essays*, New York: Monthly Review Press.

Anderson, B. (1991), *Imagined Communities*, London: Verso.

——— (2000), *The Spectre of Comparisons*, London: Verso.

——— (1999), 'The Goodness of Nations', *Nation and Religion - Perspectives on Europe and Asia*, eds. Peter van der Veer and Hartmut Lehman, Princeton: Princeton University Press.

Aristotle (1952), *Politics (Treatise on Government)*, in *Great Books of the Western World*, Vol. 9 (trans. Ingram Bywater), Chicago: Encyclopaedia Britannica.

Ashcroft, B., et.al. (1995), *The Post-colonial studies reader*, London: Routledge.

Auden, W.H. and Pearson, N.H., eds. (1972), *Poets of the English Language IV - Blake to Poe*, London: Heron Books.

Austin, J.L. (1962), *How to Do Things with Words*, Oxford: Clarendon Press.

Australian Government (2011), *About Australia - National Anthem*, Canberra: Department of Foreign Affairs and Trade, http://www.dfat.gov.au/facts/nat_anthem.html/.

Bakhtin, M. (1994), *The Bakhtin Reader*, ed. Pam Morris, London: Edward Arnold.

Barthes, R. (1973), *Mythologies* (trans. Annette Lavers), St Albans, Herts: Paladin.

Bender, G. (1978), *Angola under the Portuguese: The Myth and Reality*, Berkeley: University of California Press.

Berlant, L.G. (2008), *The Female Complaint: The Unfinished Business of Sentimentality in American Culture*, Durham: Duke University Press.

Billig, M. (1995), *Banal Nationalism*, London: Sage.

Billy Liar (1963), John Schlesinger (director), London: Vic Films.

Blacking, J. (1976), *How Musical is Man*, London: Faber.

Blake, W. (1977), *The Complete Poems*, Harmondsworth: Penguin.

Bloom, H. (1973), *The Anxiety of Influence: A Theory of Poetry*, Oxford: Oxford University Press.

Borat (2012), *Kazakhstan National Anthem Lyrics*, Lyrics Mania, http://www.lyricsmania.com/kazakhstan_national_anthem_lyrics_borat.html Accessed 24 June, 2012.

Bourdieu, P. (1984), *Distinction – A Social Critique of the Judgement of Taste* (trans. Richard Nice), Cambridge, Massachusetts: Harvard University Press.

Bowra, C.M. (1962), *Primitive Song*, Cleveland: The World Publishing Company.

Bristow, M.J. (2006), *National Anthems of the World*, 11th ed., London: Blandford.

Buch, E. (2004), *Beethoven's Ninth – A Political History*, Chicago: University of Chicago Press.

Butler, J. and Spivak, G.C. (2007), *Who Sings the Nation-State?* London: Seagull.

Casablanca (1942), Curtiz, Michael (director), Burbank: Warner Brothers.

Castells, M. (2004), *The Power of Identity*, in *The Information Age*, Vol. 2, Oxford: Blackwell.

Cerulo, K.A. (1989), 'Sociopolitical Control and the Structure of National Symbols: An Empirical Analysis of National Anthems', *Social Forces*, 68:1.

Césaire, A. (2000), *Discourse on Colonialism*, New York: Monthly Review Press.

Chatterjee, R. (2012), 'Earworms: Tunes That Stick in Our Heads', *PRI's The World – Global Perspectives for an American Audience*, Boston: WGBH Educational Foundation, http://www.theworld.org/2012/02/music-earworms/ Accessed 23 June, 2012.

Clark, R. (1822), *An Account of the National Anthem Entitled God Save the King*, London: W. Wright, Fleet Street.

Clark, M. (1992), *A History of Australia*, in *From the Earliest Times to the Age of Macquarie*, Vol. 1, Melbourne: Melbourne University Press.

Clark, M. (1968), *A History of Australia*, in *New South Wales and Van Diemen's Land 1822–1838*, Vol. 2, Melbourne: Melbourne University Press.

Coleridge, S.T. (1973), *Coleridge's Verse: A Selection*, eds. William Empsom and David Pirie, New York: Schocken.

Cone, E.T. (1974), *The Composer's Voice*, Berkeley: University of California Press.

cummings, e e (1963), *Selected Poems*, Harmondsworth: Penguin.

Cunningham, V., ed. (1982), *Spanish Civil War Verse*, Harmondsworth: Penguin.

Daughtry, J.M. (2003), 'Russia's New Anthem and the Negotiation of National Identity', *Ethnomusicology*, 47:1.

Davies, S. (2003), *Themes in the Philosophy of Music*, Oxford: Oxford University Press.

Dawkins, R. (1976), *The Selfish Gene*, Oxford: Oxford University Press.

——— (2006), *The God Delusion*, London: Bantam.

Derrida, J. (1987), *The Truth in Painting* (trans. Geoff Bennington and Ian McLeod), Chicago: University of Chicago Press.

Dickinson, E. (1982), *Collected Poems of Emily Dickinson*, New York: Crown.

Divje Babe Flute, *Wikipedia* (2013) http://en.wikipedia.org/wiki/Divje_Babe_flute Accessed 28 August, 2013.

Durant, W. and Durant, A. (1961), *Story of Civilization – The Age of Reason Begins*, New York: Simon and Schuster.

Encyclopaedia Britannica (1930), 14th ed., London: Encyclopaedia Britannica.

Eze, E.C., ed. (1977), *Race and Enlightenment*, Oxford: Blackwell.

Fanon, F. (1963), *The Wretched of the Earth* (trans. Constance Farrington), New York: Grove Press.

de Foigny, G. (1693), *A New Discovery of Terra Incognita Australis or the Southern World*, London: Dunton.

Frost, R. (1995), *Collected Poems, Prose, & Plays*, eds. Richard Poirier and Mark Richardson, New York: Library of America.

Freud, S. (1952), *Freud*, in *Great Books of the Western World*, Vol. 54, Chicago: Encyclopaedia Britannica.

Fulweiler, H.W. (1993), *Here a Captive Heart Busted: Studies in the Sentimental Journey*, New York: Fordham University Press.

Gainsbourg, S. (2006), *Live au Palace*, New York: Universal.

Gellner, E. (1983), *Nations and Nationalism*, New York: Cornell.

Gerth, H. and Mills C.W., eds. (1947), *Max Weber – Essays in Sociology*. London: Routledge & Kegan Paul.

Gesner, G., ed. (1983), *Anthology of American Poetry*, New York: Avenel.

Ginsberg, A. (1985), *Collected Poems 1947–1985*, London: Penguin.

Government of the Republic of Slovenia (2010), *National Insignia*, http://www.vlada.si/en/about_slovenia/political_system/national_insignia Accessed 23 June, 2012.

Gracyk, T. and Kania, A., eds. (2011), *The Routledge Companion to Philosophy and Music*, New York: Routledge.

Greek President's Homepage. (2012), http://www.presidency.gr/?page_id=164&lang=en Accessed 30 December, 2012.

Guthrie, W. (2013), 'This Land is Your Land', http://en.wikipedia.org/wiki/This_Land_Is_Your_Land Accessed 2 January, 2013.

La Grand Illusion (1937), Renoir, Jean (director), Paris: RAC.

Hall, J.A. (1986), *States in History*, London: Blackwell.

Harré, R. and Parrott, W.G. (1996), *The Emotions: Social, Cultural and Biological Dimensions*, London: Sage.

Harris, N. (2008), *The National Anthem*, Chicago: Heinemann-Raintree.

Hearn, J. (2006), *Rethinking Nationalism*. Basingstoke: Palgrave Macmillan.

Hidetoshi, N. (1988), 'Flag and Anthem, Symbols of Distress', *Japan Quarterly*, 35 (2).

Hobsbawm, E. (1990), *Nations and Nationalism since 1780*, Cambridge: Cambridge University Press.

Hobsbawm, E. and Ranger, T., eds. (1992), *The Invention of Tradition*, Cambridge: Cambridge University Press (Canto).

'The Internationale' (2008), *Wikipedia*, http://en.wikipedia.org/wiki/The_Internationale Accessed 23 June, 2012.

Juslin, P.N. and Sloboda, J.A. (2001), *Music and Emotion: Theory and Research*, Oxford: Oxford University Press.

Kant, I. (1952), *The Critique of Pure Reason, The Critique of Practical Reason, The Critique of Judgement*, in *Great Books of the Western World*, Vol. 42, Chicago: Encyclopaedia Britannica.

Kelen, K., and A. Pavkovic. (2010). 'Resurrection: a Tale of Two Anthems Sung by Serbs.' *Nations and Nationalism*, 42:7, London: Basil Blackwell.

——— (2012).'Of Love and National Borders: the Croatian Anthem, 'Our Beautiful Homeland', *Nations and Nationalism*, 18:2, London: Basil Blackwell.

Kivy, P. (1993), 'Platonism in Music: A Kind of Defense', *The Fine Art of Repetition: Essays in the Philosophy of Music*, Cambridge: Cambridge University Press.

Kohn, H. (1955), *Nationalism: Its Meaning and History*, Princeton: Princeton University Press.
Kristeva, J. (1984), *Revolution in Poetic Language* (trans. Margaret Waller), New York: Columbia University Press.
'La Espero' ('The Hope'), Esperanto Anthem, http://en.wikipedia.org/wiki/La_Espero Accessed 24 January, 2013.
Landau, E. (2008), *The National Anthem*, New York: Scholastic (True Book Series).
Laurence, P. (2013), 'Swiss to Launch National Anthem Competition in 2014'. *BBC News Europe*. http://www.bbc.co.uk/news/world-europe-23550915, Accessed 24 August, 2013.
Lindsay, N. (2000), *The Magic Pudding*, Sydney: Angus and Robertson.
Locke, J. (1996), *Second Treatise of Civil Government*, Corvallis: Oregon State University, http://oregonstate.edu/instruct/phl302/texts/locke/locke2/locke2nd-a.html Accessed 23 June, 2012.
Lord, A.B. (1960), *The Singer of Tales*, Cambridge: Harvard University Press.
Mackellar, D. (1911), *The Closed Door*, Melbourne: Australasian Authors' Agency.
Magoffin, R. (1983), *Waltzing Matilda: Song of Australia: A Folk History*, Qld: Mimosa Press.
——— (1995), *Waltzing Matilda: The Ballad of the Fair Go*, Cooparoo, Qld: Robert Brown and Associates.
——— (1998a), *Waltzing Matilda: The Answers*, Kynuna, Qld: Matilda Expo.
——— (1998b), *'Waltzing Matilda' and Other Nursery Rhymes*, Kynuna, Qld: Matilda Expo.
——— (1998c), *The Swagman's Story of 'Waltzing Matilda' – A Centenary Tribute*, Kynuna, Qld: Matilda Expo.
——— (2001), *The Provenance of Waltzing Matilda*, Kynuna, Qld: Matilda Expo.
——— (2005), *Waltzing Matilda Home Page*, Kynuna, Qld: Matilda Expo, http://members.eisa.net.au/~billm/Matilda1.html Accessed 5 May, 2009.
Mallarmé (1965), *Mallarmé*, ed. Anthony Hartley, Harmondsworth: Penguin.
Manne, R., ed. (2003), *Whitewash: On Keith Windschuttle's Fabrication of Aboriginal History*, Melbourne: Black Inc.
Marshall, A. (2008), 'And the Winning Anthem is…' *The Guardian*, http://www.guardian.co.uk/music/2008/aug/11/olympics2008.
Marx Brothers (2012), *Duck Soup Script – Dialogue Transcript*, Drew's Script-o-rama, http://www.script-o-rama.com/movie_scripts/d/duck-soup-script-transcript-marx.html Accessed 24 June, 2012.
Mauss, M. (1979), Techniques of the body, In *Sociology and Psychology*, (trans. Brewster B.), London: Routledge and Kegan Paul.
May, S. (1944), *The Story of Waltzing Matilda*, Brisbane: W. R. Smith & Paterson.
Meeker, J. (1972), *The Comedy of Survival: Studies in Literary Ecology*, New York: Scribners.
McLatchy, J.D., ed. (1990), *The Vintage Book of Contemporary American Poetry*, New York: Random House.
McCormick, P.D. (19), *Advance Australia Fair*, Brisbane: W. H. Paling & Co.
Mendelsohn, O. (1996), *A Waltz with Matilda: On the Trail of a Song*, Melbourne: Landsdowne Press.
'My Country 'Tis of Thee' ('America'), *Wikipedia*, http://en.wikipedia.org/wiki/My_Country,_%27Tis_of_Thee Accessed on 13 April, 2013.

National Anthem of Peru (2012), *Wikipedia*, http://en.wikipedia.org/wiki/National_Anthem_of_Peru, Accessed 23 June, 2012.

'Negaraku' (2012), *Wikipedia*, http://en.wikipedia.org/wiki/Negaraku Accessed 24 June, 2012.

Nettl, P. (1952), *National Anthems*, New York: Storm Publications.

Nichols, E., et al. (2009), 'Relationships between Lyrics and Melody in Popular Music', *International Society for Music Information Retrieval*, http://research.microsoft.com/enus/um/redmond/groups/cue/publications/ismir2009MelodyAndLyrics.

Nietzsche, F.W. (1974), *Early Greek Philosophy and Other Essays, Complete Works of Nietzsche*, Vol. 11 (trans. Maximilian A. Mügge), New York: Gordon Press.

Ogden, C.K. and Richards, I.A. (1949), *The Meaning of Meaning: A Study of the Influence of Language upon Thought and of the Science of Symbolism*, London: Routledge & Kegan Paul.

Ong, W.J. (1982), *Orality and Literacy: The Technologizing of the Word*, London: Routledge.

Oxford English Dictionary (1989), eds. Murray, James, et al., Oxford: Oxford University Press.

Pagel, Mark (2012), *Wired for Culture*, New York: Norton.

Parry, M. (1930), 'Studies in the Epic Technique of Oral Verse-Making I: Homer and Homeric Style', *Harvard Studies in Classical Philology*, 41.

Pater, Walter H. (2006), *The Renaissance: Studies in Art and Poetry*, Teddington, Middlesex: The Echo Library.

Paterson, A.B. (1921), *The Collected Verse of A.B. Paterson*, Sydney: Angus and Robertson.

Plato (1952), *The Dialogues of Plato*, in *Great Books of the Western World*, Vol. 7 (trans. Benjamin Jowett), Chicago: Encyclopaedia Britannica.

The Presidency, Republic of South Africa, http://www.thepresidency.gov.za/pebble.asp?relid=265 Accessed 1 September, 2013.

Queen (Freddie Mercury) (1977), *News of the World*, London: EMI.

Radic, T. (1983), *A Treasury of Favourite Australian Songs*, South Yarra, Vic.: Currie O'Neil Ross.

——— (1996), 'Songlines of Waltzing Matilda', *The Journal of Australian Studies*, 49, St Lucia: University of Queensland Press.

Radio Free Europe (2006), 'Kazakh Leader Changes National Anthem', Radio Free Europe/Radio Liberty, http://www.rferl.org/content/article/1064476.html Accessed 23 June, 2012.

Reddy, H. and Burton, R. (1971), *I am Woman* (single), Los Angeles: Capitol Records.

Reed, L. (1972), *Transformer*, New York: RCA.

Rumens, C. (2012), 'Pussy Riot's Punk Prayer is Pure Protest Poetry', *The Guardian*, http://www.guardian.co.uk/books/2012/aug/20/pussy-riot-punk-prayer-lyrics Accessed 24 June, 2012.

Sacks, O. (2007), *Musicophilia: Tales of Music and the Brain*, New York: Vintage.

Sadie, S., ed. (1980), *The New Grove Dictionary of Music and Musicians*, 6th ed., London: Macmillan.

Sammler, D. (2010), 'The Relationship of Lyrics and Tunes in the Processing of Unfamiliar Songs: A Functional Magnetic Resonance Adaptation Study', *The Journal of Neuroscience*, 30:10, 3572–3578.

Saussure, F. de (1986), *Course in General Linguistics* (trans. Roy Harris), La Salle: Open Court.

Saville, A. (1995), 'Sentimentality', *Arguing About Art – Contemporary Philosophical Debates*, eds. Alex Neill and Aaron Ridley, New York: McGraw Hill.

Scholes, P. (1942), *'God Save the King': Its History and Romance*, London: Oxford.

Schön, D., et al. (2005), 'Musical and Linguistic Processing in Song Perception', *Annals New York Academy of Sciences*, http://www.mus.cam.ac.uk/~ic108/teaching/perceptionandperformance/Papers1112/Music_lang_song_interact_Ann_NY_Acad_Sci05.pdf Accessed 23 January, 2013.

Scruton, R. (1997), *Aesthetics of Music*, Oxford: Oxford University Press.

——— (2009), *Understanding Music: Philosophy and Interpretation*, London: Continuum.

Searle, J.R. (1975), 'A Taxonomy of Illocutionary Acts', *Language, Mind, and Knowledge*, Vol. 7, ed. Günderson, K., Minneapolis: University of Minnesota Press.

Sebeok, T.A. (1960), *Style In Language*, Cambridge, Massachusetts: MIT Press.

Semmler, C. (1988), *The Banjo of the Bush: The Life and Times of A.B. Paterson*, St Lucia: University of Queensland Press.

Serbisyo Philippine Government e-Services Portal (2008), *Philippine Symbols*, Manila: Philippine Government, www.eserbisyo.gov.ph/Default.aspx?ssid=84&aid=1870 Accessed 23 June, 2012.

Shakespeare, W. (1943), *The Complete Works of William Shakespeare*, Oxford: Oxford University Press.

The Sexpistols (1977), 'God Save the Queen', *Never Mind the Bollocks, Here's the Sexpistols*, London: Virgin.

Smith, A.D. (2008), *The Cultural Foundations of Nations: Hierarchy, Covenant and Republic*, Oxford: Blackwell.

——— (1999), *Myths and Memory of the Nation*, Oxford: Oxford University Press.

Smith, S.F. (2012), 'My Country 'Tis of Thee I Sing', *Wikipedia*, http://en.wikipedia.org/wiki/My_Country,_'Tis_of_Thee Accessed 23 June, 2012.

The Sound of Music (1965), Wise, Robert (director), Hollywood: Twentieth Century Fox.

Sounds of the Soviet Union, http://www.marxists.org/history/ussr/sounds/lyrics/anthem.htm, Accessed 23 January, 2013.

Spellmeyer, K. (1993), *Common Ground: Dialogue, Understanding and the Teaching of Composition*, Englewood Cliffs: Prentice Hall.

Starks, R.J. (1999), 'Clichés and Composition Theory', *Journal of Advanced Composition*, 19:3, 453–464.

Stevens, W. (1982), *The Collected Poems of Wallace Stevens*, New York: Vintage.

Symphony No. 9 (Beethoven) (2012), *Wikipedia*, http://en.wikipedia.org/wiki/Symphony_No._9_(Beethoven) Accessed 23 June, 2012.

Townshend, P. (2006), 'Pete's Diaries', *The Internet Archive Wayback Machine*, San Francisco: The Internet Archive, http://web.archive.org/web/20061205225327/http://www.petetownshend.co.uk/diary/display.cfm?id=285&zone=diary Accessed 23 June, 2012.

Twain, M. (1876), 'A Literary Nightmare', *The Queenslander*, Brisbane: Brisbane Newspaper Company.

USA for Africa (Michael Jackson, Lionel Richie, et al.) (1985), *We are the World* (single), New York: Columbia Records.

'The Vegemite Story' (2011), *Vegemite*, Kraft Foods Australia, http://brands.nabisco.com/kraftvegemite/Pages/the-vegemite-story.aspx Accessed 23 June, 2012.

'Die Wacht am Rhein' ('The Watch/Guard on the Rhine') (2010), *Wikipedia*, http://en.wikipedia.org/wiki/Die_Wacht_am_Rhein Accessed 23 June, 2012.

Waldron, A. (1992), *The Great Wall of China – From History to Myth*, Cambridge: Canto.

Werb, B. (1997), *Songs of the Kovno Ghetto*, Washington: United States Holocaust Memorial Museum.

West Side Story (1961), Wise, Robert and Robbins, Jerome (directors), Los Angeles: Mirisch (United Artists), http://www.westsidestory.com/site/level2/lyrics/america.html Accessed 2 January, 2013.

Whitman, W. (1958), *Leaves of Grass*, New York: Signet New American Library.

The Who (1971), 'Won't Get Fooled Again', *Who's Next*, London: Decca.

Wilde, O. (1963), *The Works of Oscar Wilde*, London: Spring Books.

——— (2000), *The Complete Letters of Oscar Wilde*, New York: Henry Holt.

Williams, R. (1976), *Keywords*, Glasgow: Fontana.

——— (1977), *Marxism and Literature*, Oxford: Oxford University Press.

Williams, P. and Chrisman, L., eds. (1993), *Colonial Discourse and Post-Colonial Theory: A Reader*, New York: Harvester Wheatsheaf.

Wood, T. (1943), *Cobbers*, Oxford: Oxford University Press.

Woodstock: Music from the Original Soundtrack and More (1970), Kramer, Eddie (producer), New York: Atlantic Records (Cotillion).

Wordsworth, W. (1996), *Selected Poems*, Harmondsworth: Penguin.

Xing Hang (2003), *Encyclopedia of National Anthems*, Oxford: Scarecrow Press.

Yao Feng (2010), *In Brief* (trans. Hilda Tam and Kit Kelen), Macao: ASM.

Yeats, W.B. (1977), *Collected Poems*, London: Macmillan.

Zalta, Edward N. (ed.) (2012), *Stanford Encyclopedia of Philosophy*: http://plato.stanford.edu/entries/music/ Accessed 23 June, 2012.

Zizek, S. (2007), '"Ode to Joy," Followed by Chaos and Despair', *New York Times*, www.nytimes.com/2007/12/24/opinion/24zizek.html Accessed 23 June, 2012.

Zijderveld, A.C. (1979), *On Clichés: The Supersedure of Meaning by Function in Modernity*, London: Routledge & Keegan Paul.

Zubir, S. (2007), 'Oral History Interview', *1959 – Singapore's State Arms, Flags and National Anthem*, http://40years.ns.sg/portal/ns/mindef_saf_history_1950s/1959_singapore_s_state_arms_flags_and_national_anthem/ Accessed 27 August, 2007.

Index